Pursuing Obedience

How to "Want to" When Your "Wanter" Doesn't Want to

J. W. Phillips

ISBN: 978-0-9968545-1-1

DEDICATION

謹將此書獻給姍玫摯愛的弟弟們

葉昇泰

葉附岱

葉東其

願 上帝的愛與你們同在

Table of Contents

Chapter 1

There's No Other Way

Obedience has a pivotal importance for our spiritual growth. Yet, despite this importance, obedience school in America has become a concept for poodles and not people. One has to wonder why that is, for the problems *people* have with obedience are far more perverse than what Fluffy will ever have!

Extensive research indicates that even in the church, where one might think moral living is elevated, the track record for obedience isn't exactly impressive. The lamentable legacy of many is that sinning keeps winning in their lives, despite repeatedly renewed vows—preceded by clenched-teeth resolve and followed by red-eye remorse. Even today, the serpent's hissing continues to indict—*s-s-sin*! And these are not trumped-up charges.

Many investigative studies document what individual experience confirms: Most church members don't know how to stop sinning.[1] And not only do they not know how, but they seriously doubt there can be a sustained victory over the downward drag of sin. Well! The outcome of this conclusion is obvious enough: What God calls carnal, they call normal.

So deeply entrenched is this problem—its cause and course seemingly irreversible—that resistance to God's remedy for righteousness was bound to surface. To counteract their defeats in this area, people started claiming their defeats were inevitable. So, after only a few syllables of presentation, all proposed solutions were routinely shut down, each sacked and dumped in the nearby disposal of discarded ideas.

The predisposition to stand stout against any "victory-over-sin" formula, especially those from a cliché Christianity, activated without fail. With eyebrows arched in skepticism and eyes rolling in disdain, these views about victory were dismissed with a sneer and snort, faster even than UFO stories from a bunch of Arkansas farmers.

But if we could only restrain this instinct and allow at least some reflection on the issue, would we not agree that an obedience school that utilizes Scripture for its curriculum makes sense? If sin is both honestly faced and accurately assessed, then in that context the viability of obedience school deserves due consideration.

As we shall discover in this book, the dynamics of obedience are a bit more complicated than what many Christians think. This is why the greatest of all the apostles, the man who wrote more than a fourth of the New Testament, confessed one day—not in passing, but with utter anguish—that he didn't know how to be good (Romans 7:18). Didn't know how to be good? This esteemed theologian?

It seems that what eluded the great apostle two thousand years ago is not a problem for most Christians today—or at least that's what they think.[2] To them, therefore, instruction in obedience isn't a perceived need.

Reinforcing disinterest in this topic is the hugely popular penchant of settling for "the settled for life." Choosing the present life, not the promised life, many Christians live somewhat normal lives: outwardly moral, inwardly lacking, blending easily with culture and seldom with Christ.

So are people who live this way happy? Not really. Permitted and protracted sin triggers very serious consequences, after all. Some of these consequences being:

- Disobedience blocks the felt presence of God

- Disobedience makes faith impossible and the promises of God unreachable

- Disobedience invites Satan to have a romping, stomping good time at our expense

- Disobedience puts us outside the boundaries where God can bless

- Disobedience terminates prayer, so none of our petitions will be answered

- Disobedience feeds our flesh until it become a monster we intensely dislike

- Disobedience strands us in a going-through-the-motions "churchianity"

- Disobedience puts a chokehold on the Word and a muzzle on praise

One might think that consequences like these would be painful enough, and certainly motivational enough, to put every believer on a search for increased obedience. What should further incentivize this search, one would think, is the immense joy obedience ultimately provides. Jesus talked about a joy that is full, a joy that will remain, a joy that no one can take away.

This linkage between consistent obedience and constant joy isn't coincidental but, according to Scripture, is actually causal.[3] Strongly affirming this perspective, Andrew Murray wrote, "Holiness is essential to true happiness. If you would have joy, the fullness of joy, an abiding joy which nothing can take away, be as holy as God is holy. Holiness is blessedness."[4]

The idea of sustainable joy seems implausible to many people because they believe emotions aren't governable. To them, feelings do what they do: They yo-yo up and down. The tide comes in; the tide goes out. Sometimes we're on the mountaintop; sometimes we're in the valley. So true joy, they say—that inner elation of spirit that finds its source in a serene and supreme confidence in God—is a rare and fleeting commodity.[5] Its arrival is unusual; its departure is not.

Several possibilities account for the "dips" and "drops" in our happiness—our track record of inconsistent obedience being the most likely among them. It is in this context that the old hymn said it well: "Trust and obey, for there's no other way to be happy in Jesus, but to trust and obey."

Yet, we have tried to find some other way. Not because we have been all that calculating. The greater problem is Christians being propagandized by the world about what happiness is and isn't. The world has its own ideas about how to become happy, and obeying God isn't one of them! Hence, disobedience is often overlooked as the prime suspect for the theft of one's happiness.

Our lack of focus on the obedience issue has caused a dense haze to settle in, one that obscures what our life could be like if only a more consistent obedience were in place. Our unexamined assumptions about obedience—especially when it comes to how attainable and sustainable it is—have set us up for the low level of happiness we have come to accept as "reality."

The aforementioned Andrew Murray, perhaps the greatest devotional writer ever, disclosed the chronic misery he experienced, even years after his conversion. Speaking to the Keswick Convention in 1895, Dr. Murray testified that after a decade in the ministry "... there was dissatisfaction in my heart and restlessness inexpressible." Sitting in his little room at night, Andrew Murray used to ask himself, "What is the matter? Here I am knowing that I am justified in the blood of Christ, but I have no power for service."

Reflecting on those earlier years, Murray later said, "My thoughts, my words, my actions, my unfaithfulness— everything troubled me. Though all around thought me one of the most earnest of men, my life was a deep dissatisfaction."

In analyzing this awful predicament—so private, so painful—this well-known pastor repeatedly inquired about its reason with a desire determined to do something about it. It wasn't until many years later, however, that he was able to pinpoint the answer: "I had never learned, with all my theology, that obedience was possible."[6]

And so it is with many Christians today! They think progress in obedience can only be one that ranges from utter defeat to a near stalemate, wherein sin wins sometimes and sometimes the believer does. You will notice that in this paradigm of thought sin has been reduced only slightly: from a constant victor who won *always* to a formidable competitor who wins *often*.

By minimizing God's provision for righteous living, believers project a low level of living that eventually becomes daily reality. Like the Apostle Paul in his day, and like Andrew Murray in his, they simply have no idea how to obey God.

Throughout his ministry Jesus stressed the importance of obedience, yet he gave special attention to its importance at the very end. That he did so, particularly at *this* point in his ministry, is quite significant. Because whenever a person is about to die, and knows that he is about to die, he will not spend his final hours in frivolous conversations.

During better days of health one may occasionally do this, but once the end draws near and an aura of death has entered the room, the trite and trivial are not likely to be entertained—this due to the obvious fact that final hours and last words are almost always reserved for what matters most. So, with this observation in mind, it is instructive to examine what Jesus had to say when the time came for him to face his death.

Upon examining Jesus' final words in the 14th chapter of John's Gospel, we discover that the one concern uppermost on his mind had to do with the obedience of his disciples. With laser-beam intensity Jesus riveted his attention on this issue—very specifically, very directly, employing almost identical wording *four times*!

To gain greater clarity about why obedience *is* so important, we would do well to go back to that night when obedience endured its most stringent test and in the end secured its most impressive victory.

As we immerse ourselves in this chapter (and thereby allow the dynamics that went on that night to become increasingly real to us), the feverish rapidity of these repetitions will convey a passion, and declare an urgency, that should put every student of Scripture in its grip.

This quadruple stressing of the obedience theme is further supported in the last half of this chapter by the Lord's ten-point teaching on how to obey—especially when the decision to do so is undergoing an all-out challenge and the motivation for doing so is susceptible to a fast fade-out.

This emphasis on obedience, and the failure factors that keep us from it, deserve our utmost attention today—well before the final hours and last gasps of declining health! But, sadly, this attention hasn't been forthcoming from the church. Christians today haven't been all that impressed with the optimal importance of this extraordinary subject. Too often, it seems, believers have to come to the very edge—of disaster, or even life itself—before they are finally willing to focus on life's most critical issue, the obedience necessary for an abundant life.

It is in this vein, I'm afraid, that the following story may one day describe us.

The countdown had begun. Fingers were nervously poised over the very buttons that could unleash a nuclear holocaust upon all the habitable earth. But then ... just moments before the "awful awful" ... the two sides hesitated. Sobered by a prospect neither side had ever faced before—the end of all life: plant, animal and human—national leaders called for a forty-eight-hour truce. Recognizing both the shortage of time and the enormity of the problem, they summoned the most brilliant minds available to see if there was some way this impending destruction could be averted.

At the disposal of these sage contemplators of the geopolitical scene, men and women of exceptional genius whose expertise extended to many spheres of knowledge, was a gigantic computer that could be programmed with the most advanced wisdom known to man

Finally, after contemplating the most cutting-edge insights, these intellectual elites completed their computer programming; and, when finished, they submitted the following questions: How can we save our world? How can we live in peace? How can we live with purpose and pleasure and increasing respect? These were not academic questions, to be sure, but were questions asked of desperate men.

Slowly, the calculations were made until finally—with television broadcasting this event to the entire world—the following printout was given:

I am the Lord your God.
You shall not make any graven images.
You shall not take the name of the Lord your God
in vain.
Remember the Sabbath and keep it holy.
Honor your mother and father.
You shall not kill.
You shall not commit adultery.
You shall not steal.
You shall not lie.
You shall not covet.

The Ten Commandments! Think of it: Thirty-five hundred years ago, slaves from Egypt went traipsing off into the desert; and in less than three months they came to possess a document so free of national peculiarities and so articulate of human responsibility it has emerged as the only good sense way for men and nations to live.

But this, quite clearly, is not the way we have lived! "The modern man," says Sir Oliver Lodge, "is not worrying about sins, still less about their forgiveness."[7] Instead, allowing the ordinariness of what he calls "real life" to numb him, he negotiates his day as if there were nothing amiss. With a systematic disregard for both the unseen and the eternal, he neglects the voice of conscience and every summons it makes to reflect, repent, and repattern.

Even in the church, with all of its impressive programs and its high tech efforts for spreading the gospel, the track record for obedience is alarmingly disconcerting. Thomas Chalmers, the nineteenth-century Scottish theologian, declared, "Sin is that scandal which must be rooted out from the great spiritual household over which the Divinity rejoices ...."[8] Tolerated sin results in diluted faith and a distorted testimony.

When commenting on this dilemma, A. W. Tozer observed:

Christians habitually weep and pray over beautiful truth, only to draw back from that same truth when it comes to the difficult job of putting

13

it into practice. The average church simply does not dare to check its practices against biblical precepts. It tolerates things that are diametrically opposed to the will of God, and if the matter is pointed out to its leaders they will defend its unscriptural practices with a smooth casuistry equal to the moral dodgings of the Roman moralists.[9]

Those compromises many Christians make, and those rationalizations they subsequently adopt, may deceive those willing to be deceived, but they can never withstand the scrutiny of Scripture. What gives such deception so much plausibility, though, is its near-universal acceptance by a church too much influenced by the world it was supposed to transform. Popular preachers choose to edit God, virtually ignoring his call to holiness while emphasizing their views about happiness.

Even some of the more fervent churches in our midst, resonating to a revelation other generations missed, also stumbled in this matter of simple obedience. Pursuing mighty exploits, they overlooked daily obligation. In his book, *Winning the Invisible War*, E. M. Bounds observed:

Many Christians are so enthusiastic over some marked advance, or some higher elevation gained, that they become enchanted with the beautiful and lofty regions ... and are unconscious of their loss. Instead of pressing on with tireless steps, they cover the future with their imaginations. Then, while their minds are filled with fantasies of their advanced position, their feet have slipped backward, and they are in the valley again. They are so happy that it is almost impossible to bring them to their senses ....

It is good to have singing and shouting sanctification. But if it is not joined by marching and fighting faith, it will sing and shout itself as thin as a ghost and as dry as a desert.[10]

As for those who make an idol out of feelings, J. C. Ryle said, "Insensible almost to themselves, they take up a kind of hysterical, sensational, sentimental Christianity ...."[11] They are more concerned to fly high in ecstasy than to walk straight in obedience.

The Bible presents a progressive revelation; and the Holy Spirit who ministers this revelation does so with a progressive illumination. For example, when Adam made his exit from Eden that day, he had no idea that there would ever be such a thing as a cross, a church, a call to evangelize, and that consummate glory awaiting the redeemed around the Messianic banquet table.

Nevertheless, from Eden onward the key concern has always been obedience. Nothing in the ongoing revelation of God, or in the progressive illumination by the Spirit, was ever intended to distract from this issue. To the contrary, all that God later revealed, and all that the Holy Spirit later ministered, only reinforced what was ever most on the heart of God—our need to obey him.

The Importance of Obedience

If we were to revisit the Garden of Eden with all of its luxuriant foliage and sweet smelling aromas, we would see that more than Hawaii, Tahiti, or some other place of exotic enchantment, the garden described in Genesis was uniquely a paradise on earth. But what was the one prerequisite for remaining there? Obedience! As long as Adam obeyed the Lord, life in that perfect environment could continue. However, when Adam did what the Lord told him not to do, he was immediately banished from the garden and was never allowed to return.

Significantly, when turning from the front of our Bibles to the back, we find these words recorded: "Blessed are those who do his commandments, that they may have the right to the tree of life, and may enter through the gates into the city" (Revelation 22:14). Interestingly, the very tree spoken of in Genesis had somehow, during the interval between prehistory and post-history, been transported to our permanent home, heaven. So who are the ones, according to the Bible, who have access to this tree? "Those who do His commandments." Whether we talk about Eden or heaven, the condition for residency is exactly the same—obedience.

Some people have the idea that the Old Testament teaches about law, whereas the New Testament teaches about grace. Consequently, under the sway of this overly dichotomized view, their response to the New Testament's assertion that salvation is by grace and not works is to say "Thank you, Lord" and refuse to do any!

Apparently, they never noticed the next verse in this passage which says we are saved *unto good works* that God foreordained before the foundation of the world for us to walk into (Ephesians 2:10). Hence, good works—and the obedience that implies—is very much a part of the New Testament message.

G. D. Watson remarked that "there never was a time when good works were so scare in proportion to the amount of religion professed."[12] Offering one explanation for this phenomenon, Tozer astutely observed, "To escape the error of salvation by works we have fallen into the opposite error of salvation without obedience."[13]

When it comes to obedience, the priority never changes. The Old Testament tells us *what*; the New Testament tells us *how*. However, there should be no confusion about the fact that obedience, from Genesis to Revelation, is crucial to our salvation in several respects.

The Accomplishments of Obedience

In the first place, obedience is immensely important because our salvation was itself secured by obedience. Referring to the Lord Jesus, Philippians 2:8 says, "... he humbled himself and became obedient to the point of death, even the death of the cross." In contemplating this verse, it's important to realize that the obedience cited here included more than a willingness to go to the cross. Gethsemane's "not my will but Thine be done" never would have been uttered had Jesus not first lived a perfect life.

The sacrifice for mankind's redemption, remember, had to be an unblemished lamb. Accordingly, just one act of disobedience, however slight and seemingly insignificant, would have disqualified Jesus from dying a Savior's death.

16

While the presence of sin in his life might still have allowed him to die a hero's death or a martyr's death, it would not, it must be stressed, have permitted a Savior's death.

Obedience is also crucial to the increasing intimacy with God that salvation enables. In his book, *The Spirit of Christ*, Andrew Murray asserts, "God's own Son could only maintain his relationship with the Father and experience his love and life by obedience." Moreover, according to Murray, the relationship Jesus had with the Holy Spirit was also contingent upon a consistent obedience.

> After a life in holy humility and obedience for thirty years, he spoke that word of entire consecration, "it becometh us to fulfill all righteousness" (Matthew 13:15). Then he gave himself to baptism for the sins of his people, and he was baptized with the Spirit. The Spirit came because of his obedience.[14]

The notion that unconditional love will assure access to God and intimacy with God has never been true, not even for God's own Son. The prerequisite for divine intimacy, even within the Trinity, is righteousness. Knowing this principle to be true, Jesus told his disciples, "If you love me, keep my commandments" (John 14:15). For to sever obedience from love, as we in the modern world have done, distorts love and dislodges obedience. This is an outcome A. W. Tozer repudiated when he wrote: "... the final test of love is obedience. Not sweet emotions, not willingness to sacrifice, not zeal, but obedience to the commands of Christ."[15]

Atomizing this truth in order to support it, Andrew Murray wrote:

> Obedience is not knowledge of the will of God, not even approval, not even the will to do it, but the doing of it. Knowledge and approval and will must all lead to action ...
>
> I may know what is good and yet not approve it. I may approve and still not will it. In a certain

sense I may will a thing but even so, may lack the energy or self-sacrifice or power that will arouse me to actually do that thing. Thinking is easier than willing, and willing is easier than doing ... God wants his will done. This alone is obedience.[16]

The main reason obedience is the litmus test of love can be attributed to this fact: Every protected and protracted sin, whether it takes the form of an act or an attitude, or whether it transgresses by omission or commission, declares what our lips would never declare and what our mind would never think—"Jesus, I really don't love you that much."

To ally ourselves with what sent Jesus to the cross is hardly an expression of love! Oswald Chambers said, "It is possible to be grossly selfish in absorbing the salvation of Jesus, to enjoy all its benedictions, and never follow him one step."[17]

Whatever else can be said about this type of response, it certainly isn't love. And therefore G. D. Watson was correct in his observation, "Obedience is the supreme test in the life of faith, and the love of obedience is the highest of all."[18] This is also why Luther said he would rather obey God than do miracles."[19]

It is curious, sometimes, to observe how this charge of lovelessness will be debated by the ones it rightly labels. To prove this, just examine the way people confess their sins. In an almost cavalier way, they'll admit their shortcomings, acknowledging that, yes, they did do wrong; and, yes, they did transgress God's standards. But then in the next breath they'll wonder why anyone would want to make a federal case out of this. Isn't it only human to sin?

Actually, it isn't. We must always keep in mind that Jesus was the one who was fully human—yet he never sinned! To sin, therefore, isn't just being human; it's being less than human. To take refuge in this "to-sin-is-only-human" rationale shows no grief about one's past and, really, no expectation of a much improved behavior in the future. It conveys instead a surface and shallow acknowledgment, so typical of the callous heart.

John 14:21 further addresses the relationship between obedience and intimacy with words that establish their connection to be crucial and not coincidental. Jesus said, "He who has my commandments and keeps them, it is he who loves me. And he who loves me will be loved by my Father, and I will love him and manifest myself to him."

Jesus, for many people today, is little more than a religious icon—at best a historical memory, and worst only an idealistic abstraction. But those who want Jesus to be more real to them must come to grips with why he isn't. It has to do with those crossroad decisions they keep making where self gets indulged and the Word of God gets ignored.

What must be considered more carefully is what the poet called "the road not taken"—because that road, so seldom traveled and at first glance so uninviting, is precisely where Jesus will lavish and ravish the believer with his soul-satisfying love. What an awesome prospect! The very heart of God touching our heart! And, better still, the inner qualities of that heart actually intersecting our life!

Another benefit of obedience is the way it qualifies believers to participate in ministry. Significantly, when I Timothy, chapter 3, sets forth the prerequisites for certain positions of ministry, it had much more to say about obedience than it did about giftedness. And similarly when II Timothy, chapter 2, discussed those vessels of honor useful to the Master, it first insisted that everyone who names the name of Christ must depart from iniquity. In other words, if we're going to name the name, especially in the ministry we're attempting to undertake, we must walk the walk.

This was a point God made exceedingly clear during the beginning days of Israel's history. Saul, Israel's first king, was told by the prophet Samuel to completely destroy the Amalekites, the nation's perennial enemy—including all their livestock! But when Samuel returned to Israel's campsite, he heard the bleating of sheep, a proof-positive sign that Saul had not done what the Lord told him to do.

The feeble excuse Saul used for preserving these sheep was that they could be used for worship. It was all for religious reasons, he piously intoned. Really? Saul would dare tell the prophet that?

Under a sudden compulsion from heaven, Samuel then told Saul in no uncertain terms, "Obedience is better than sacrifice." Moreover, because Saul thought nothing about amending the Lord's instructions, he got his pink slip *that day*! Saul was summarily dismissed from his exalted position as Israel's king.

Now, one has to wonder that if God would do that to a king, is he going to be more lax and lenient with us? No, what happened to Saul was hardly an overreaction on God's part, or some arbitrary object lesson designed to warn believers who would read about it centuries later. Subsequent history has clearly shown: The Lord *will* set aside those believers who cannot be trusted to obey him. Thomas Goodwin, the seventeenth-century Puritan scholar, said "... it is best to obey God in all things, at all times, and in all conditions ...."[20]

So how important is obedience? Obedience, the residency requirement for Eden, is also the residency requirement for heaven. In fact, it was through obedience that our salvation was secured; and through obedience that we can gain an unhindered fellowship with God, a ministry for God, and—get this—an increased value to God.

Speaking through Moses more than thirty-five hundred years ago, God set forth this last point by saying, "If you will indeed obey my voice and keep my covenant, then you shall be a special treasure to me ...." (Exodus 19:5).

So how would you like to be someone of immense value? Someone who brings the Lord extraordinary pleasure? Someone whose stock is soaring high in heaven? If this is your desire, then know for a certainty that obedience is *the* key, the most important essential, without which the pleasing of God is altogether impossible. Affirming this perspective, Charles Finney said, "God makes sincere and full-hearted obedience the one unalterable condition of his favor."[21]

It is true that obedience isn't always easy. There will be forces that come against us that can overwhelm whatever willpower we can muster. It is during these times that evil plots hatched against us will require a far greater revelation than what human ingenuity could ever conceive—that is, if the cunning deceit in those plots is to be exposed and the devious designs of those plots are to be thwarted.

The good news, though, is such a revelation already exists! For it was during that climatic episode in Jesus' life—when the forces of evil mounted its greatest momentum and unleashed its fiercest attack—that Jesus gave his disciples a revelation critical to obedience. This revelation teaches believers how to "want to" obey when our "wanter" doesn't want to. That may not be the most elegant way to put it, but it does make the point.

For too long, Christians have been accepting defeats that never needed to come, and thus have been robbed of blessings that would have made their life so much better. This spiritual malaise will cease, however, once they seek to understand, and then implement, the very motivations that brought victory to Jesus.

To examine the biblical record is see that Jesus was acutely aware of the temptations that would come to him, and it was this awareness that helped prepare him. All too often, though, believers today seem unprepared. Once caught by surprise, they'll then find themselves perplexed, as if such opposition has to be mistake for which God must now give an account. A. B. Simpson wrote:

> Most persons, after a step of faith, are looking for sunny skies and unruffled seas. When they meet a storm or tempest, there are filled with astonishment and perplexity. But this is just what we must expect to meet if we have received anything of the Lord.
>
> The best token of his presence is the adversary's defiance, and the more real our blessing the more certainly will it be challenged.[22]

Speaking quite bluntly about the matter, F. B. Meyer asked:

> Do you think that the prince of hell was pleased when you forsook him for your new master,

Christ? Certainly not! At the moment of your conversion your name was put on the proscribed list, and all the powers of darkness pledged themselves to obstruct your way. Remember how Satan hated Job; does he not hate you? He would vent on you the hatred he has for your Lord, if he might.[23]

And should the Spirit of God fill you one day, think not that Satan will then retreat and cease his siege against your soul. He won't. Instead, he'll double down in his defiance, seeking to undo what just happened to you. Why? Because as a Spirit-filled believer, you have become a danger to him. This is exactly what happened to Jesus, about whom Samuel Chadwick wrote:

His baptism furnished the opportunity and the basis of the temptation. The order is inevitable and universal. Being full of the Spirit does not bring immunity from temptation but exposure to it ... Every man's Pentecost is the signal for Satan to gird himself.[24]

It was immediately after the baptism that Jesus encountered Satan in the wilderness. The attack came sooner, not later, because the interval of time Evil may use to strategize against us wouldn't work against Jesus.

You and I, even today, are scarcely acquainted with the seething hatred of Satan. No doubt, the viciousness of his plots would send most believers today into a fast retreat. Therefore, according to Jessie Penn-Lewis, "God mercifully hides us from the malice of Satan and evil spirits until he gets us close enough to himself to endure the awful sight, and even then he allows us only faint glimpses ...."[25] We are told enough, however, to begin our preparation and to establish our defense. Likewise, the Lord Jesus sought to prepare the apostles for all the obstructions to obedience they would encounter in the garden and at the cross.

Determined to benefit from this preparation, we will now revisit the Upper Room and Gethsemane, intent on receiving what the apostles themselves missed at first—the very strategy that brought the greatest victory this world would ever see, even when the odds against it were enormous and the motivation for achieving it were under the most devastating assault.

Reflection Questions

1. Which consequence of disobedience is more recent in your life?

2. Which consequence of disobedience has been more frequent in your life?

3. Which accomplishment of obedience resonates the most with you? Please explain.

Chapter 2

The Spirit's Strength

Obedience isn't always easy. And while we wish it weren't true, there are times when we don't even want to obey. Deeper down we do, but competing with these deeper-down desires are a multitude of other desires. Contrary desires! Compelling desires! And at times controlling desires! So how are we to obey the Lord when the situation is practically screaming at us to give in?

D. H. Lawrence said that no inspiration will get "weak, impotent, vicious, worthless and rebellious man" beyond his own limits. According to Mr. Lawrence—the English novelist, poet, and playwright—man simply doesn't have it within him to obey the laws of God.[1] According to many, these laws set a standard the ungodly can't meet. Even the godly Kierkegaard seemed to identify with this sentiment when he lamented, "It is so hard to believe, because it is so hard to obey."[2]

This predicament surfaces more often than we would like to admit. We would do well, then, to learn from Jesus *how* we can stand strong whenever circumstances coalesce to weaken our will and to divide our loyalties. The strategy we have used in the past seems not to be working. So maybe we should another strategy.

Jesus is indeed our example here, because no one ever faced what he faced. All the conspirators of eternal ruin invaded the Garden of Gethsemane that night. There was never a night—before or since—when the fires of temptation raged more ferociously, or the forces of hell were unleashed with greater abandon.

The might of the Roman army was never an issue to our Lord, a point made clear by the way manifested glory flattened every soldier there. Much more the issue was the intense battle within the soul of the Savior: Would the Suffering Servant extend his suffering *this* far? Or would Jesus disqualify himself from this mission by refusing the Father at the very end? Important for us to see is that obedience, even for the Son of God, was the issue.

While on his way to Gethsemane and then to Golgotha, Jesus had a lot to say about obedience. His quadruple stressing of the obedience theme (vss.15, 21, 23, 24) was motivated by the tremendous blessings obedience can bring, as well as by the terrible consequences disobedience can bring. So, not wanting his disciples stranded in a going-through-the-motions "churchianity," Jesus identified ten specific ways his disciples could obey him, the first of which we will consider next—the Spirit's strength.

The Coming of the Spirit

It is significant that after stressing the importance of obedience in verse 15, Jesus then spoke of the Holy Spirit's coming in verse 16. The rationale for this sequence is obvious; for unless the disciples could lay hold of a power greater than self can generate, the return to old, cold ways was sadly certain.

To examine further what Jesus had to say about the Holy Spirit in this passage is to make some very astounding discoveries. For example, the word "Helper" in verse 16 (elsewhere translated as "Comforter" in other versions of Scripture) comes from the Greek word *paraclete*, which means "to come along side." Instead of diagnosing our difficulties with detachment, the Holy Spirit, having much more compassion than that, will rush to the rescue!

Charles Finney pointed out, "... the Holy Ghost is not far away in some remote quarter of the universe where you cannot reach Him, but is present, and needs only be made welcome ...."[3] Our struggle with obedience, therefore, need not be an isolated one, because he who has overcoming

26

power will come to our side—not just to hold our hand and pat our little head and tell us how much better heaven is going to be, but to make all his resources available for challenges we are now having to face.

The very fact that Jesus uses the masculine, third person, singular pronoun to describe the Holy Spirit is also important. This means that, contra the *Star Wars* injunction: "the Force be with you," the Holy Spirit, who has more power than *Star Wars* ever thought about, is a person, and not just some mysterious power. F. B. Meyer weighed in on this point, saying:

> There is no need for me to prove or attempt to prove that the Holy Ghost is a person. In the Greek, though the name for the Holy Ghost is neuter, it is followed by a personal pronoun, *autos*, which could not be used unless the Holy Spirit was a person.[4]

Borrowing from the older King James Version of the Bible, many ministers from earlier centuries were fond of speaking about "the Holy Ghost" (usually with a certain quiver in their voice whenever they did so). But this, too, is somewhat misleading, once the biblical record is examined. The Third Person of the Trinity isn't a spook or ghoul.

Keep in mind that the King James Version of the Bible was translated about the same time Shakespeare was writing his plays. Prominent in Shakespearean English then was this fascination with apparitions, or ghosts. Still, one mustn't think of the Holy Spirit in terms of Casper the Friendly. The Holy Spirit is hardly a floating white-sheet phenomenon! He is actually every bit as personal as Jesus is, or as the Father is.

When Jesus said he would pray for another helper, the Greek word for "another" used here is the word *allos*, which means another of the exact same qualities. The first helper, of course, was Jesus. But because he was about to leave, Jesus told his disciples that there was another helper coming—one possessing the same power, the same wisdom, the same love, the same everything. However, there would be four important differences, differences we must now delineate.

First, although Jesus was present in a physical way, the Holy Spirit would be present in a spiritual way. Jesus ate and slept and put on clothes, but the Holy Spirit, when he came, wouldn't do any of those things. This means that if one were to leave out cookies and milk for him, like children do for Santa each year, the cookies and milk would still be there in the morning. Therefore, the way Jesus manifested himself on earth was distinctly different from what was to follow, the abiding of the Holy Spirit.

Second, while Jesus' sojourn on this earth did come to an end, the Holy Spirit, Jesus said, will never leave us. Upon entering our hearts at the time of conversion, the Holy Spirit will abide—which among other things means to stay put. How long will the Holy Spirit remain in the heart of the believer? Jesus answers that question in verse 16—forever!

Third, unlike the Lord Jesus who only lived among *some* believers, the Holy Spirit dwells with *every* believer. It doesn't matter whether that believer lives in the city or in the country, is a third world citizen or a citizen of a superpower, is a titled person with much esteem or is someone this world never heard of, the Holy Spirit, with equal affection and the utmost devotion, will abide within each believer in the same way.

Interestingly, that word "abide," used in verse 16 to describe the Holy Spirit, is also used earlier in this chapter to describe the mansions in glory God has for us. This indicates that the Holy Spirit isn't just coming for a weekend visit, but is coming to take up permanent residence.

Fourth, while Jesus, during his three-and-a-half year earthly ministry, was *with* believers, the Holy Spirit—during this new dispensation, this new stage of God's salvation economy—will actually be *in* the believer, Jesus said. Now I hope that an overfamiliarity with the truth hasn't dulled its wonder for you. Think of it! The Holy Spirit, having all the qualities of Jesus, actually living *inside* a believer!

Ephesians 3:22 says that we are a dwelling place of God in the Spirit. I Corinthians 6:19 says that our physical body is the temple of the Holy Spirit. Ephesians 3:19 says that any believer—not just the pastor of a megachurch or some world traveling evangelist, but any believer—can be "filled with all the fullness of God."

Now, as you think about obeying God, do you think that maybe, just maybe, the indwelling Holy Spirit could make a tremendous difference?

An Astounding Admission

One of the most amazing admissions in recorded history is found in Romans, chapter 7, verse 18, where the greatest apostle of all time acknowledged the unthinkable—that he, this first-rate theologian whose intellectual prowess soared stratospheres beyond his peers, didn't know how to be good.

Didn't know how to be good? Paul, one of the brainiest brains the world has ever known? This man who had the equivalent of two doctorate degrees by the time he was twenty-one! This man who had studied under Gamaliel, the greatest theologian of his day! How is it even possible that *this* man, steeped in the highest expression of ethical wisdom and conversant with the loftiest thoughts of monotheistic religion, could be so totally and pathetically clueless, especially about a proposition as basic and elementary as this?

Why, ask the little children—indeed, ask them one and all—and they'll tell you that it's no problem for them. *They* know how to be good! One can even undertake a survey that asks every adult this question. And I guarantee you that almost everyone will say the same thing: namely, that while they may not always do good, they most assuredly know how to be good, once they make the commitment.

So, again, how could it be that this man should find himself being so utterly stumped by an issue that for everyone else was a nonissue? Actually, as we previously pointed out in this series, this wasn't true of Paul. The man in Romans 7 depicts a sincere, zealous, unconverted Jew. Even so the idea of not knowing how to be good is shocking to us, because we have the idea that when it comes to obedience, there's nothing magical or formulaic about it. To us, the proposition is really quite simple: Either one says "yes" to the Lord and obeys, or one says "no" to the Lord and disobeys. It's all a matter of willpower! But is it?

An oversimplification like this is dangerously flawed for several reasons: first, because it greatly overestimates what the will can achieve; second, because it badly underestimates the spiritual forces that come against one's will; third, because it inevitably lowers the standard of what "good" really is; and fourth, because it summarily dismisses all the resources God has provided for a life of consistent, God-glorifying obedience.

Paul disclosed to gain victory over that downward drag of sin by explain four laws: 1) the law of God; 2) the law of the mind; 3) the law of sin and death; and 4) the law of the Spirit. So let's seek to understand next what these four laws mean.[5]

The Law of God

The law of God, as Paul uses it here, means more than the Ten Commandments. This term really refers to every command of Scripture binding on the believer today. While the demands and commands of the law can be debated, resisted, or set aside, the law (even if the response is one of rebellion) still doesn't go away. And that's because the moral "oughtness" God put in our hearts resonates with only his law and not with anything else with which we might seek to replace it. Like a Timex watch, the law can suffer terrible abuse at our hands, but even so it "keeps right on ticking." The dominion the law has over us simply can't be dislodged! Indeed, there is a very real sense in which the law doesn't break—we do!

Paul described the law of God as holy, just, and good (Romans 7:12). That is, no amendment will improve it and no deficiency can be found in it. The law reflects God's nature, in that it sets forth principles that explain how God himself lives. For example, God would never lie, steal, or covet. And further: He would never seek to gain an advantage for himself by wronging another person.

Have you ever stopped to think what it would be like if this weren't true? What if the Lord God of the universe were as impish as the mythological gods of Rome and Greece?

What if he threw tantrums, or lashed out in retaliation, or sought to gratify himself in crude, carnal ways? Can you imagine what it would be like if a god like that were running the whole show?

Thank heaven, this isn't the case! Our God is righteousness personified, and that's why he cannot—and he will not—sin!

A correlate of this truth—that the law is holy, just, and good—is that the law, even when looking at it from a selfish point of view, is still the best way to live. The law is God's way of fencing off the territory where you and I need to be so he can bless us. Those who dismiss Sinai's commandments as a "decalogue of don'ts" are missing the point. Properly understood, the forbidding sounded forth by God's law shouldn't trigger a foreboding, a dread of consequences. This forbidding, instead, was motivated by God's desire to see every one of his children abundantly blessed.

The Law of the Mind

The second law Paul refers to in this passage is "the law of my mind" (Romans 7:23). This law acknowledges a person can "delight in the law of God according to the inner man" (Romans 7:22)—respecting it, revering it, and even be revved up to do it. And yet, what he deep down wants still doesn't occur! Andrew Murray said:

> My mind may be most active about religion. I may preach or write or think or meditate, and delight in being occupied with things in God's Book and in God's Kingdom; and yet the power of the Holy Spirit may be markedly absent."[6]

Even a believer can read the Word, study the Word, memorize the Word, and teach the Word; but although the Word is both chased and cherished, the Word he spends so many hours translating does not in the end translate him. Why?

The gap between what we know and what we grow isn't accounted for here because truth was shuffled off to the attic of intellectualism or sent down to the basement of planned neglect. There is another factor that can neutralize the truth. And every believer has experienced it.

In attempting to explain the law of the mind, Paul tells us how he delighted in the law and purposed to obey it. It is altogether possible, though, to know and know and know; and yet what we know, even though we sought it with passion, doesn't change us. This observation certainly lines up with what James says about the engrafted Word being able to salvage our souls. That word within us can be exactly God's answer for some area of struggle in our life. Nevertheless, the saving, the healing, the delivering that word can provide may not have happened. And again we have to ask the question, why?

In response, it must be pointed out that facts in the brain, even if they are biblical facts, do not constitute a renewing of the mind. The renewing of the mind, which Scripture says *will* change us completely (Romans 12:2), involves much more than replacing faulty data with correct data. This is why the Bible let us know, as far back as Joshua, that there must be continual meditation, visualization, verbalization, and implementation of God's Word before that Word can then take on the "charged up" dynamic that that word "renewed" conveys.

A major part of this perplexing picture includes the fact that Word-to-soul transactions failed in the Old Testament and they will fail today. The Word *must* connect with our spirit if it is going to produce lasting change. Activating mental capacities alone is insufficient.

Apparently, what Paul was operating on, at least during this stage of his life, was something less than what God set forth for Joshua. The law of the mind pointed Paul in the right direction, and it even motivated him to want to go in that direction—*but* it was powerless to get him there. The biggest reason this was so was attributable to another law, what Paul called "the law of sin and death" (Romans 7:23).

The Law of Sin and Death

This third law was more like a scientific law rather than a legislative law. This distinction requires an explanation.

Congress can pass a law establishing 70 miles per hour as the speed limit for the country. But even though this law was passed with almost unanimous consent, those who abide by it will find nearly everyone else on the highway whizzing by at much greater speeds.

By contrast, a scientific law is operational no matter what people think or attempt to do. Take the law of gravity, for example. A person can shout his shrilled denunciations against this law, and may even attempt to defy it as he steps off the roof. But guess what? He's going down, down, down at breakneck speed! Scientific laws, unlike legislative ones, always dictate results. And in much the same way, the law of sin and death always kicks in and does its damage.

The law of sin and death, simply stated, is this: At the very point Paul resolved with all his heart to obey God, saying, "This time I mean it, God! This time I'm not going to fail!" something rose within him that triggered this inexplicable nosedive into defeat. Even though the willing and resolving on Paul's part were sincerely and seriously voiced, they were, nevertheless, overcome just as easily as fire reducing cellophane to instant ashes.

According to Paul, even though the law of God produced the desire to obey, it also stirred up the very forces that would disobey (Romans 7:7, 8). Somehow (just how it isn't easy to explain), the lure of the forbidden aroused these formerly dormant desires to do exactly what the law said not to do.

In medicine, this might be called an aversive reaction. This is outcome is the opposite of what a particular dosage of medicine was supposed to produce. Instead of sedating, for example, the medicine may cause some people to become extremely anxious.

In further explaining this phenomenon, Paul said there was an alien sin force within him that rendezvoused with his phantom self, the flesh. I say phantom self, because twice Paul said, without censure from heaven, that it was "not I" (Romans 7:17, 20). Yes, Paul was responsible for any sin he committed. However, contrary to those who say we have two natures, Paul was saying the flesh was not in any way a part of his true identity. It was a force he had to contend with, the residue of an old nature that had vanished. This, by the way, has enormous implications for strategizing obedience, as we shall discover in a later chapter.

The important point is that well-intentioned flesh—however informed, however inspired—cannot obey God, especially if it depends on truth floating around in the shallows of the mental. If willing flesh and an assemblage of accurate truth could have pulled off the victory, Paul would have surely succeeded—for no one tried harder than he! Or was more determined than he!

Yet, inexplicably, he failed! Indeed, he failed so miserably that he finally came to the place where he saw that no further attempts, similar to the ones he had been making, could possibly succeed. Therefore, what we see next is a scene we thought we would never see—a zealot giving up! And in giving up, being reduced to copious tears as he cried, "O wretched man that I am! Who will deliver me ...?" (Romans 7:24).

Now, we have to ask ourselves: At the time Paul spoke these words, was he just having a bad day? The answer to this question can be given quickly: It is an emphatic no! Something far deeper, something much more profound, was at work. Paul actually came to the end of himself, as he finally realized (to speak anachronistically) that no other book, speaker, seminar, or doubling of efforts on his part could bring about the success he desired. Accordingly, Paul had no other option but to get off the road he had been on for such a long time and, if possible, to find another road.

The road Paul had been traveling was the road of self—to be sure, a dedicated self, a consecrated self, but still and all, self. Instead of yucky flesh (such as a more notorious element might demonstrate), or plain vanilla flesh (such as most people within the church manifest), Paul exhibited a USDA Grade-A Choice flesh—impressive, informed, morally sensitive, exceedingly diligent; but, because it was flesh, it had to die.[7] Commenting on this fact, Jack R. Taylor echoed a thought A. B. Simpson had offered a century before:

> The Holy Spirit is the Great Undertaker who
> finally brings us to the place to which God has

34

assigned us; namely, the sharing of Christ's tomb. But He cannot bring us to participate in the crucifixion-life without our consent. We must consent to die.[8]

What encourages this consent is the very experience Paul had. For once a person experiences the futility of his flesh, especially when he is aspiring to so much more within the moral realm, that futility will cause him to finally hate the source of it all (his self-life, the flesh) and will bring about this eventual willingness to die.

In his book, *The Complete Green Letters*, Miles Stanford notes: "Our hatred of self is actually developed and strengthened during our miserable years of slavery to it. We never realize the necessity and value of Romans 7 failure while we are in its throes."[9]

It really does no good at all to lament the feeble, fragile, non-fruitful qualities of our self-life, because that's just the way the self-life is; and no program of improvement or repair is going to change that. By the same token, to think that we can rid ourselves of this self-life by the very powers that we already know the self-life doesn't have is logically ludicrous.

With regards to such an attempt, John Owen, the Puritan theologian, said this: "Mortification from a self-strength, carried on by ways of self-invention, unto the end of a self-righteousness is the soul and substance of all false religion."[10] The alternative, Owen insisted, has to be along more biblical lines. "The Spirit alone is sufficient for this work. All ways and means without him are useless. He is the great efficient. He is the One who gives life and strength to our efforts."[11]

Unfortunately, when many people read of Paul's struggles, they often draw a false conclusion, thinking to themselves: If the great apostle struggled this way, is it any wonder their own progress isn't any better? They then conclude, quite falsely, that this must be the way it is in this life. We may want to obey, we may try to obey—and certainly it is good that such a desire is in our hearts—but because we are Adam's offspring, after all, perfection won't come until we go to heaven. Even though the effort is worthwhile—and

God, who surely sees our hearts, approves our attempts—we might as well know from the beginning that we're not going to be all that successful.

But is this true? No, it's not at all true, as Paul makes very clear when he talks about another law. The idea that obedience is only an ideal but not a functional, doable goal is widely believed by an unbelieving church. While progress is deemed possible, success (in an ongoing sense) is not.

The Law of the Spirit

In Romans, chapter 8, verse 2, Paul says that "the law of the Spirit of life in Christ Jesus has set me free ...." Here, the apostle declares that at long last that internal civil war struggle ended! What's more, when Paul got free, the biblical record makes it clear that he stayed free! But how did he do it? Explaining his victory requires understanding this law of the Spirit.

To understand what the law of the Spirit is we must recall the words that God spoke to two of his prophets more than seven hundred years before Bethlehem. God told Jeremiah and Ezekiel that one day he was going to give men a new heart and a new spirit that would have his laws written within. In promising this, God was really saying that men would have a new nature, a nature empowered to satisfy every demand of the law in a way that well-intentioned flesh could never do. As it turned out, this new nature was nothing less than the very life of Jesus (Colossians 3:4) indwelt by the Holy Spirit (Romans 8:2).

The lesson Paul finally learned is that it is one thing to *receive* the Holy Spirit, as every believer has (Romans 8:9); however, it is something quite different to have the life of the Spirit in him *released*. The release of the Spirit, which corresponds to the filling of the Spirit, means that the divine life within will flow out, unmixed with the dross and alloys of fleshly impurity. What will instead manifest is the very life of Jesus. And can that sin? Never!

This is why the Scripture says, "Walk in the Spirit and you shall not fulfill the lusts of the flesh" (Galatians 5:16). One dynamic eliminates the other. They don't mix.

36

Seeing the broader perspective, Stephen Charnock declared, "Christ came to take away sin, the guilt by his death, the filth by his Spirit ...."[12] By both these means sin is effectively removed.

Andrew Murray is right: "There are two lives—the self-life and the Christ-life; I must choose one of the two."[13] Making this precise point, Ruth Paxson contended:

> The Christian life is not merely a converted life, nor even a consecrated life, but it is a Christ-life. Christ is the Christian's center; Christ is the Christian's circumference; Christ is all in between. As Paul put it, "Christ is all in all."[14]

When we say that Christ's life has come into us to displace our life, we do not mean that the believer's faculties are somehow suspended and that his personality has been banished. We simply mean that when the Spirit fills, the very character qualities that pulsate in the heart of Jesus become operative in us: his love, his peace, his joy, his desire to please the Father, his desire to minister to others and, above all, his desire to worship. All this begins to flow in a way that human gusto and gumption could never produce.

"God's way of working," wrote Hannah Whitall Smith, "is to get possession of the inside of a man, to take the control and management of his will, and to work it for him. Then obedience is easy and a delight ...."[15] Our will is finally exercised only at the impulse of God's will (Philippians 3:13), which the Holy Spirit propels.

John Hunter compared "the law of sin and death" with the downward pull of gravity, and "the law of the Spirit of life in Christ Jesus" with the law of aerodynamics. Mr. Hunter explained: "The law of gravity will fight hard to hold the huge plane on the ground. But the power put forth from the four jets will bring into operation the new law of aerodynamics."[16] One would never think that a tube of metal weighing 150 tons could ever glide in the air. But even a universal law such as gravity can be reversed if a greater law supersedes it.

Interestingly, the Holy Spirit, who is the Bearer of Jesus' life, is also called "the Spirit of holiness" (Romans

1:4). This unusual phrase tells us not only that the Third Person of the Godhead is holy, but also that all holiness that finds its place in us originated with him. Therefore, if we don't want another inning of sinning, we're going to have to recognize that the supreme need of the Christian life is this release of the Holy Spirit.

Such a release—which will happen suddenly, not gradually—will become an ongoing, very dramatic experience in which you will actually feel the presence of Another inside you. You will know that what is coming out of you didn't originate with you, nor will it consummate with you. It came instead from God—fully tested by Jesus, approved by the Father, and borne by the Holy Spirit, who is also the energizer of its release. Charles Finney wrote, "The soul never in any instance obeys in a spiritual and true sense, except it be thus influenced by the indwelling Spirit of Christ."[17]

It is only under this governance by the Holy Spirit that the life of obedience is possible. All other approaches—however well-intentioned and naively undertaken—are doomed to fail. A. B. Simpson said, "The secret of pleasing God is to possess God, and let him possess you; for he gives what he commands and enables for that which he requires."[18]

It is this great fact that the apostle finally came to learn. But he never would have learned it had he kept believing what everyone else was believing, that knowing how to be good was easy. It wasn't until Paul concluded he was on the wrong road, and that he really didn't know how to be good, that God could finally get his revelation to this man—a revelation that answered a question that most people never ask how am I to be good?

Not until this question gets asked, and asked with an intensity that has to have an answer, can God's answer become a life-giving revelation. Should the question never come, or if it does come makes only an intellectual inquiry, then the answer will remain unknown.

The critical point not be overlooked, though, is this: No one—absolutely no one—will *ever* ask this question until finally it becomes clear just how high the standard is, how formidable the enemy is, and how weak and wicked the self-life is. Indeed,

- it is not until we see that the standard is sky high and that God will never lower it or grade on a curve,

- and not until we see how cruel and cunning the enemy is and how he, with great ease, has ensnared even the greatest of God's prophets,

- and not until we see how self has no defenses of its own against the onslaught of this enemy, that we will finally see our need with a clarity that causes us to cry out with that strange mixture of desperation and determination, "How am I to be good?"

Yes, only *then* can we join the great apostle on a road that we, like he, never knew existed. It is, in fact, the only road that leads to a God-pleasing obedience, with all of its accompanying joys and unrivaled blessings.

So is this the road you are now on? Or are you just learning about this road? If the latter response is true of you, it's time to get off the road you've been on. For the obedience Jesus requires is impossible without the Holy Spirit's filling. Which is exactly why this teaching on obedience mentions the Holy Spirit first.

Pursuing obedience is a doomed venture unless the Holy Spirit releases his righteousness with supernatural power. The fickle and flawed righteousness we crank out has already been exposed by Scripture and exploited by Satan. Yet this pattern need not continue even one more day! For there's another way to live, about which most believers do not know, but now you do!

And you'll know it even better as the Holy Spirit enables this revelation to shine with increased brightness into your life—to the point revelation becomes motivation, and motivation becomes operation.

Reflection Questions

1. Have you experienced the struggle Paul discussed in Romans, chapter 7? Please explain.

2. Have you thought, like most people have, that you know how to be good and that knowing how isn't your problem?

3. What did you learn from this chapter that you didn't know before?

4. Have you experienced a setting free by the "law of the Spirit"? If so, please share your testimony?

Chapter 3

Heaven's Hope—Part I

When it comes to altering behavior or motivating change, studies show the carrot is better than the stick and that rewarding is more effective than punishing. While the consequences that deter do have merit, greater motivation is generated by a hope that inspires. It is indeed hope that most effectively summons our best efforts—much more so than any punishment, threatened or applied.

As the Bible uses this word, hope is not a synonym for a wish—some lame, vain, wouldn't-it-be-nice outcome about which we have no assurance. Instead, hope is a robust word invigorated with unimpeachable integrity. What the Lord promised, this integrity guarantees, the Lord will fulfill.

And just here may we ask: Is there *any* promise that exceeds what the Bible says of heaven? The prospect of a better job, a nicer house, a new circle of friends, or even that long-awaited dream vacation can hardly compare with eons of continual bliss and uninterrupted joy. Contemplating such a future, A.W. Tozer wrote:

> The true Christian may safely look forward to a future state that is as happy as perfect love wills it to be. Since love cannot desire for its object anything less than the fullest possible measure of enjoyment for the longest possible time, it is virtually beyond our power to conceive of a future

as consistently delightful as that which Christ is preparing for us.[1]

Think of it! To be in the presence of Jesus and out of the presence of sin has to be profoundly better than any hope this world has to offer. John Wesley said, "I am a creature of a day, soon to drop into eternity; I want to know one thing, the way to heaven."

Upon gaining this knowledge, and then treasuring the assurance it affords, our time in this world will be viewed in a radically different way. Chief among these altered perspectives is this: The person rightly assured of heaven will not have an addiction to the pleasures of earth.

While heaven's hope does provide a powerful motivation for obedience, what is also true is that a hope not contemplated—indeed, a hope practically forgotten—will exert little-to-no motivation for change. And this is precisely the status into which the hope of heaven has fallen today.

Dave Hunt points out: "No matter how beautiful, peaceful, and joyful someone believes heaven may be, rare is the person for whom it is *desirable* until death can no longer be postponed."[2] G.D. Watson certainly thought this to be the case when he wrote a century earlier, "The great body of nominal believers never think about obtaining a soul fitness for heaven till the hour of death."[3] One commentary on Matthew's Gospel further addresses this same point:

> How many people are there who never thought of heaven until someone died? So long as they were prosperous, and life smiled, they were content. They had no need of another world and no eyes to see it, for it takes need to give us the eyes.[4]

Goethe, the great German writer, practically sanctioned this postponement of thought when he wrote, "We may well leave the next world to reveal itself to us in due time, since we will soon enough be there and know all about it. Leave the next world to reveal itself in due time!"[5] Instinctively, though, we know Goethe's advice can't be correct. Yet, it may be the advice most people follow.

In his book, *Mere Christianity*, C.S. Lewis acknowledged:

> Most of us find it very difficult to want heaven at all—except in so far as "heaven" means meeting again our friends who have died. One reason for this difficulty is that we have not been trained: our whole education tends to fix our mind on this world ....[6]

But Tozer said, "... if we believers were as spiritual as we ought to be, we might be looking forward to death with a great deal more anticipation than we do."[7] Amplifying this thought, Tozer wrote: "... the difference between a believer living on this earth or being promoted into the presence of Christ is the difference between 'good' and 'far better.'"[8]

This deficit in our training—wherein we fixate our focus on this world, keeping heaven out of view—can hardly find scriptural support. For the first thing Jesus spoke about was heaven (Matthew 5:3). And when it came to the end, the biblical record makes it clear that heaven was still on his mind (Matthew 28:18). In fact, in the fourteenth chapter of John's gospel, where Jesus provided ten motivations for obedience, we see that after this stipulation about the Spirit's strength came this subsequent emphasis on heaven's hope.

Most of us, at some time or another, are bound to ask the questions: What will become of me after death? Will I cease to exist? Will I spin out into oblivion? Will I remain buried in yonder grave? Will I spend an endless eternity in physical pain? Will I go to heaven? The weight of these questions far exceed whimsical wondering; these questions need answers.

But to not even ask them raises concerns about how such density of mind and vacuity of thought can be so oblivious to the obvious. In his book, *Pensees*, published eight years after his death, Pascal wrote:

> Nothing is so important to man as his own state, nothing is so formidable to him as eternity, and thus it is not natural that there should be men

43

indifferent to the loss of their existence, and to the perils of everlasting suffering.[9]

Completely unnatural though it be, Pascal then described a man "who spends so many days and nights in rage and despair for the loss of office, or for some imaginary insult to his honor" and yet "knows without anxiety and without emotion that he will lose all at death." How can this be?

For his part, Pascal couldn't hide his astonishment: "It is a monstrous thing to see in the same heart at the same time this sensibility to trifles and this strange insensibility to the greatest objects. It is an incomprehensible enchantment and a supernatural slumber ...."[10]

In one sense, wrong answers studiously considered, have much more merit than a complete lack of consideration due to disinterest. Because doesn't Scripture compel a man to think? Paul, for example, bid believers to think about the possibility of no historical resurrection. "If Christ be not risen from the grave," Paul hypothesized in theoretical candor, "then we are of all men most miserable." For if there is no resurrection, and hence no heaven, hopelessness becomes the believer's only valid option.

Bertrand Russell well described such hopelessness when he wrote:

> No fire, no heroism, no intensity of thought and feeling can preserve an individual beyond the grave ... all the labors of the ages, all the devotion, all the inspiration, all the noonday brightness, are destined to extinction in that vast death of the solar oyotcm ... the whole temple of man's achievement must inevitably be buried beneath the debris of a universe in ruins.[11]

Glaciers of gloom will chill the landscape of any person who sets aside Scripture, the Savior, and the supernatural—all of which Bertrand Russell in fact did. No one can be happy if this philosophy is accepted. We will either amend the philosophy or the philosophy will end us.

A life of utter meaninglessness is virtually uninhabitable to the thinking man, offering no domicile for his spirit and no reward for his labors. However, when Jesus came to this world, he heralded the certainty and enormity of heaven's blessings.

In his book, *Whatever Happened to Heaven?* the author Dave Hunt declared:

> One cannot read the New Testament without seeing its heavenly orientation. Heaven was continually on the heart of our Lord and it was the context for everything he taught the disciples. He made it clear that he was calling them to turn their attention and affection and interest from this world to heaven, from what had been their earthly home and hope to his "Father's house" from whence he had come and to which he would soon take them.[12]

Following this precedent and pattern, the emphasis on heaven must be restored in the hearts of believers today, for whom it was intended to bring an enormous courage—even the courage to obey.

The Place

If I were going to make a big move to some faraway place, I would want to know as much as I could about that place—in advance! For me, occasional speculations would never do! I would want answers to such questions as: What does this new home of mine look like? What are the people like who live there? What will I do once I get there? The reason I would ask these and other questions is because any move across a continent, or across an ocean, is bound to change my circumstances, my relationships, in fact my entire outlook on life.

So what would it be like to move to a place so far away no boat or plane could get you there? And what would it be like to stay in that place—not for months, years, or decades—but for multiplied millennia? Can you imagine how life-altering this would be? Thoughts like these have to peak

45

one's interest in heaven! "But wait a minute!" the skeptic might interrupt to challenge. "How do we know that heaven really exists? No one has ever come down from there, or back from there, to tell us about it!"

In his book, *The Case for Biblical Christianity*, E.J. Carnell acknowledged this perspective when he wrote:

> Scoffers dismiss the hope of heaven as an innocent but fruitless projection of wishful thinking. They grant that it would be nice to think that good people have nothing to fear, but where is the evidence for this belief? Jesus has come and gone, and things continue as they were from the beginning.[13]

However, those who speak this way (and unfortunately many do) have to be put on notice. Because in Acts 7:55 we are told that Stephen looked steadfastly into heaven; and when he did so he saw Jesus standing on the right hand of God. Moreover, II Corinthians 12:2 tells of Paul being caught up in the third heaven.

Paul's words here hardly support the Mormon assertion that heaven is divided three ways—the terrestrial, telestial, and celestial, each representing in a lesser-to-greater degree the blessings of heaven. No, in biblical cosmology the first heaven is where the birds fly; the second heaven is where the sun, moon and stars orbit; and the third heaven is where God lives. It is certainly possible that when Paul was stoned at Lystra, he had his homecoming to heaven reversed, whereupon he returned to earth to complete his mission.

Further credentialing the doctrine of heaven are the assertions Jesus made. In John 3:13, Jesus referred to himself as "he who came down from heaven." In John 6:12, Jesus said it flat-out, "I came down from heaven." So there you have it, from the lips of our Lord: He came from heaven!

Now, heaven, as Jesus speaks of it here, isn't a temporary stopover, a resting place for those about to be recycled to earth. The doctrine of reincarnation may reward the good turtle who tried to cross the interstate with, say, a future life as a philosopher; but before Jesus was born, he—ever and always had lived in heaven, higher than the highest in all of creation, the recipient of adoring worship from throngs of angels—ever the beloved of God! In Revelation 1:18, Jesus speaks to John from heaven, saying, "I am he that lives and was dead ...." He came from heaven. He returned to heaven. His place of departure became his destination.

You see, all the grave diggers in the world couldn't dig a hole deep enough to bury eternal life. And all the coffin makers in the world couldn't construct a coffin formidable enough to contain eternal life. Therefore—because of what Stephen saw, Paul experienced, and Jesus testified to—this teaching about heaven is more than wishful thinking or mere speculation. The doctrine of heaven is rooted in reliable, infallible, eyewitness testimony.

Heaven ... what is it like? Is it just a state of mind? No, not merely that, because Jesus said, "I go to prepare a *place* for you ...." In rebuttal to this supposed literalism, some people contend, "But wasn't Jesus simply continuing the myth popular in his day?" And the immediate and decisive answer to that question is—no, he was not, for in this same verse Jesus ruled that idea out when he said, "... if it were not so, I would have told you" (John 14:2).

Jesus *wasn't* limited to first-century Palestinian thought. If there weren't an actual place called heaven, then Jesus would have corrected what was popularly believed, just as he had been faithful to do with other topics wrongly perceived by men. Heaven, therefore, *is* a place!

W.A. Criswell, formerly the pastor of First Baptist Church in Dallas, wrote:

> There are some who say that heaven is "a state of mind," "a fancy," "a dream," "an abstraction," "an idea," "wishful thinking," "a figure," "a sentiment." But, the Bible testifies that heaven is as real as the home in which you live and the city in which you dwell.[14]

Those who tell us that we shouldn't think of heaven as being "up" or "down" seem to forget that those who saw

Jesus depart this world saw him go up. The biblical record doesn't say that Jesus, standing on the Mount of Olives, suddenly vanished. Theoretically, that could have been the report. But instead we are told that five hundred people saw Jesus ascend into the clouds; and that while they were gazing up, two angels spoke, saying that in the same way Jesus left he would return. So, whatever amending thoughts valid science may offer, its validity will be impeached if the conclusion set forth speaks of heaven as another dimension and therefore not a place.

The Excitement of a City

In describing the place called heaven, the Bible presents two contrasting pictures.[15] One picture is that of a stimulating city offering lots of things to do (Revelation 21:2). To me, this picture of a city is a lot better than that one which has a believer floating on a cloud with a harp! The ethereal, antiseptic heaven of Hollywood—where everyone walks slowly, rotates their heads mechanically, stares their weird "other worldly" stares and speaks somber profundities in a whispered monotone—is not a place where I want to go! Far preferable to me would be God's busy, bustling city booming with life!

In Revelation 3:12, we find Jesus calling heaven "the city of my God." This appellation conveys affection, pride, a sense of belonging—something million dollar ad campaigns try to stir up, only to see their promotion diluted by the harsher realities of life, such as drugs, traffic, and crime.

Problems such as these won't ever plague God's city, though, because Revelation 21:2 calls it "a holy city." Now, if that isn't a contradiction in terms! A holy city ... where? When we think of the city, we think of shady politicians, bribable policemen, the sleazy halls of prostitution, and those dark alleys where gang members hide out.

Can you imagine a city where no evil is going on—where there are no judges, no jails, and nothing punitive, restraining, and remedial? Can you imagine a city where everyone has the joy of the Lord, where everyone is filled with the Spirit, and where everyone has an overflowing love toward other people?

48

It is no wonder Jesus spoke of this place with such great affection!

Hebrews 3:14 speaks of heaven as "a continuing city." In other words, it's not one of those cities with relics and remnants that speak of a past glory, a city that time has passed by but the tourists still visit. The reason there will never be any merchandising of memorabilia in this city is because there won't be any decay or deterioration in this city! Other cities may have to consult the dusty past to find what was best about their city, but this one never will! Heaven is as remarkable today as it was in the beginning.

Revelation 21:21 tells us the streets of this city are made of pure gold. Literally? Maybe, but probably not. Remember, gold is said to be the king of metals, that which has the greatest value. Could it be, then, that by using this metaphor of gold, God was saying, that for which you and I will pay an exorbitant price—and then preserve with fastidious care and display with infectious pride—doesn't even compare with what heaven has to offer? Why, we paved our streets with that stuff!

Scripture likens this old world of ours and all it has to offer to a footstool. Of course, a footstool is hardly a cherished piece of furniture. By looking at it, one would never be able to guess what the mansion or the rest of the estate looked like.

Expanding this thought for our benefit, John Bate wrote these words:

> Let a man take a survey as far, as wide, as deep and as minute as his mind will enable him of the beauties, the sublimities, and the magnificence of all the works of God, and of man, as they lie out on the broad surface and in the great depths of the earth, and ask, if such are the glories which compose and enshrine the footstool and the vestibule, what must the glories be which adorn and compose the palace—the abode of his throne? If the workmanship of the outer court is so superb, what must that be which is exhibited in heaven itself? [16]

That part of the created order we are privileged to see is immensely impressive! Language often fails us when it comes to describing what we see in nature. At best, our words can suggest enough to encourage the reader to supply his or her's own imagination to envision the reality we're trying to describe. So what sensations will we experience when we finally see with our own eyes all that heaven has to offer? Pretty exciting, right? The city!

The Bible also tells us that gates will surround the city. Commenting on these gates, John MacArthur writes:

> The existence of gates implies that people are able to leave and enter the city. Don't think the city *contains* us. It will be our home, but we will not be confined there. We will have the infinite universe to travel, and when we do, we will go in and out through those gates.[17]

What an adventure that will be! There are many people who would have loved to travel extensively while on earth but money or time didn't allow them to do so. There should be no great regret about this, however, because travel itineraries we earthlings can't even imagine will be ever available to us in ages to come! So—just one more highlight in the city of God!

The Contentment of the Garden

There is another picture of heaven different from the first one we just considered. This picture is more rural, rustic, bucolic, and beautiful. The pastoral charm of the countryside is depicted in Scripture with enchanting appeal.

Whenever people conjure up their visions of paradise, their visions never include honking horns, frantic work schedules, an ornery public, and merchants shouting their wares. Instead, a quieter scene is envisioned—not unlike the place where it all began in the Garden of Eden.

Luxuriant foliage, chirping birds, the smell of springtime in the air with just the right mix of the sun's warmth and the coolness provided by a gentle breeze! As Charles Finney put it, "Its rivers and flowers and fruits combine everything that can regale the senses and charm the taste."[18] Ah, to be able to lay back and absorb into your soul the beauty of all that surrounds you—swaying trees, rippling streams, the animals at play.[19] Why, this is more like it! *This* ministers to you! Wouldn't it be great to stay *here*?

As in the Garden of Eden (Genesis 2:10), the Bible tells us that in heaven, too, there will be a river, a river of life that refreshes and nurtures and gladdens. In John's gospel, Jesus makes a contrast between the waterholes of this world (which in time dry up and can never in any sustained way satisfy) with God's river of living water (John 4:13,14; 7:37, 38). But to appreciate better the meaning conveyed by this contrast, you might want to ask yourself this question: What percentage or portion of your life is mere existence, as opposed to abundant life? How often are you treading water, clocking in time, and operating on instinct, versus being touched by God, used by God, and drawn by God into soul-satisfying fellowship with him? Could it be that you and I are far better acquainted with existence than we are with life?

Well, consider the opposite of this: What if every moment of our lives throbbed with meaning, pulsated with joy, so there was no humdrum existence? This is exactly what the River of Life has to offer.

Also in heaven, we are told, is the Tree of Life (Revelation 22:2), which like the river we just described was similarly represented in Eden. You will recall that the psalmist likened the godly man to a tree planted by the river of life which brings forth fruit (Psalm1:3). Now, if this fruit constitutes the nine character qualities spoken of in Galatians—love, joy, peace, patience, etc. (Galatians 5:22, 23)—that would have to mean that there won't be any inner turmoil or any strained relationships in heaven, since the ceaseless partaking of this fruit would prevent all that.

Back in Genesis, chapter 3, we find a most unusual verse, at least in terms of its Hebrew grammatical structure. This verse has God speaking after the fall, after man's banishment from the garden, and just before the angels had been stationed with their flaming swords east of Eden. Verse 22 reports God to have said this regarding man: "And now lest he put out his hand and take also of the tree of life, and eat, and live forever—"And there the verse stops, an incomplete sentence, the abhorrent thought too awful to contemplate, much less to articulate!

Had this verse continued, it would have said something like this: What if sinful man somehow got access to this tree and then *in that condition* lived on and on forever? What a perplexing, painful prospect! In contemplating it, you might want to ask yourself: Would you want your present life to last forever, or would something around threescore and ten sound better to you? For many of us, taking the good with bad isn't an arrangement we want continued.

In contemplating this question further, perhaps you would have to admit that one or more areas in your life are gradually getting worse. While the deterioration may be imperceptible to you and perhaps to others as well, what do you suppose these faults are going to look like in a thousand years? In a million years? In two million years? Like a monster, that's what! And that's why God sent the angels, the fire, and the swords! It was due to this very fact: For sinful people to live forever would be disastrous!

The garden—a place of restful repose for those who have been redeemed from sin and self and can now partake of this unguarded and ever available tree. You want the fruit of love? Yes, it is yours! You want the fruit of joy? Yes, that is also yours! You want the fruit of peace? By all means! This and much more are yours to enjoy as you partake of the fruit from the Tree of Life.[20]

What is especially good about this place called heaven is that we won't have to choose between the stimulation of the city and the relaxation of the country. The respective appeals of each are both going to be ours, since there is going to be a coordinated rhythm between the two—the energy and excitement of the city, and the tranquility and serenity of the country.

As you meditate on heaven, contemplating its reality and endless joys, what stirrings of heart occur? Are you less frantic to grab this world's goodies and more inclined to make decisions from heaven's point of view? Is your approach to temptations different? Your stamina for trials upgraded? The setting of your affections on things above more consistent? And is your determination to please Jesus locked in?

No doubt, with assurances of heaven encouraging, you can accelerate your strides toward obedience, bypassing every detour that once sidetracked you.

We will continue our meditation on heaven in the next chapter with an agenda to let heaven's hope topple every rival to lordship and to elevate every desire that has heaven for its source.

Some may wonder if heaven is too good to be true, but, let me ask you, if there were no heaven, would you believe that God is true? A perfect God with a perfect heaven makes perfect sense! And thankfully Scripture fortifies this belief with impressive testimony.

What we must continue to consider, though, is how we can obey God more perfectly than we do. And in this regard, our vision of heaven should be kept in the center of our thinking. The primary reason being: Many motivations for obedience are based on heaven.

So, as with Jesus when he was on earth, it should also be true of us: We do what we do on earth with heaven on our mind.

Reflection Questions

1. Prior to reading this chapter, did you think about heaven very much?

2. After reading this chapter, will you think about heaven more frequently?

3. What images of heaven mean the most to you?

Chapter 4

Heaven's Hope—Part II

Whenever temptation tries to sink its hooks, we are more likely to take the bait if the lure seems near while heaven seems far away. This is no surprise, because how one frames the picture usually predicts the outcome. If we frame it so we see only the immediate, we'll react one way. But if we frame it with an eternity perspective, we'll react differently.

By enticing our souls with God's picture of heaven—as a city and as a garden—we experience the strong surge of hope needed to clarify the desirability of heaven and thereby sustain our pursuit of it.

Of course, it isn't just the place of heaven that will satisfy so immensely but also the people of heaven. Thomas Watson wrote, "In the kingdom of heaven, we shall have sweet society with glorified saints."[1] Writing in the twelfth-century, Bernard of Cluny gave thought to the social joys of heaven, saying:

> I know not, oh, I know not
> What social joys are there.
> What radiance of glory,
> What joy beyond compare.

On earth, we also seem not to know this—not because imagination fails us, but because our heart does. Lamenting this fact, G.D. Watson wrote:

One of the sorrows that comes to a humble and tender heart in this life is the clash of religious souls, the misunderstandings and strife between those who really love Jesus, and the scarcity of broadhearted and intelligent charity and fellowship. "We shall know each other better when the mists have cleared away."[2]

The Bible says that we shall know even as we are known. According to Watson, this means there will be "the mutual, whole-hearted appreciation of each other's character and history, and of the variety of graces and gifts."[3] Anticipating this happy day, Watson declared, "No imagination we now have can calculate the delicate and multiplied joys we shall have in heaven, flowing out from the appreciation of all the varieties of the saints of all ages."[4]

J.C. Ryle extended this thought when he wrote:

We shall see apostles, prophets, patriarchs, martyrs, reformers, missionaries, and ministers, of whom the world was not worthy. We shall see the faces of those we have known and loved in Christ on earth, and over whose departure we shed bitter tears.

We shall see them more bright and glorious than they ever were before. And best of all, we shall see them without hurry and anxiety, and without feeling that we only meet to part again. In glory there is no death, no parting, no farewell![5]

Isn't that good? And just think: When these relationships are restored, our love for each other, due to our glorified status, will greatly increase.

According to Chrysostom, the fourth-century archbishop who was known as the "golden-mouthed orator," believers "shall have such a resplendence of beauty on them that the angels shall fall in love with them."[6] This glory within shall even manifest physically, making our reunion with loved ones far sweeter than we ever imagined.

The ultimate blessing, obviously, will be seeing God, in whose presence we will more immediately and intimately dwell. G.D. Watson said that all else "are but twilight joys, are but the outer fringes of earthly bliss, compared with that ecstatic awe, the ineffable gladness of seeing the face of God."[7]

"To see the face of God," Watson declared, "... is the climax of all vision in the universe. Nothing in creation can surpass or equal the seeing of the face of God."[8] And so it was for good reason that Thomas Watson declared, "The soul is never satisfied till it has God for its portion, and heaven for its haven."[9]

Since heaven is a physical, geographical, identifiable place, and since the citizens of heaven are both totally changed and completely contented (their employment being their enjoyment), what practical implications does this splendid scene offer us today?

Actually, the implications it provides, instead of being secondary in scope, are of primary importance. For the biblical view of heaven will vitalize vision, encourage effort, promote purity, and develop discipline. Briefly, let's examine each of these benefits in turn.

Vitalizing Vision

Ephesians 2:6 says that the believer on earth has already been raised to sit in heavenly places in Christ Jesus. As such, the throne privileges the believer has are more than enough to make a lasting impact on our world.

To be sitting in heavenly places means to have access to the astounding resources of God. What kind of resources, you ask? In Ephesians, chapter 1, the Spirit of God answered this question in a way that shocks our sensibilities even as it excites our faith.

Verse 19 introduces this subject when it talks about the greatness of God's power. Verse 20 clarifies this greatness when it says it is the same power that raised Jesus from the dead. Verse 21 then says this power is far greater than what all the demonic powers have. Verse 22 speaks of the victory Jesus and his church will have on earth. And verse 23 tops it off by saying that all of God is in us.

In writing these truths, Paul got so excited he wrote a sentence nine verses long! Almost breathlessly, the apostle lays it all out. One can almost see, upon reading this sentence, how fast Paul's pen must have been racing and how flushed his face must have been once he completed so inspiring a thought.

This elaboration on power is preceded with a request for wisdom, knowledge, revelation, understanding, and enlightenment. These stacked terms, each addressing a different aspect of knowing, are passionately petitioned so believers could get the blinders off so as to see more clearly what God has called us to. Because if we don't see it—and indeed many Christians today do not—then what could have been, and should have been, will not and cannot happen. Instead of moving in the flow of God's vision and operating in the power of God's resources, Christians will be wandering this earth with a vague sense God has something for them to do. But for reasons unknown to them, they can't figure out what it is.

Vision determines everything! Our life will be no more, and no less, than the vision we have. Our goals, our methods, our relationships, our circumstances, how we see ourselves, how we solve problems—in fact, all that constitutes life is decisively impacted by vision!

So what if our eyes did get opened, and what if we did have this mind-convicting, heart-motivating, vision-lifting perspective of sitting in heaven right now—so connected to the Lord of glory that we knew his death-defying, demon-defeating, kingdom-establishing powers were ours to use—would that make a difference? Do you suppose with this vision gripping our lives we might be dreaming different dreams, and making different plans?

I should say so! Instead of looking up hopelessly whenever something intimidating challenged us, we, composed and courageous, would be looking down with that more-than-conqueror's spirit.

Scripturally, this vitalizing of vision is premised on the fact there *is* a heaven. Take that factor out of the equation and nothing else Paul said in this passage would be true. The foundational premise is: The clearer our thinking, the more we realize how important heaven is and why other blessings require its eternal existence.

Encouraging Effort

A second contribution of the heavenly perspective is that it encourages effort. Scripture amplifies this truth in I Corinthians, chapter 15, by discussing the resurrection of the believer and our subsequent entrance into heaven. Having once set forth these twin truths, this chapter concludes by saying, "Be steadfast, unmovable, always abounding in the work of the Lord, for as much as you know that your labor is not in vain in the Lord" (I Corinthians 15:58).

The challenge of diligent and dedicated labor is given here because nothing better stimulates someone to this kind of faithfulness than a strong vision of heaven.[10] You've heard the complaint that some people are so heavenly-minded they are no earthly good. Well, history offers a different testimony. The documented past proves that the people who valued the next life most made the greater contributions to this life. A Christian never works so well, or fights so valiantly, than when he or she is captured by a strong hope for heaven.

But to live life with such impact and purpose, E.M. Bounds insisted:

> The Christian soldier must put heaven strongly in his head and heart. He must see heaven, feel heaven, and keep heaven in the heart at all times. He will stand with unsteady step if heaven seems far off. He will fight feebly if heaven is dimly seen. [But][11] the full sight of heaven will give strength to his loins, zeal to his faith, glory to his future, and victory to his present.[12]

One man who knew this truth well was David Brainerd, an eighteenth-century missionary to the Indians in upper state New York. Braving an inhospitable forest where diseases and other dangers lurked, David Brainerd launched out where few dared to go. In doing all this, he died before his thirtieth birthday—but not before exhibiting a passion that exceeded his peril! Onward was his direction because upward was his perspective.

So what exactly kept him going when the temptations to quit were many and severe? We are not left to guess. David Brainerd wrote a journal documenting his innermost thoughts. This journal, never intended for human eyes, has become a devotional classic today, largely through the efforts of Jonathan Edwards, who was David Brainerd's father-in-law (and in whose home David Brainerd died).

You may feel uneasy about reading someone's private journal, but the great Jonathan Edwards interpreted the propriety of doing so when he had this journal published. In one journal entry, David Brainerd wrote: "... my soul longed for an arrival in the heavenly country, the blessed paradise of God. Through divine goodness I have scarce seen the day for two months, in which death has not looked so pleasant to me."[13] So inspired by this vision of heaven, David Brainerd gave himself even more nobly to the conversion of what other people called "savages."

In reading a daily account of his life, we are struck by these repeated references to heaven, such as this one: "My thoughts were much in eternity where I love to dwell." Now by putting this in the present tense, we are made to know how real heaven was to David Brainerd. The reason these meditations could rally his heart is because, as E. M. Bounds once put it, "An eternal heaven of unsullied purity, of unalloyed bliss through endless years, is a doctrine which enables man and honors God."[14]

The journey to heaven isn't easy, especially when God takes us down character-building roads we never would have chosen. J.C. Philpot, the nineteenth-century English preacher, described the journey God plans, which in some ways we would rather not take:

> We are willing to walk to heaven; but not to walk there in God's way. Though we see in the Scripture that the path to glory is a rough and rugged way; yet when our feet are planted in that painful and trying path, we shrink back; our coward flesh refuses to walk in that road. God

therefore, as a sovereign, brings those afflictions upon us which he sees most fit for our profit and his glory, without ever consulting us, without ever allowing us a choice in the matter. And he will generally cause our afflictions to come from the most unexpected source, and in a way most cutting to our feelings—in the way that of all others we would least have chosen—and yet in a way which of all others is most for our profit.[15]

The question, then, is this: Will we accept the cross applied to our life and let it become the master-passion of our life? We said we would when we agreed soon after our conversion to take up the cross. But is that our position still? Are we today experiencing higher levels of Christ's risen life because we have consented to lower levels of his crucified life?

F.J. Huegel wrote:

... if we have built upon some other foundation; if we have hardened our hearts to the irresistible wooings of Golgotha; if we have been unwilling to accept its eternal verities regarding God and sin; if the awful plunge of the God-Man into the abysmal ocean of human woe has not moved us to true repentance; if we have not joined the universal chorus that sings the praise of the Crucified—could heaven mean anything to us? Would we be out of place?[16]

The reciprocal dynamics of dying and rising will cycle through at God's direction, and at some point with our permission, thus fashioning for the believer the very life the resurrection intended to produce. This sanctioned suffering of God is one, F.B. Meyer said, that "looks a hundred times into the abyss, and suddenly sees angels sitting."[17] Is this your experience, too? Or does such talk seem altogether foreign to what you have known?

As we think about our current progress and how our life measures up with the biblical mandate given in I

Corinthians 15, we have to ask ourselves: Are we steadfast, or are we pretty quick to quit? Are we unmovable, or do we embrace all these ready-made excuses for flitting about? Are we abounding in the Lord's work, or are our efforts more token and occasional?

G.D. Watson said, "Notice how children in their play will begin a dozen enterprises in a day and leave them all unfinished at night."[18] But the child of God with heaven on his heart won't live his life with fits and starts, with sudden enthusiasm followed by aborted efforts. So, again, the question: Have we matured enough in the Lord to remain steadfast?

If these questions stab us with conviction and leave us stuttering unsatisfactory replies, then we should consider the turnaround factor of the heavenly vision; for this alone is able to motivate a steadfast, unmovable, abounding work for the Lord.

Tozer wrote with conviction on this point when he declared, "It may be said with certainty that Christians who have lost their enthusiasm about the Savior's promises of heaven-to-come have also stopped being effective in Christian life and witness in this world."[19] But this must not be!

Promoting Purity

The heavenly vision also helps believers in daily life because of its power to promote purity. In this regard, Philippians 3:19 characterizes enemies of the cross by saying, "Their end is destruction, whose god is their belly, and whose glory is their shame—who mind earthly things." Unfortunately, this capsule-like characterization fits not only the Hollywood jet-setter and the suicidal rock star, but also many people living in Middle America. These flesh-driven people, so controlled by their bodily appetites and their self-serving desires, are so tuned into earthly things they will compromise almost anything to get billboard recognition.

Titus 2:12 speaks of denying ungodliness and worldly lusts. Yet, how easy it is to be caught up in the value system of the world. For everywhere we turn—at school, where humanism is espoused; at home, where the immorality of TV desensitizes us; at work, where we see a generation lost to God—we are pulverized by worldliness, the very thing that Titus 2:12 says we are to resist. In the words of S. D. Gordon, "Temptation will come with the subtlety of a snake, with the rush of a storm, with the unexpected swiftness of a lightening flash."[20] So how are we to effectively resist?

Significantly, the next verse, Titus 2:13, says we are to be "looking for the blessed hope, and the glorious appearing of the great God and our Savior Jesus Christ." For it is as we look and long for him who is the essence of heaven that our hearts become enraptured by a reality superior to all the appeals of this world. Therefore, what once dazzled us with its glitter will soon seem yellow and tarnished when compared with the brighter prospects of heaven.

Amy Carmichael wrote, "He that shall be our bliss when we are there is our Keeper while we are here ...."[21] And this vision of heaven will help make it so!

Many people will struggle and strive against their flesh, hoping against hope to sedate—at least for a little while—the monster of self. In this same vein, they'll try to break free from their addictions to this world, even though their body-trembling, perspiration-producing withdrawal isn't at all easy. How much easier it would be, though, if heaven were in view! Because with heaven in view the self-life will shrink, and the world's temptations will diminish with far less struggle.

Thomas Goodwin, the great Bible expositor of the seventeenth century, put it succinctly: "The more thou desirest heaven, the more holy thy heart is ...."[22] The end-result is something which for a long time you never thought you would have—purity!

Along these same lines, a vision of heaven can greatly motivate the believer today to develop discipline. Romans 14:12 proclaims that each of us will give an account of our life before God. More specifically, II Corinthians 5:10 says believers will appear before the judgment seat of Christ, where we will be judged—not in terms of heaven or hell (because obviously that issue has already been settled), but in terms of how we lived our life after we became a Christian. Were we obedient? Were we attempting to please God? Were we extending faith? Were we depending on his Spirit? Our answers to these questions can be revealing.

Upon evaluating every word, deed, and thought expressed or experienced in our life, the Lord will then give rewards to those who earned them, rewards that will greatly determine what heaven will be like. G. D. Watson wrote, "We are saved by faith, but our rank in the kingdom of heaven, our future degree of blessedness, our crown, the size of our immortality will depend on our good works, including our good works toward God in obedience to him ...."[23]

As we think about the judgment that will come and the eternal heaven that awaits us, the discipline we exercise down here makes total sense. In his book, *Jesus, Author of Our Faith*, A.W. Tozer wrote:

> I can only hope that you are wise enough, desirous enough and spiritual enough to face up to the truth that every day is another day of spiritual preparation, another day of testing and discipline with our heavenly destination in mind. For as I hope you have already seen, full qualification for eternity is not instant or automatic or painless.[24]

Do understand that heaven won't be the same for every believer. The believer who lived a casual, carnal, careless life won't have the same capacities to enjoy heaven as does the believer who lived a self-denying, Spirit-filling, kingdom-enhancing life. True, while both believers will be happy, one believer will be much happier than the other.

Aware of these differences between Christians and their respective capacities in heaven, C. S. Lewis observed, "The joys of heaven are, for most of us in our present condition, 'an acquired taste'—and certain ways of life may render the life impossible of acquisition."[25] Also commenting on these differing capacities for enjoying heaven, Richard Baxter wrote:

> The eye of flesh is not capable of seeing, nor the ear of hearing, nor the heart of understanding

heaven and its glories. But there the eye, the ear, and the heart are made capable. Else how could we enjoy those things in heaven? The more perfect the sight, the more delightful will be the beautiful object. The more perfect the appetite, the sweeter the food. The more musical the ear, the more pleasant the melody, and the more perfect the soul, the more joyous these joys, and the more glorious these glories.[26]

When Jesus said that we could lay up for ourselves treasures in heaven (Matthew 6:20), he made it clear there was an investment we could make that wasn't susceptible to rust or robbery, one offering a greater return than any investment this world can generate. Therefore, if we have our eyes fixed on the greater gain promised by heaven, this objective to live obediently before the Lord won't be as hard to achieve as we first thought.

As good as heaven is, which language and current knowledge fail to apprehend, heaven can't be reduced to a travelogue for tourists. Heaven has a much greater attraction than that! Hence, Charles Spurgeon's testimony on this point bears repeating:

To be forever with the Lord is my idea of heaven at its best. Not the harps of gold, nor the clouds unfading, nor the light unfading, is glory to me; but Jesus, Jesus himself, and myself forever with him in nearest-and-dearest fellowship.[27]

It is the heart that wants this fellowship, and wants it now, that will turn away from anything that hurts this fellowship. To this kind of heart, the heart that loves Jesus and can think of heaven only in terms of being with him, obedience is easy.

By the way, it is in the fifteenth chapter of Revelation that we learn about the harp of God. G.D. Watson said, "The harp of God is the ability to praise God."[28] It is making melody in the heart, which the Holy Spirit enables (Ephesians 5:19), that composes and conducts this praise.

This melody, that begins on earth but flourishes uninterrupted in heaven, is the very fellowship Spurgeon extolled and Jesus desires.

Music for the Messiah! Songs for the Savior! Oh, to be in that place as a fervent worshipper! Finally, the deadly duality of conflicting desires will be over and the heart-purity we longed for will last.

Affirming the truth that Jesus did indeed prepare a place for us, James S. Stewart then asked, "But what if we are not prepared for the place?"[29] This is not a question to be sloughed off, or a question to be summarily dismissed soon after its introduction. For as we think about the heaven our rewards will enable—that realm of living where the enhanced capacities bestowed on us increase our eternal joy—at issue is not the preparation Jesus made for us on the cross, since that part of the preparation is settled and need not be called into doubt. At issue is the preparation we are making for the greater glories of heaven.

As we reflect on this, we must ask ourself: Is there Scripture-stipulated merit in our lives that God can reward? And is there the kind of discipline, and effort, and purity manifesting that pleases God?

It is, I submit, the hope for heaven that will get us prepared! Tozer acknowledged a view of heaven "where we are kind of glorified butterflies waving our wings gently in the zephyrs that flow down from the celestial mountains."[30] Such useless floating, though, won't happen there, and should not happen here if the preparation provided by God has its intended effect.

Instead, our "flight" will have an agenda, specific in direction and special in destination. Unlike all those other flights where people arrive exactly as they were when they departed, we will be changed—gloriously and eternally changed—becoming at last fully ready to meet our God!

Reflection Questions

1. What thoughts come to mind, what desires begin to develop in you, as you think about the social joys of heaven?

2. Which of the three motivations for obedience presented in this chapter appeals to you the most?

Chapter 5

Identity's Influence

As we consider all that God commands and all the Holy Spirit has personally prompted us to do, would we want to see the latest printout detailing our track record for obedience? Most of us would just as soon not face the record. The avoidance that kicks in does pose a question for us, though: For why is our obedience track record like this?

Imagine that in this coming week there were no compromises, no rationalizations, and no harboring of any secret sins but that we, filled with the Spirit and fed by the Word, were bold in our faith, passionate for souls, and zealous for good works. Now if somehow, some way, that happened next week, would next week be better than the week before? Of course, God would be pleased and others would be impressed, but the point is: Would *we* be happier? Far happier, right? A glow and gladness would radiate that weren't there before!

Well, then, if the life of obedience is much more satisfying than the life of disobedience, why was last week, and the weeks and months preceding it, the way they were? Another way to ask this same question is this: Why do we find ourselves perpetually trapped in a lifestyle we really don't want?

There are, no doubt, many answers to this question, answers Jesus supplied while on his way to die for our sins. What we're studying in this book, remember, is tested-in-the-battle truth. The blood sweat of Gethsemane convincingly proves that. The temptation to disobey wasn't deflected with supernatural ease that night, but was excruciatingly real. And yet, in the end, Jesus did prevail, and by so doing authenticated forever these ten strategies for obedience we are now attempting to understand.

The strategy that we will focus on in this chapter deals with the way self-image affects our obedience.

Your View of You

Do you know why most people never experience a sustained victory over sin? *It's because they never thought they would, and also because they never thought they could!* Having embraced that "what a worm am I" theology (which teaches that even after conversion the child of God is still a sinner), these people live what they believe. Those confessions declaring "I-sin-every-day become a self-fulfilling prophecy.

The axiom—if you see you as you, you will be you—isn't just a tease or a tautology, because the image you have of yourself is crucial to spiritual growth. What you see is precisely what you'll be! And it is for this reason God doesn't want you accepting an image of yourself based on past performance.

To think of yourself in terms of past decisions, habits, and failures is to neutralize the desired outcome of II Corinthians 5:17, which speaks of the believer becoming a new creation—and of old things having passed away, and of all things having become new!

So what passed away—just our sins? No, the very nature that produced those sins passed away. Romans 6:6 says the old man was crucified. Did you get that? Dead! Gone! Annihilated! Obliterated! So settle this in your thinking. Your old man doesn't exist anymore!

Is this what you believe to be true? Or have you been thinking that somehow your old man survived the crucifixion and didn't exactly die? Many people think they have both an old man and a new man. One reason they think this way is because Ephesians 4:22 tells us to put off the old man, thus prompting the obvious question: Why would Scripture tell us to put off what doesn't exist? This is a fair question. What this verse really means, however, is that we're not to allow the residue of past programming to weasel back into our lives, whose source, the old man, is now gone.

According to Martyn Lloyd-Jones, the infinitive "to put off" in verse 22 is one of result. That is, we are to act consistent with what Jesus accomplished at Calvary. Colossians 3:9 says, "... you have put off the old man with his deeds." Did you notice the words here? "Have!" *Past tense*! The spiritual schizophrenia that says you are part sinner, part saint doesn't come from Scripture. The Bible says something quite different: that you are a new creation— period!

Significantly, when referring to the old you, the Bible says "you died" (Colossians 3:2) and "were buried" (Romans 6:4). So this notion that the old you survived crucifixion, climbed out of the grave, and is yet alive today has to be inaccurate. The hyphenated, bifurcated humanity that assumes a Christian is both unregenerate and regenerate is not the teaching of Scripture, and really makes no sense.

If one contends the old nature dies later, at the time of our physical death, then it must be asked: Where does Scripture ever say that? And the answer is: Scripture never says that! The death of the old nature was achieved on the cross and then made applicable to the believer at the time of conversion. To say otherwise runs contrary to Scripture. Moreover, it inevitably burdens the believer with a low vision of the Christian life. This "half and half" stuff (old nature and new nature) becomes a self-fulfilling prophecy of chronic sin failure.

Nathaniel Hawthorne wrote a parable he titled "The Holocaust." This parable tells the story of an attempt to finally rid the world of all evil. In pursuit of this goal, men inspired by a holy zeal gathered to start a bonfire, into which every imaginable evil was cast.

The devil drew near, and viewed their work with much consternation. The fire grew! The smoke soared! And shouts of victory were heard near and far! As far as these people were concerned evil had become a thing of the past. But as the crowd walked away that night gloating over their success, the devil's face suddenly brightened. "I am not done yet," he declared. "They have forgotten one thing. They have forgotten to throw in the human heart."

But what those in this parable forgot, God did not forget. Because when Jesus went to the cross that day, he didn't just die *for* us, but he also died *as* us, thus terminating the Adamic nature that had sinned into existence what God never created. Unwilling to supplicate, negotiate, or indoctrinate that old nature of ours, God chose the more radical option: to terminate it!

Yet, it is obvious *something* inside the believer is causing a lot of problems. So if it's not the old man, what is it? It is what the Bible calls the flesh, or what might be rightly called our phantom self. Did you know that the Bible has more to say about the flesh than it does about the devil? Perhaps this is true because the flesh is capable of almost anything the old man is capable of. Unlike the devil, who isn't omnipresent, the flesh is always with us. And also, unlike the devil, the flesh is actually inside us. Proximity and constancy, therefore, make the flesh a formidable foe.

The flesh is a residue of the old nature, now vanquished and vanished. It is an alien sin force with which we must contend—but it not who we are, or even part who we are! This is why, when commenting on the misery of manifesting sin, Paul twice said, "It is not I" (Romans 7:17, 20). Whereas the old nature totally defines a non-Christian (they are that and nothing but that), the flesh doesn't isn't in any way belong to the believer's true identity. It is alien to our identity.

There are at least two other distinctions between the old nature and the flesh. First, the old nature has no capacity for God (according to Romans 3:11, the old man isn't even looking for God), but the flesh *can* desire to please the Lord. Jesus acknowledged as much when he said the flesh is weak but the spirit is willing (Matthew 26:41). Jesus never denied the flesh could be willing; for, unlike the old nature, the flesh can be perfectly willing. While the flesh is obviously weak (in that it can't do what God desires), it *is* willing!

Peter's announcement that he would stand strong even if all the other disciples failed is an example of willing flesh.

Peter's subsequent betrayal of the Lord is an example of weak flesh.

Another discrepancy between the two—the old nature and the flesh—is this: Romans 6:6 declares that the old nature is extinct, but according to this verse the flesh isn't extinct. The Greek word for "destroyed" in this verse (referring to the body of sin, our flesh) simply means sidelined, put out of commission, or brought into remission. Unlike the old nature, the flesh is never rendered extinct; yet, it can be overcome by fillings of the Holy Spirit.

While ministering in the Upper Room where the Holy Spirit would later descend, Jesus spoke of our true identity in the most exalted, elevating way. In verse 17, Jesus said of the Holy Spirit that he "will be in you." In verse 20, Jesus said of himself, "... you will know that *I* am ... in you." And then in verse 23 Jesus said the *Father* is going to be in you, too. Do I understand what Jesus was saying? I understand it enough to be shocked!

According to A. W. Tozer: "The eternal plan was not to bring God down to man's level, but for the Son to take humanity up into God. Thus we are to be joined in the beauty and wonder of the theanthropic union—God and man in one."[1] Andrew Murray, supporting this point of view, similarly observed, "... God's one object was to dwell in man, making him partaker of his goodness and glory."[2]

Does this not astound you? That God became a man is a momentous miracle too unfathomable to comprehend. But that the story ends with humanity brought into the Godhead is an even greater miracle. Jesus' words in verse 20 illustrate the point, "... I am in My Father, and you in me, and I in you." Had these words come from any other lips, we would have dismissed them as heretical, thinking the relationship between Jesus and the Father is so infinitely beyond what we'll ever know, there's no way that *we* belong in this verse!

Colossians 2:19 declares that "in him (meaning Jesus) dwelt all the fullness of the Godhead bodily." This truth we can partially understand. But when Ephesians 3:19 speaks of believers being "filled with all the fullness of God," that reduces us to speechless wonder. How can this be? We, here on this earth, full of God?

Any attempt to explain the theanthropic union will certainly be inadequate, yet the fact remains that our new nature, what may be accurately called our real self, is nothing short of divine life (Colossians 3:4), in that the very character attributes of Jesus have been put into us. If this is what we received, the implications for obedience are huge.

A Paradigm Shift

Most believers view the Christian life as a ceaseless attempt to uproot bad habits, bad attitudes, and anything else offensive to God, and then through diligence and desire to replace all these with the righteousness of God. Hence, for many people, the Christian life is a step-by-step, principle-by-principle, obedience-by-obedience climb; until at some point, after a lot of knowing and doing, one is finally made conformable to the image of God.

It must be emphatically stated, however, that the Christian life is *not* a matter of us attempting what Jesus already achieved! To the contrary, the Christian life is *his* life—not just being revered by us, or imitated by us, but actually flowing through us!

In his book, *Forever Triumphant*, F. J. Huegel wrote:

> Give up the fight if in your own strength you have been struggling to gain a victory which you seem never quite able to achieve despite prayers and tears and effort and consecration ... You don't have to climb this stony, thorn-infested, unscalable mountain. You can begin at the top.[3]

And the reason you can begin there is because the perfect life of Jesus is already inside you! Ephesians 4:24 says the new man was created in righteousness and true holiness. Consequently, your job is not to duplicate what Jesus already did. Your job is to let the Holy Spirit release the life of Jesus already inside you.

In his book, *Limiting God*, John Hunter explained:

> ... my daily Christian life is a moment by moment experience of receiving Christ. Whatever

72

problem, fear, anxiety, temptation or frustration comes into my life, it isn't my job to meet it. My job is to expose the whole situation to Christ Jesus the Lord and then to walk believing that what he has promised he will perform.[4]

This doesn't mean being passive, as we put our lives on automatic pilot and sing out *que sera sera*. But it does mean we will believe for the Lord's wisdom and grace to flow in us, even as his life within us flows. This approach is very different from simply letting God help us. For God to offer help, as he did in the Old Testament, is one thing, but for the released life of the Lord to replace what had formerly been our life is quite another.

The doctrine of the new nature is at the heart of the New Testament. Dr. Charles Hodge, the nineteenth-century professor of theology from Princeton University, said, "The secret of holy living lies in the doctrine of the union of the believer with Christ."[5] For all the ideals to which we aspire are in that life, a life that serves not as a model but as a source.

Any attempt to replicate the virtues of that life through dedication and consecration will fail. Acknowledging this fact, Dr. Hodge explained that "we are made holy not by the force of conscience, nor of moral motives, nor by acts of discipline, but by being united to Christ ...."[6] A. B. Simpson fully agreed, saying, "This is still the secret of divine holiness. It is union with Jesus, abiding in Jesus, dependence upon Jesus every moment and for everything."[7]

This road to holiness, however, is not the road most Christians walk. Most Christians—instinctively, habitually— will try to do the best they can—and if their efforts appear to be coming up short, they'll then ask God to help. But, given the context of such prayers, this request puts the Lord in a dilemma: For if he does answer prayers like these, he'll be keeping those who asked him on the wrong road longer!

A vast portion of the church spends a lifetime on that road. Indwelling sin is a reality to them; the indwelling life of the Lord is not. Oh, they know the words, and would never attempt to debate them. But this knowing isn't experiential.

Releasing the New Nature

The alternative to fleshly obedience is the continual releasing of our new nature. Instead of trying to achieve a victory of our own, we are to recognize, in the words of Huegel, that "The Christian victory is nothing more nor less than the amen of faith to the great all-comprehensive victory which Christ consummated at Calvary."[8]

To attempt a victory on our own will result in a surface and shallow outcome, a victory that is cosmetic, at best. The appearance of victory may be impressive—from a distance! But a closer inspection will discover the ugly truth: Defeat is covered with mounds of caked and cracked Pharisaical makeup.

Ever aware of feeble attempts to fashion a victory of our own, Ruth Paxson asked:

> What is the real, inward meaning of "victory"? Well, it does not mean mere outward control over the expression of sin, but a definite dealing with the inner disposition of sin. Real victory makes a change in the innermost recesses of the spirit that transforms the inner disposition and attitude as well as our outward deed and act.[9]

This is a change no Christian can make, nor is called upon to make. Jesus already achieved victory for us when he gave us his nature, so why reinvent the wheel? Our need is to get what he already put in us released. It is not to attempt the doomed enterprise of changing our inner life through intense dedication.

So how does this new nature release happen? We know how it happens initially, through the baptism with the Holy Spirit, but how does it happen after that? The Scripture identifies three ways. First, by experiencing the presence of God; second, by extending our faith during a time of trial; and third, by letting our self-life die.

To understand the dynamics in view here, let's further examine each of these ways. There's some unpacking that needs to be done, if clouds of confusion are to be dispelled.

Released Through Knowledge

Colossians 3:10 says the new man is renewed through knowledge. In this context, the word "knowledge" means more than a mastery of biblical concepts or an understanding of theological abstractions; instead, it primarily means an intimacy with God transmitting divine disclosures. This is the kind of knowledge Paul had in mind when he spoke of his eventual "face to face" dwelling with God in glory, at which time he said, "I shall know just as I also am known" (I Corinthians 13:12).

Realizing there was a greater knowing of God than could be attained on earth, Paul expressed his passion for moving into this realm when he said, "that I might know him ...." (Philippians 3:10). What Paul really wanted was not the documentation that comes from history, or the precepts that come from philosophy, but an immediate, experiential knowing.

And yet, do not the apostle's words surprise us? After all, Paul had as direct an encounter with the Lord as anyone will ever get that day on the Damascus Road. And soon after this experience Paul isolated himself in the desert of Arabia for an extended period of time just so he could have this unhindered intimacy with the Lord. Moreover, the book of Acts chronicles how Paul had one encounter with God after another. So, after all these years and experiences, why would Paul still identify this as the number-one need in his life?

Before responding to this question, we must first recognize that what we see in Paul is exactly what we saw in Jesus. After hours of strength-sapping ministry, Jesus would pray well into the night, and sometimes all night. Keep in mind that Jesus had been living with the Father for millions and billions and trillions of years! There was never a time when the two were ever apart! Consequently, we might think that a little time away wouldn't be such a devastating prospect. But, oh no! More than ever Jesus just had to be with him! There was no need for a break in the relationship.

The psalmist helped us understand this phenomenon when he wrote, "O, taste and see that the Lord is good ...." (Psalms 34:8). This passionately presented invitation by the psalmist makes a lot of sense when we begin to contemplate how exceedingly good God is. For who could love us more than the Lord does? Has anyone given us more than he? Is there anyone with a better personality? Is there anyone with greater wisdom? Is there anyone with greater power? No, no, no, and no! Jesus is the strongest, wisest, most loving person in the whole universe!

Actually, if any one of these attributes were found prominent in another person, we would immediately understand why people want to be with that person. For we all want to be with a person who brings the best out of us. And can anyone do this better than Jesus?

Scripture says as we behold the Lord, that seeing will result in a transformation of our being "from glory to glory" (II Corinthians 3:18). This means to be in his presence causes our real nature to rise and release. A fact Paul must have discovered through personal experience, because after his rendezvous with God in the desert, he said, "It pleased God .... to reveal his Son in me."

Isn't this an intriguing way to put it? What was revealed to Paul in that desert was not the God of the Old Testament, nor the Jesus who ministered in history, nor the Lord enthroned in glory, but the indwelling Lord! The very life of Jesus inside him! It is this life, and this life alone—the life resident in our new nature—which is holy. Therefore, to experience God at this level, and to know him like this, is the one sure way to live a consistently obedient life.

Released Through Faith

A second way the new nature rises and releases is through faith. II Peter 1:4 talks about the great and precious promises, through which we can be made a partaker of the divine nature. However, to claim these promises so that they successfully manifest requires faith. The mere fact that God inspired these promises and that Scripture reports them doesn't mean they're coming true.

Remember, God promised that generation of Jews that made it out of Egypt that they could inherit the Promise Land. But as we now know, almost every one of them died in the wilderness and never spent one day in the land that had been promised. A. B. Simpson asked:

Was there ever a more pathetic story than that of the tribes that marched behind the pillar of cloud and the flame, that came right up to the gates of Canaan, and yet right there at that very threshold failed to enter in? Was there ever a sadder spectacle than those ancient millions turning back into the desert day after day and year after year, in that endless round of fruitless wandering until at last they perished in the sand?[10]

Hebrews 4:2 explains precisely why this failure occurred when it declares that "the word which they heard did not profit them, not being mixed with faith ...." Therefore, after wandering in the wilderness without purpose, they died off like a bunch of flies on a hot August day. In fact, all but two of them went to an early grave.

The one factor that accounted for these early deaths? Not trusting the One who led them out to lead them on! In the end, it was fear, and not faith, that had determined their destiny.

The promises of Scripture represent God's blessings, secured at a great price and extended now in his open hands. But if we won't reach out by faith and receive these blessings, then these blessings will never manifest in our lives.

Knowing this, the Lord summons us to go out on a limb, and if need be to go out on a leaf, to become so childlike in our expectation we will believe only him and not all the evidence that seems to refute what we're believing. There is something about this transaction—as we answer his call and leave our safety—that causes self to die, the Lord to be magnified, and our new nature to flow with force.

Conversely, if we won't go out on a limb—preferring reason to revelation and the causes of self more than the causes of God—then we won't experience God (because he's out there on that limb where we wouldn't go).

Moreover, we won't see the promises profiting us, either, (because we wouldn't mix our faith with them), and we won't find our new nature being released (because the forces of flesh will have prevailed within us). Failure to exercise faith transactions terminates desired outcomes.

Released Through Self-Life Crucifixion

A third way the new nature rises and releases is through the dying of our phantom self, the flesh. Andrew Murray wrote, "... in death alone the life of God will come; in death there is blessedness unspeakable."[11] G. D. Watson amplified this point when he wrote:

> Surely it is a great blessing to loathe sin, and a still greater blessing to loathe that particular sin which has done us the most damage. It is God's design that we should have the most perfect victory where we have been the weakest. This requires a limitless crucifixion of self and a complete possession by the Holy Spirit.[12]

Lesser measures would have been permissible had the flesh been less formidable. But for the new nature to manifest, and for new nature victories to occur, the crucifixion of one's self-life is necessary.

By definition, resurrection has to occur in a cemetery, right? But if there's no dying, how can there can there ever be a resurrection? It was precisely this dying Paul had in mind when he first spoke of "the fellowship of his suffering" after speaking about "the power of his resurrection" (Colossians 3:10).

Thoughts of the resurrected life hold much appeal for the believer, especially when it becomes known, finally, that this life is available on earth. To this day, unfortunately, most people don't know that. However, we can only access this life to the extent we permit the dynamics of the cross to be activated in our lives.

Jessie Penn-Lewis explained this point when she wrote:

> Your spirit cannot dwell and move and live in God unless you are willing to let the Holy Spirit apply the death of Christ's cross to you, and cut and cut until, as Peter says, "you are judged according to men in the flesh" so that you might "live according to God in the spirit" (I Peter 4:6).[13]

The reason the Lord asks all those who would follow him to take up their cross is because that's all they can do. They can't crucify themselves any more than they can raise themselves to new life. But if they will take up that cross, as a sign of their willingness for the Lord to put them on it, the Lord will do the rest.

The resurrected life that sees the believer seated in the "heavenlies" (Ephesians 2:6), identifying with the ascended Christ and beginning even now to rule with him from there, can only become a functioning reality when the believer maintains and deepens his identification with the crucified Christ.

The connection between the cross and the throne is not singularly one of sequence. For the cross and throne are subsequently conjoined as reciprocal and even simultaneous realities. Reciprocal in this life as the dynamics of the cross gives access to the dynamics of the throne. Simultaneous in the next life as we see the Lamb upon the Throne (Revelation 5:6). Can you imagine such a scene—a throne of such stunning glory, and sitting upon it a little lamb?

The sixth chapter of Romans also connects the cross and the throne when verse 5 declares that we are to be planted in his death if we are to be strong in his life. Jessie Penn-Lewis offered valuable insight into this verse when she wrote:

> You are to be planted, to be rooted, to be deep down in his death, so that nothing can tear you out—so that not all the forces of hell can draw you out of your deep-rooted place in his death; "baptized," "planted *into his death*."[14]

The new nature will only be words to you, and hardly daily experience, unless you discern the distinctions Paul was careful to make. The word "planted" suggests a garden and not a grave. The reason we are to be planted into the Lord's death is because any dying we do—however noble in aspiration and sacrificial in cost—won't accomplish the spiritual victory to which we should aspire. Only the death of Jesus won the victory sufficient to release divine life!

Therefore, instead of attempting to win a victory of our own by future endeavors of consecration, we are to identify with the victory already won, and then agree—by the heart remade at Calvary and subsequently made tender by Calvary—to die to everything that necessitated Calvary: sin, self, and Satan.

The power to do this isn't one of self-effort; for we're to be strong in the Lord, the Bible said, and in the power of his might. But this power—the power of resurrection and newness of life—is only released when we give God permission to draw us, through identification first and implementation second, to the cross of Jesus.

Consider this question: Had television cameras been present the very moment Jesus was raised from the dead, would these cameras have transmitted pictures of Jesus struggling and striving to be raised to new life? No, that wouldn't have been the scene depicted. Jesus was the recipient of resurrected life; he wasn't the source of it.

Had we been present that first Easter morning, we would have been surprised by how calm and noiseless this whole operation was. And the same principle is true of us: Resurrection is more a miracle from God than a product of our efforts. It is something God does for us; it is not something we do for God.

It is clear, then, that if we want sin, self, the devil, and the world to do a fast fade-out in our lives, then the power of the cross is our only option. Anything less than that—however appealing it may be to others, and whatever accolades it may bring to us—will leave these destructive forces in position to prevail over us still.

Paul Billheimer said the cross is the safest place to be; for while pinioned to that cross, he said, all the hyphenated sins—self-love, self-desire, self-ambition, self-pity—will be put out of business. This, then, will allow a life full of the Lord's anointing to emerge.

Further encouraging the discovery of one's real self, author G. D. Watson wrote:

You will find out, like the most of us find out, that in carrying out the principle of your obedient

80

heart you will have to suffer; and that very suffering simply proves to angels and devils that you are true. God knew you were true from the very beginning, but God wants you to know you are true.[15]

All scripturally-sanctioned suffering undertaken the right way helps the believer to discover through firsthand experience new dimensions of their real identity.

The Record Doesn't Lie?

When this new life—indeed, divine life, the essence of your new nature—finally manifests, you may be tempted to wonder, "Is this really me?" In response, the devil will leap on the scene to tell you it isn't you. He'll attempt to convince you that these feelings will soon go away, and that the divine invasion is only temporary.

In the devil's ongoing attempts to get you to forfeit your filling, he will then send accelerated accusations, trying to trigger a fastidious search for all that is wrong in you. With each possibility cited, he will seek to pot-mark your soul with blemishes too many and too severe to cover up— and then magnify it all with his mirror suddenly thrust in your face!

Then comes his big announcement, "*This* is you!" he will say. "See it—and don't try to deny it! The record doesn't lie!" Oh? And is this what God would say?

There are several passages in Scripture that offer a remarkably different accounting; and in reading them, even the believer is surprised, if not somewhat perplexed.

For example, Romans, chapter 4, verses 20-22, makes a statement about Father Abraham that seems to make no sense at all.

He did not waver at the promise of God through unbelief, but was strengthened in faith and gave glory to God, and being fully convinced that what he had promised he was also able to perform. And therefore it was accounted to him for righteousness.

81

Upon reading these words, it is *we* who are tempted to waver, stagger, and stumble. Talk about revisionist history! How could the Lord say such things about Abraham?

Had an on-the-spot reporter questioned this assessment, she would have asked, "What about Hagar? Do you remember the way Abraham and Sarah panicked, and how they decided to get their long-promised offspring through Hagar, Sarah's handmaid?" Why, the Middle East is a boiling political cauldron today, all because Abraham and Sarah wouldn't trust God to fulfill his promise!

Very likely, our on-the-spot reporter would also bring up that episode recorded in Genesis, chapter 17, where God showed up in person one day to assure Abraham that he was going to be a father of a nation. And how did Abraham respond? The Bible tells us that Abraham fell on his face and laughed!

Little wonder, too. With Sarah being a half-century beyond childbearing years and Abraham himself being a hundred years old, this message from God seemed preposterous! Abraham didn't stagger at the promise, you say? Why, he fell over backward and howled at it!

More than once we see these eyebrow-raising assessments of the Lord that cause us to wonder how statements like these can be made. In the Old Testament, for example, we are told David was a man after God's own heart. He was? This man who committed adultery and murder, and then lied about it for a whole year? This man with seven wives who was hardly a great father and had to face out-and-out rebellion within his own family? How can a man like this be singled out for such a high compliment?

In the 17th chapter of John's Gospel, we see Jesus giving yet another astounding assessment when he said of his disciples, "They have kept your word." They have? What about their panic during the storm, and their pettiness in the Upper Room, and their scattering when persecution came, and their unwillingness to relate redemptively to those of another race? How are we to account for evaluations like these?

Actually, there is only one way to account for them, and it is this: When God saw the deepest deposit in the hearts of

Abraham, David, and these disciples, he recognized what was of God, and what through eternity would endure, and then with the breath of kindness he blew the rest away.

The record doesn't lie? No, but the record *can* be expunged! For he who is gracious enough to remember our sin no more will see what the Accuser doesn't want us to see—our true self, our new nature! And on that basis, he will extend heaven's warmest welcome, offering astounding accolades no saint ever thought would come.

What God does in these assessments is precisely what we ought to do, too. Instead of becoming a part of a Satan-inspired scrutinizing of the record, we should look for the good, marking out those times when the new nature in us did manifest, and when faith was released, and when our circumstances were changed, and when the Lord was glorified.

Not for one moment should we retain in our memory what God has forever removed from his. Learning the lesson of past failures is all that is required. What we must not allow is for these memories of past sins to undermine our current understanding of self.

Just know, now and always, that while the facts the devil assembles against us may be correct, his interpretation of what those facts mean is not at all correct. Philip Yancey wrote:

> Sociologists have a theory of the looking-glass self: you become what the most important person in your life (wife, father, boss, etc.) thinks you are. How would my life change if I truly believed the Bible's astounding words about God's love for me, if I looked in the mirror and saw what God sees?[16]

If we saw ourselves as God sees us, the Accuser's attempts to stamp our self-image with his incriminating indictments would be thwarted. What we would instead see would greatly encourage us to be who God says we really are. In this way, identity's influence would inspire an obedience that never would have been possible so long as the devil's accusations—for too long unwittingly believed—were echoing in our souls, compounding the damage once done, despite the assessment of God.

Summing up this point, Martyn Lloyd-Jones wrote, "There is a new nature in you, and that new nature must show itself. It shows itself in obedience and righteousness and holy living; it does not show itself by continuing in sin."[17]

To the extent we think sin is normal, the new nature becomes unreal. And to the extent the new nature seems vague and abstract, it can be axiomatically stated that sin is not only our companion, but, too often, our master.

It can be distressing to hear someone say to the church that we all need to know is who we are in the Lord, only to then hear an explanation from them that proves they don't know. Our true identity is not forensic only, wherein legal ramifications of the cross are cited and what is true of our new position in Christ is enumerated. Saying only these things sets up the scenario where the white robe of righteousness is placed over souls mired in the mud of sin. And this is not what Scripture teaches!

A cover-up like this deeply dishonors the sin-solution God provided. It is not just our *position* but it is our actual *condition* that changes. The new nature God gave us was created in righteousness and true holiness (Ephesians 4:24). So the robe of righteousness will be put around that.

If we think our righteousness is only positional and not actual, then this will mean: 1) We will exile ourselves from the realm victory lies (the righteousness of God deposited in our new nature); and 2) we will severely marginalize that victory every day on earth.

Our track record for obedience simply won't change like it could, and like it should, until we have a functional understanding of the new nature. Capacities embedded in our new nature *must* be utilized if we are to live a holy life. But if we don't know how to use these capacities, sin will be more formidable in its aggression against us than it ever has to be.

Imputed righteousness, whereby we get credit for the perfect life Jesus lived, saves us from the guilt of sin, but it does not save us from the power of sin. It is imparted righteousness, the righteousness of God put in our new nature, that has this power to overcome sin—consistently, completely, and convincingly!

To believe only in imputed righteousness, therefore, is to distort Jesus' role as our Advocate, so he becomes the skilled lawyer who gets the guilty off. However, the victory God has provided for us includes imparting his righteousness today. I hope you understand this truth, for it is far more honoring to God, and far more reflective of New Testament facts, to say that Jesus is our Sanctifier, and not just our Advocate.

The victory already won by the Lord, accessed through our new nature, is infinitely better than the victory we are trying to win through functions of our soul—the mind, will, and emotions. The contrast between these two approaches to daily righteousness is so profound! One leads to many discrediting defeats; the other leads to consistent obedience.

Are you beginning to understand the difference between these two approaches? It is so important that you do, because it is only if we know who we are, that we can live like he wants. But if we don't know who we are, our progress will be one where once the devil defeated always, but now he defeats us often.

Living *this* way dishonors God, disgraces grace, and demeans major portions of the gospel. The full gospel promises more.

To see who you really are opens opportunities for obedience beyond what you formerly thought was possible. Whereas the compromised life bogged you down in defeat and therefore limited the way God could use you, successful obedience will qualify you for greater challenges and thus a much greater kingdom-of-God impact.

Reflection Questions

1. How are you helped by the realization that the old man in you no longer exists?

2. How are you helped by the realization that the flesh isn't even partially you?

3. How are you helped by learning that the new nature put inside you at the time of conversion is entirely you?

4. Have you experienced the new nature being released in you upon activating one of the three strategies identified in this chapter? Please explain.

5. How will you use God's assessment of Abraham's obedience and Jesus' assessment of the disciples' obedience in your life?

Chapter 6

The Father's Fellowship—Part I

What was the single biggest factor that kept Jesus from sinning? To answer this question, one would have to examine what happened in the Garden of Gethsemane. The temptations throughout Jesus' ministry were many and severe, but they were never more severe than what occurred that night. For that was the night of the final countdown, the time when the "go" or "no go" decision would at last be made.

At stake that night was the redemption of mankind and, of strategic importance, the defeating of the devil. Prior to this night, the devil's empire had been on a collision course with the kingdom of God. This evil empire, menacing and malicious, had been wreaking a terrible vengeance on earth. But the time had come to determine which of these two supernatural governments would survive.

As Jesus went to the garden that night, he crossed the Brook Kidron where the blood of the Passover lambs flowed from the temple on Mount Moriah down through a constructed trough into this brook. It is estimated that more than a quarter of a million lambs were killed at this season of the year.

The path Jesus walked that night hardly resembled the decorated corridors of the carpeted, modern day church with its lovely air-conditioned prayer room, soft lights, well-placed devotional books, and cushioned chairs. What Jesus saw instead was blood—an ominous foretelling of *his* blood! And not a small smattering of blood, but a blood flow that testified of lives emptied and ended.

Because it was in a garden that the first battle had been lost, it was only fitting that a garden would be the scene for the war that would be won. But it wouldn't be won easily! Read the biblical record and you will see that this was the closest Jesus ever came to defeat. When Jesus spoke the words, "let this cup pass from me," the angels, if they were watching from the portals of heaven, must have looked at each other with great consternation.

"Was Lucifer going to win? Were thousands years of redemption history going to end in failure? Would the Son refuse the Father?" The possibilities seemed imponderable.

The Father's Suffering

When it comes to understanding what occurred in the deepest part of the garden that night, the fourteenth chapter of Mark's gospel is particularly enlightening. According to verse 34 in this chapter, Jesus acknowledged, "My soul is exceedingly sorrowful."

Jesus never used words lightly, so this had to be a sorrow that shook him to the inner core! Never before had such sorrow been felt! Indeed, so intense was this sorrow Jesus vigorously pressed the Father to put an end to it!

In verse 36, Jesus cried, "Abba, Father." Now, one can only imagine how that pulled at the heartstrings of God, for nowhere else in Scripture do we see Jesus uttering this double designation, "Abba, Father." But on this night, summoning all the feelings he had, Jesus cried out to his Father in the most pitiful, heart-wrenching way And these feelings, no doubt, exerted more impact on the Father than he had ever experienced before!

Put yourself in the Father's place. The joy of your life and the recipient of your deepest love is crying out to you not to let him be sacrificed like this. And since you do have the power to stop his pain, the question is .... will you? Will you put a stop to all this undeserved vengeance and save your Son from what murdering men wanted to perpetrate? Or will you let contemptible men do their worst? The decision required was not without an agonizing awareness of its exorbitant cost.

Imagine further that your Son—in the grip of this precedent-setting, soul-shattering pain—actually *tells* you (as verse 36 plainly states), "Take this cup away from me." In reading these words, it is clear the pressure is now escalating to an unfathomable and non-quantifiable degree. Engulfed by this sorrow, your Son isn't asking anymore; he's crying out telling you! So how are you going to respond? Can you continue to withstand his pleadings, pleadings you have never heard before?

The Son then brings theology into this conversation when he reminds you that "all things are possible." Surely, your Son implores you (as both mind and heart make their respective appeals) that in the omniscience and omnipotence of your being, there has to be a way out of this!

So how are you holding up? Can you keep letting this insane hatred toward uncompromised virtue go on? And if so, how *can* you? Isn't your love for your Son an overriding factor more decisive than anything else?

The lickety-split way we quote Jesus' words—"Father, let this cup pass from Me; but not my will but thine be done"—causes us to completely lose its meaning. Just as fast as the one breath duration it takes us to quote these words, glossy fiction replaces brutal fact. What we must be made to see is that in ways as mysterious as they are upsetting, Jesus came to the very edge. Sin, indeed, was terrifyingly close!

And what kept Jesus from it? As we examine the biblical record, the answer doesn't elude us—it was his fellowship with the Father! The greatest part of Jesus' pain was not the nails, the thorns, the spear, and the ridicule. No, what sent Jesus into such convulsive anguish that night was the fact that as the sin-bearer of the world his fellowship with the Father, for the first time in the eons of eternity, would be cut off.

This immanent outcome was one where the Father would turn away, the Holy Spirit would take flight, and Jesus would cry out in abandonment. The excruciating anguish that erupted cannot be explained. E. M. Bounds described what occurred that night: "Angels retired, heaven hushed its music, and all was draped in silence. All creation trembled in awe while Satan's dread power was allowed to expend its dark forces on heaven's Anointed One."[1] Never before and never again would anything this awful occur.

As we pause and get our bearings, seeking respite from such rarefied heights, as well as from such despondent depths, let's succumb to an oversimplification by bringing this principle at work in the garden into a more common domain.

A Father's Moral Influence

All across our land, in homes where the father has exerted a strong moral influence through both example and expectation, many a son and daughter have found that influence to be one of their strongest deterrents against sin.

Whenever temptation turned up the heat, what had been ingrained in these children, and what was esteemed so greatly by them, rose with a mighty momentum so that, for them, the temptation was quickly quenched and the victory was convincingly won. A. B. Simpson said, "A true child will cherish his father's wants and interests and would avoid everything that would throw a shadow of reproach upon his name."[2]

Of course, most homes don't have a father like that. In a day where a high percentage of children are born out of wedlock and an increasing number of families are led by a single parent, many children don't have a father on the scene at all.

Deeper down every child wants a father worthy of respect and emulation. Dick Gregory described his own feelings about this in this autobiographical account.

It was on a Thursday, the day before the Negro payday. The eagle always flew on Friday. The teacher was asking each student how much his father would give to the Community Chest. On Friday night, each kid would get the money from his father, and on Monday he would bring it to the school. I decided that I was going to buy me a Daddy right then. I had money in my pocket from

90

shining shoes and selling papers, and whatever Helene Tucker pledged for her Daddy I was going to top it. And I'd hand the money right in. I wasn't going to wait until Monday to buy me a Daddy.

I was shaking, scared to death. The teacher opened her book and started calling out names alphabetically.

"Helene Tucker?"

"My Daddy said he would give two dollars and fifty cents."

"That's very nice, Helene. Very, very nice, indeed."

That made me feel pretty good. It wouldn't take too much to top that. I had almost three dollars in dimes and quarters in my pocket. I stuck my hand in my pocket and held on to the money, waiting for her to call my name. But the teacher closed her book after she called everyone else in the class.

I stood up and raised my hand.

"What is it now?"

"You forgot me."

She turned toward the blackboard. "I don't have time to be playing with you, Richard."

"My Daddy said he'd ..."

"Sit down, Richard, you're disturbing the class."

"My Daddy said he'd give ... fifteen dollars."

91

She turned around and looked mad. "We are collecting this money for you and your kind, Richard Gregory. If your Daddy can give fifteen dollars, you have no business being on relief."

"I got it right now, I got it right now, my Daddy said ..."

"And furthermore," she said looking right at me, her nostrils getting big and her lips getting thin and her eyes opening wide, "we know you don't have a Daddy."

Helene Tucker turned around, her eyes full of tears. She felt sorry for me. Then I couldn't see her too well because I was crying, too.

"Sit down, Richard."

And I always thought the teacher kind of liked me. She always picked me to wash the blackboard on Friday, after school. That was a big thrill. It made me feel important. If I didn't wash it, come Monday the school might not function right.

"Where are you going, Richard?"

I walked out of school that day, And for a long time I didn't go back very often. There was shame there.[3]

Isn't this sad? How desperately little Richard wanted a daddy! But to all the Richards of this world, God has said that he will be a "Father of the fatherless" (Psalm 68:5)—that is, the provider, the protector, and the standard-bearer of their homes, as well as the encourager of their dreams and the comforter of their hearts. Losing a father need not be what it appears. For there is One who will draw close to undertake beyond what any earthly father could ever do.

The Importance of God Being Our Father

Although the idea of God being our father didn't originate with Jesus, it is significant that Jesus always called God Father and never called him anything else. A. W. Pink declared, "Nothing is more calculated to warm the heart and give liberty of utterance than a realization that we are approaching our "Father.""[4]

Philosophers and theologians have entertained different thoughts about God. To Aristotle, God was "Pure Actuality." To Barth, he was "The Wholly Other." To Bultmann, he was "The Beyond in our Midst." To Tillich, he was "The Ground of Being." To Teilhard, he was "The Omega Point." To Otto, he was "The Numinous." To Altizer, he was "The Kenotic One." But in contrast to all these abstract, honorific designations, Jesus called God "Abba," a child's name for "Daddy."

According to John Owen, the eminent Puritan theologian, "Abba is the Syriac or Chaldee name for Father, then in common use among the Jews ...."[5] But while it was common in its usage for earthly fathers, it was not at all common as a reference for God. The Jews viewed God in a more honorific, transcendent way. And haven't we done the same thing? Addressing this tendency, Horatio Bonar wrote:

> We are apt to associate God only with what is cold and abstract and ideal; ourselves with what is emotional and personal. Herein we greatly err. We must reverse the picture if we would know the truth concerning him with whom is no coldness, no abstraction, no impersonality.[6]

Alexander Maclaren said that "monarchs often called themselves and seldom were" ... the father of their people.[7] It took none other than Jesus to add this important understanding of God as our Father. And we can be grateful that he did, because as Samuel Chadwick wrote, "It makes a tremendous difference when the soul realizes that God is ... not a shrouded mystery, but a living personality, not an unsympathetic embodiment of power but a loving and tender Father."[8]

Think of the alternatives, then contemplating the consequences these have: What if Jesus had chosen another name instead, such as Captain—Captain of the Lord of Hosts? Can you imagine how our view of God would have been radically altered had Jesus kept calling him Captain?

Hannah Whitall Smith wrote:

> In the Old Testament God was not revealed as the Father so much as a great warrior fighting for his people, or as a mighty king ruling over them and caring for them. The name of Father is given to him only a few times there, six or seven at the most; while in the New Testament it is given about two-hundred or three-hundred times.[9]

Before going to Gethsemane that night, Jesus spoke of that which was so much on his heart—the abundant provision available to these disciples to keep them spiritually strong. Included in these ten provisions was this most amazing and marvelous mystery, that which had meant so much to Jesus—the Father's fellowship. If the disciples would only obey, then, Jesus said, the Father would love them, indwell them, and manifest himself to them (John 14:21, 23). Hence, that which represented the greatest motivation in Jesus' life could as well become the greatest motivation in their lives.

To strengthen the intended appeal of this truth, let's consider who the Father is, as we contemplate two of his attributes.

Our Father's Power

The Sovereign of the Skies is a God of incomprehensible power, a fact that is obvious even to the least reflective ones among us. Frederick W. Faber observed, "To the savage on whose inobservant mind no phenomena are forced but those of power—such as the storm, the flash, the sea, the sun, the wind—the Creator is simply a Spirit of Might."[10] That such might is possessed by a heavenly Father, a beneficent Being who loves the savage and sophisticate alike, is beyond the grasp of an unenlightened mind.

94

While it is indeed good to have a strong father (as opposed to a weak and ineffective one), it is simply past comprehension to think our father is the strongest man in the universe! Ephesians 4:6 speaks of "one God and Father of all, who is above all ...." Jesus said, in John 10:29, that the "Father is greater than all." How much greater, you ask? Try this one on for size. Jeremiah 32:17 says, "Ah, Lord God! Behold, you have made the heavens and the earth by your great power and outstretched hand. There is nothing too hard for you."

The famous astronomer Sir James Jeans says that there are more than a hundred billion stars just in that part of the universe we know. In our galaxy alone it would take light traveling at the rate of 186,000 miles per second 80,000 years to cross from one side to the other. And that's just our galaxy! No one knows how many other galaxies there are! The Keck telescopes on Mauna Kea in Hawaii have increased our estimate exponentially by the discovery of millions of more galaxies. So with this credential in mind, do you think that a God who can do all this could solve your problem?

Whenever times get tough and we are suffering "according to the will of God" (which means this isn't a suffering we brought on by our own sinful actions, or a suffering we foolishly thought God sanctioned), we should commit our souls to him "as to a faithful Creator" (I Peter 4:19). Do you see the practical implications of this? When confronted with difficult problems, we can go to our Father with surging confidence, because it was he made a universe so vast and marvelous no scientist has even begun to discover all he did. We do know this, though: With such demonstrated power twinkling their testimonies in the sky, Jeremiah had to be right—nothing is too hard for him!

In Isaiah 44:24, the Lord declares, "I am the Lord who makes all things, who stretches out the heavens all alone, who spreads abroad the earth by myself." So with a double emphasis punctuating the point, God is making it clear that creation wasn't done by some committee!

Planet Earth—8,000 miles in diameter, 25,000 miles in circumference, with its majestic mountains, dense forests, vast oceans, and breathtaking views—is the work of the greatest botanist, engineer, chemist, astronomer, and artist all rolled into one.

What if your earthly father was the greatest—well, take your pick of any of these professions—wouldn't that make you proud? For good reasons, you would have enormous respect for his unequaled achievement! But just think: Your heavenly Father is the greatest at *everything*!

I know such lofty thoughts have a way of floating out of the real world in which you and I live. So let me try to bring it closer to home. Romans 4:17 says that God "calls those things which do not exist as though they did." This means that way back in eternity past, there was a time when there was no earth, or sun, or moon. But then one day God Almighty stood on the portals of heaven and let loose his booming voice commands; whereupon—presto!—there they were, spangling the whole universe, planets galore with their dazzling lights!

Now, picking up on this precise thought but transferring it to a different realm, I Corinthians, chapter 1, says:

> But God has chosen the foolish things of this world to put to shame the wise, and God has chosen the weak things of the world to put to shame the mighty, and the base things of this world and the things which are despised God has chosen and the things which are not to bring to nothing the things which are (I Corinthians 1:27, 28).

As with the original creation, the Father today is in the business of transforming what is not into something full of his glory. So if you have done your share of foolish things— good news! You're a perfect candidate for the Father's transforming work! And if you are weak and at times sinful— rejoice! You are exactly the kind of person in whom God has chosen to bring about awesome change! And there's more good news! God's wonder-working power isn't just seen in science; it can actually be seen in *you*—if you'll let him do it.

Ephesians 3:20 declares that our heavenly Father "is able to do exceedingly, abundantly, above all that we ask or think ...." This verse reminds me of those times as a boy when I would make my Christmas list of favorite toys. When Christmas morning arrived, I would open my presents, only to discover that what I received was better than what I had requested. Had I known about some of these toys, I certainly would have put them on my list—but I didn't even know about them.

This is the kind of experience the child of God can have, because what the Father is seeking to give us is even better than what we are asking for—"exceedingly, abundantly" better!

Have you ever stopped to think what it might be like if God was a typical holy man—pious, commendable in character, but out of the loop when it comes to power? What if the only thing he had to offer were sweet prayers, provoking thoughts, and affectionate embraces?

Aren't you glad your Father in Heaven can't be ignored like that as the powers that be trot him out for opening ceremonies but then routinely ignore him just as soon as their staged smiles begin to fade?

No, the movers and shakers of this world are themselves going to be moved and shook whenever the Father, who will not be put off, intervenes to exert his power.

For those who have given even a modicum of thought to how vulnerable we are in life, the power of God has been more appreciated. In his book, *Our Own God*, G. D. Watson described our situation.

> We find ourselves in contact with great, giant forces that could at any moment destroy our life; wind could blow us down, water drown us, the fire burn us, the cold freeze us, the gases strangle us, gravitation crush us, the darkness blind us. We can no more manage these elements on a worldwide scale than we could create a world, and yet we walk serenely through these huge giants like Daniel resting supremely in a den of hungry lions, because we instinctively trust an unseen

and omnipotent God to regulate these elements and to take care of our littleness and ignorance.[11]

Were it not for God's protection, we would be defenseless and our peril would be predictable.

Contemplating the great forces of nature and the restraints our God has put upon them, caused missionary to the Muslims Lilias Trotter to offer this diary-entry on November 5, 1895. Sitting by the seaside in Eastbourne, England, Lilias witnessed the waves crashing to shore, one after another, all furious in their assault. Inspired by what she saw, she wrote:

> Oh with what joy it came as one watched themselves hurling themselves with all their might and succeeding in doing nothing but washing a few tiny pebbles a few inches and dragging others back in their place—such power and such impotence![12]

The power of our Father is on display every day to those sane enough, and sensitive enough, to see it. And because of this power, that which would oppose and thwart can do pitifully little.

Our Father's Wisdom

Another attribute of our heavenly Father is his wisdom. Do you know how many wise men there are on the earth? You won't have to consult a "Who's Who" to find the answer to this question. The Bible tells us—just one! I Timothy 1:17 speaks of "God *who alone* is wise." And that makes sense when you think about it, because respected authorities who have expertise in one area will invariably be found woefully lacking in another area.

Maybe you have had the experience of attending a meeting where all the advice being dispensed sounded so good. Insights were flashing, momentum was building, things were clicking and connecting in a marvelous way when, suddenly, the speaker made a remark that jolted you. "What!" you thought to yourself as you began to process what was said, "How could he possibly believe something as double dumb as that?"

Tony Compollo once observed how interesting it can be to sit in a college classroom and hear some PH.D rattle on. These professors, he said, can sometimes say the most ignorant things and never think or blink twice.

Granted, what the Lord reveals may also jolt us at times, but in a different way. Like one coming out of the dark and into the light, God's truth may bring its discomfort and need to adjust. But, upon further reflection, we will conclude that what he said is considerably more credible than the contaminated thinking that had been bouncing around in our brain.

I Samuel 2:3 asserts that "the Lord is a God of knowledge." This word 'knowledge' is in the plural in the Hebrew language; so some older translations, wanting to make this point clear, translate this word as "knowledges." This means that our Father in Heaven doesn't have a specialty, really. Music, medicine, history, psychology—he knows everything about all of these subjects! He even knows the number of hairs on our head—which for some people doesn't exactly require a calculator to count!

By contrast, our knowledge is infinitesimally small. G. D. Watson conveyed a sense of this when he wrote:

> We cannot see a single hour ahead of us, and yet we know that we shall go on moving forward, either in this life or in another state of being, for hours, and days, and years, more countless than the drops of water into the sea. As we look out in thought over the endless ages which stretch away before us, and think of what is to become of these countless centuries, it is almost enough to take our breath, and make us quiver with questions of possibilities that are to come.[13]

Our pursuit of knowledge is limited by many factors—ability, opportunity, desire, time, and space, to cite a few. For example, I have a cousin who is brilliant nuclear physicists. He travels all over the world giving lectures and participating in symposiums. However, because of my limitations in both math and science, I could never do what he does.

My son, on the other hand, is quite proficient in deep sea diving—an expertise I will never have simply because I'm not interested in it. I do have a desire to know more about Asia. Yet, there is so much about Asia that I don't know—largely because I don't live there. To some extent, therefore, it is opportunity that has limited me—opportunity not obtained, whether desired or not.

Just now, as I am typing this manuscript on the computer, I couldn't tell you what is happening three doors away from me. Why? Because I'm not there. So in this instance, my knowledge is limited by geography, by space.

Often, my knowledge is limited by time. In truth, I know next to nothing about the past and even less than that about the future. However, because God is the Great I Am, before whom there is no sequencing of time, time doesn't present a problem. For him, the past and future are ever and always a part of the eternal present.

Actually, none of these barriers that limit us, limit him in the slightest. He is a God of knowledges!

Psalm 147:5 makes a slightly different point when it declares that "His understanding is infinite." This means that not only is God in possession of all the facts, but he also understands the significant nuances each fact and how all these facts relate.

Isaiah 40:28 tells us that "His understanding is unsearchable." By contrast, those who might want "to pick my brain" will glean whatever is there soon enough. But there is no computer, or system of computers, that could come anywhere close to storing all the Father knows.

There are times when I am puzzled, perplexed, confused. Try as I might to understand the coalescing of certain circumstances, on my own I can't understand them. Should I conclude, therefore, that life is an inscrutable mystery having no discernible purpose? Tozer wrote:

Just because I, finite man, do not understand everything that God, the infinite does, is no reason to doubt God's purpose. I may go into someone's workshop and see all the tools and gadgets that are important to the man's work. I may see laying on the table, for instance, a little tool that I can make nothing of and have no understanding of its purpose. But in the hands of the craftsman, that little tool has a well-defined purpose and does what it's supposed to do.[14]

The Father knows what I don't know; and for that I can be grateful, because this knowledge is activated for my welfare, always! If I'll just keep that thought in mind, I'll stay away from an offended spirit during those times when the pressure is on and I am perplexed.

Now, if all this impressive knowledge meant that God was a horn-rimmed nerd, some wide-eyed genius type whose mind is off in the stratosphere somewhere, we probably wouldn't find this profile particularly appealing. But Matthew 6:4 says something very intriguing to the believer, "Your Father ... sees in secret."

Those things about you which others don't know, and you may not even know, are completely known by him. Those weak linkages in a chain of events that didn't seem to be a chain, the Father sees. That hidden motive, those words which seemed to mean the opposite of what was really intended, that unexpected coming together of former adversaries—the Father saw and wasn't surprised.

J. H. Jowett could see the blessedness of this truth when he wrote, "He who knows my worst has more hope for me than they who know my best."[15] Isn't that good? Matthew 6:32 says that "your heavenly Father knows" your need. What suppression has covered, and what ignorance has kept hidden, is totally clear to the Lord. In fact, Isaiah 66:18 quotes the Father as saying, "For I know their works and their thoughts ...." Everything they've ever done, everything they even thought—the Father knows it all!

As we contemplate the wisdom of our Father, so essential for our victory, we are prompted to turn to him and him alone, especially when the conflict begins. Important for us to know as we do so are these questions posed by Dr. Jowett: "Is He intimate with my peculiar weaknesses? Does

He know where the hedge is thin and vulnerable, and where my life is most easily invaded and defiled? Does He know where defenses are more especially required?"[16]   And does he know how my particular battle can be won?

Illustrating by historical analogy, A. B. Simpson helped answer these questions:

> It has been lately stated that the great Von Moltke, who planned with such signal success the victorious campaign of the German army against France, had been ready for many years for that expected event. And when one night an orderly knocked at his door with a message from the king that war was imminent, he simply directed the orderly to go to a certain pigeonhole in his office where he would find all the directions to the different commanders with all the necessary papers ready for instant delivery. And there they were, the plans of the campaign, plans of fortresses, orders to generals of divisions, all ready; and then he turned over and quietly went to sleep. He had been ready for years.[17]

And with far greater brilliance God has long been ready for the battle you and I must fight!

Many years ago, there was a television program called "Father Knows Best." This program featured the family of one Jim Anderson who was everyone's ideal for a father. He was wise, gentle, caring, and understanding. And when the show's writers graced him with humor and humanity, they secured for themselves a long-running TV show.

Who wouldn't want a father like that—the kind of father who makes his children feel secure and loved? Dr. Jowett says of the Heavenly Father, "He not only knows; he feels. He responds to the need which he discerns. He can be 'touched with the feeling of our infirmities.'"[18] What most people wished they had, but unfortunately do not have, is clearly seen in the biblical portrait of God.

Contemplate next this hypothetical: If you had a father incredibly brilliant, amazingly wise, and totally tuned into your situation, wouldn't you want to spend a lot of time with him? Jesus did! And the same will be true of you, too, once the biblical portrait of the Father becomes a revelation to you.

Not wanting to part company from the Father, ever, you will resist the devil and every temptation he sends your way. You will stand long and strong against all that could hinder your fellowship with him—which certainly, and most obviously, includes sin. In this way, your victory will have been secured not by some brilliant strategy, or by some stirring of the emotions, or by some flexing of a resolute will, but by your love for the Father. A love that caused you to think differently, feel differently, and act differently.

Wanting fellowship with the Father, you chose that which would promote this, and rejected that which would demote it. Each faculty of the soul was first empowered, then aligned, so that your fellowship with the Father remained, no matter how ominous those obstacles threatening its extinction.

Once the day of trial finally ended and the higher ground of moral victory offered its spectacular view, you knew—absolutely knew—Father enabled this victory. For without him, and without that gravitation of soul that simply had to experience more of him, victory wouldn't have come.

Reflection Questions

1. On a lesser to greater scale of 1-5, to what extent does your desire to fellowship with the Father factor in to your decisions to resist temptation? Please explain.

2. Which of the two attributes of the Father discussed in this chapter appeals to you the most as you wrestle with your most challenging temptation? Please explain.

Chapter 7

The Father's Fellowship—Part II

Professor A. J. Gossip, who pastored during the last half of the nineteenth-century, once preached a sermon titled, "When Life Tumbles In, What Then?" Good question, even for the religious people in Scotland. In dealing with this question, Gossip described an unusual painting hanging in the National Gallery. The painting depicts someone else in attendance that day at Golgotha besides those Scripture mentions.

> Christ hangs upon the cross in a dense darkness; and at first that is all one sees. But, as one peers into the background, gradually there stands out another form, God's form; and other hands supporting Christ, God's hands; and another face, God's face, more full of agony even than our Savior's own. The presence, the sufficiency, the sympathy of God, these things grow very real and very sure and very wonderful.[1]

Always the Father! The center and circumference of Jesus' life! The supplier of his strength, the source of his wisdom, the subject of his highest affection! "The love of Calvary," James Stewart wrote, "was more than the love of Jesus; it was the love of God the Father."[2] Likewise, Samuel Chadwick declared, "All that it cost the Son to redeem the world it cost the Father. He suffered in the suffering Son."[3] Not physically, but intensely, nevertheless.

The relationship Jesus had with his Father was *the* most critical factor in his victory over sin. And the same *could* be said about us. For if our relationship with God is steadily strong and immensely rewarding, the appeal of sin to our heart will range somewhere between minimal to nonexistent. But if we are detached in our relationship with God, we can be sure that temptation has already begun to incubate, and that in some way will soon manifest.

When most of us were children, we couldn't imagine the evil we would one day do. Had someone approached us while we were still on the playground to review a checklist of potential evil, we would have denied right and left that we would ever do such things. So what happened? Two factors sum it up: Our love for the Father grew cold while the fires of temptation became increasingly hot.

Actually, there is an interrelatedness between these two factors, because we never would have gotten so close to the fires of temptation had not our love for the Father first grown cold.

Recognizing how important it is to nurture our love for the Father, we would do well to remind ourselves of how lovable he really is. Alexander Maclaren, the esteemed pastor from Scotland who preached for many years in nineteenth-century England, observed that "the conception of the divine nature is no doubt infinitely deepened, made more tender and more lofty, by the thought of the Fatherhood of God."[4]

Prompted by this insight, we will contemplate next various father-roles of God that benefit the believer.

The Giver

One of the main functions of a father is to provide for his family, to take care of physical needs, to make sure the family is protected. So we might ask: In what ways has our heavenly Father undertaken to fulfill this responsibility in our lives?

James 1:17 offers a wonderful commentary on this point when it declares, "Every good gift and every perfect gift comes down from the Father of lights, with whom there is no variation or shadow of turning." This term, "Father of lights," refers to the suns and stars we discussed in the previous chapter. As the earth does its rotations, the light will be blocked and, for us, darkness will result. This doesn't mean that the sun has lost its light. It just means, because of the earth's turning, night must inevitably fall.

In contrast to what is going on in outer space, the Father's generosity toward us won't ever be eclipsed by his turning—or ours! Even if we disappoint him, grieve him, resist him, or out-and-out rebel against him, there is still this outpouring of goodness, kindness, and mercy, which is given, the Bible tells us, to lead us to repentance (Romans 2:4).

It would be an overstatement, however, to say the faucet of his goodness is fully turned on, no matter what. For willful sin can certainly deprive us of God's intended goodness—at least for a season in our lives. Yet, when the historical record is complete, there will be ample evidence to show how graciously good God was even when sin had been wrongly welcomed into our lives.

In Matthew 7:11 Jesus said, "If you then, being evil, know how to give good gifts to your children, how much more will your Father who is in heaven give good gifts to those who ask him!" This suggests that as great as the gap is between his goodness and our evil (and that gap is considerable), so also is the gap between his giving and our giving. Matthew says God offers "much more." James says it is "perfect." And while the extent of his giving can't be fully known, we know enough to affirm: God's giving far surpasses what our limited knowledge discloses.

In contemplating the generosity of God, consider first his faithfulness to supply our daily needs. Jesus taught us to pray to the Father "give us this day our daily bread." The words "this day" emphasize we are dependent creatures. Despite intellectual achievements, and all our philosophical thoughts, we, like the animals under our control, have to eat. Every day, and several times a day, we are brought into daily reminder that we need God to sustain us.

The bread we are encouraged to petition means more than a loaf of carbohydrate intake; it refers instead to all our material and physical needs. What a welcome balance this emphasis brings to the ethereal, transcendent dimensions of some religions! In contrast with the religions of the East, Christianity is practical enough to focus on bread.

We may not have appreciated—at least not at first— how shocking the scripture is that reported: "The Son of Man came eating and drinking ..." (Matthew 11:19a). But what a scandal to some! Eating and drinking? *God*—a consumer, just like us? Those in the Mediterranean world considered matter and flesh sources of evil. So how insidiously incongruent it was to be told God became flesh! Flesh? One mustn't ever focus on the material, but on the spiritual! That message that had been ingrained in them from youth.

Contrary to this philosophy, Scripture repeatedly affirms the importance of the material! Indeed, far from ignoring our material needs, or addressing them with repudiation and disgust, God graciously supplies these needs, and even urges that these needs be made a part of our prayers.

What if Jesus said such requests were too trivial for divine attention? What if he instructed us to restrict our requests to world evangelism, or to the dominion of God on earth, or to the expansion of his kingdom in a culture increasingly infected by evil?

Or, worse still, what if the Lord of Glory had expressly excluded the mundane things of daily life from our prayers? What if everything physical and financial in nature were prohibited during prayer?

In response to these questions, Helmut Thielicke remarked:

We would all be orphans, dear friend, if that were so. Only in our Sunday best and with scrubbed and shining faces could we dare to pay an occasional visit to our stepfather, hiding our calloused hands and the lines of care upon our faces. Then we should have to conceal from him all the little joys and sorrows of our life, only to find ourselves in the next moment terribly forlorn and alone again as soon as we were outside the stepfather's audience chamber, and every day life came flooding back upon us with renewed force.[5]

Due to the Father's great love for us, this is not a dilemma we will ever have to face, because, as the hymn writer very well put it, "God will take care of you. All you may need, he will provide."

In addition to material needs, God offers an array of gifts that far excel what any shopping catalog advertises. For example, II John, verse 4, says that the commandments came from the Father, commandments that are "holy and just and good" (Romans 7:12). Now, this may not impress you as a great, whoop-to-dee gift, but consider what our world would be like if he who ran it was more like that basketball coach who said, "Boys, if you can't win fairly, *win!*"

What if God thought evil was sometimes funny, and that losers were to be dismissed with snickering disdain? Or what if it were cleverness that impressed him, instead of goodness? Can you imagine how our lives would lose hope under a governing like that?

Consider further: What if God had no expectation that we should become holy, and therefore never brought this subject up? What if there were no commandments, no communication of any sort on this topic, but only pity as we lived out our pathetic, sinful lives?

When viewed in this context, the commandments of God can rightly be called a gift. These commandments bring clarity where confusion would have existed, moral insistence where unprincipled compromises would have prevailed, a summons to integrity where whispered invitations to do evil would have been common.

Standing strong against the baser instincts of man, these commandments shine brightly into eyes which at first couldn't see, and reverberate loudly into ears which at first couldn't hear. In these ways, the commandments exert an influence without which history would chronicle a record of compounding evil and untold misery.

These commandments also declare the authority of the Creator over his world. Instead of a negotiating that says,

"Let's make a deal," the Almighty God—negotiating nothing!—declares, "This is the deal!"

The commandments of God are subject to no revision, amendment, or exceptions of any kind. Not because God is harshly authoritarian, but because what he set forth at Sinai was perfect from the beginning. Any changes to these commandments, or other commandments subsequently given, would diminish the benefits of these commandments.

Now a person could inventory all that money can buy and never come up with a gift as good as the next one we will consider. According to I John 4:14, the Father gave us his own precious Son. Think of it: If the Son hadn't come, we would have no deliverance from our sins (Hebrews 9:12), no inheritance of eternal life (John.3:16), and no promises to claim for daily life (Ephesians 2:12).

To better grasp what that situation would be like, consider what has happened to almost every Jew alive today. There was a time when Jews had a feverish expectancy that the Messiah would come. But not anymore. The modern-day Jew has given up on a coming Messiah. And having done so, all they have left are exemplary ethics, the skeleton of ancient traditions, and the distractions of this world. Without a Messiah to hope for, confidence in the future—and, really, confidence in God's involvement in the present—all too quickly dissipates.

But as the born-again believer knows this belief in a coming Messiah retrieves hope from the ash bin of discarded promises and vitalizes these present days with unspeakable joy. Jesus—our Savior from the power and penalty of sin, whose life indwells us and redefines us—is God's greatest gift to us.

But what also amazes us is that we are the Father's gift to Jesus! Indeed, so valued was this gift it was prominent in the mind of Jesus when he approached death (John 17:6, 9, 24). These multiple mentions by Jesus had major significance, for they envisioned a day of shared glory with him. As the Father's love gift to Jesus, it was decided by God's grace that we would inherit the throne Lucifer couldn't get and a nature above that of the angels. His descent into death caused our ascendancy into the bridehood of Christ.

Oh, my! Our minds, our hearts, can scarcely contemplate being treasured to this extent. All this because the Father gave us Jesus, and then gave us to Jesus!

What else did the Father give us? As we further inventory his gifts, we learn from Acts 1:4 that he who convicts, inspires, teaches, energizes, indwells, and seals us unto the day of redemption, the Holy Spirit himself, was a gift from the Father. Imagine what our life would be without the Holy Spirit. Why, without Holy Spirit, the words of the Bible would be just that—only words. The life Scripture promises, therefore, would remain tantalizingly out of reach. At the same time, Jesus himself would be far less precious to us, were it not for the Holy Spirit who lifts him up. Like a car without an engine and a balloon without air, ours would be a limp, lame life going precisely nowhere—*if* we didn't have the Holy Spirit.

Still another gift given to us by the Father is seen in the I John 3:1 declaration, "Behold, what manner of love the Father has bestowed upon us that we should be called the children of God." The word "behold" in this verse is a word full of excitement, a word demanding complete and immediate attention.

The word "manner" means something foreign, unheard of, and out of this world. So by putting us into his family, God has given us his nature, his resources, and a destiny that far exceeds anything we could have ever dreamed of!

In this life, a person can waste a lot of time discovering that fame, fortune, and the goodies of this world don't and won't satisfy. However, if we ever get a vision like John had, we will be just as thrilled as John was about what the Father has given us. Moreover, once we realize what blessed beneficiaries we are, the motivation to please the Lord will grow exponentially in our hearts, and thus strengthen our ability to obey him.

Not to be overlooked in this promise of the new nature is the blockage this reality should demolish for people who have a difficult time believing God really loves them. Theologically, they know the Bible says he does, and that the Bible must be right. But emotionally they have a difficult time receiving this love because what they see in themselves isn't very lovable. But, you see, God loves what he gave, and what he gave is the new nature. This new nature is the very life of Jesus (Colossians 3:4), a life which totally defines who we are (II Corinthians 5:17). Now, once the believer's eyes are opened to see who they really are, the receiving and returning of the Lord's love will be greatly accelerated.

The Lover

There are fathers in this world who do a good job providing for the physical necessities of life, and they may even do a good job with setting standards and following through with needed discipline. But what they do not do nearly as well is simply love their children.

Unfortunately, more than a few people think of God as aloof and distant, or as being easily upset and often grieved, especially when he thinks about them! The problems these views present are certainly obvious—for who would want to rush into the arms of a father like that?

The Bible presents a very different view of God. The Apostle John found the Lord so approachable he actually laid his head on the Lord's shoulders during the Last Supper. John never directly identified himself by name in the gospel he wrote but always referred to himself as "the disciple whom the Lord loved." John just couldn't get over this love!

Henry Scougal, the Scottish seventeenth-century professor from the University of Aberdeen, wrote glowingly about this love, saying:

> Nothing is more powerful to engage our affection than to find we are beloved ... to have the love of one who is altogether lovely, to know that the glorious Majesty of heaven hath any regard for us, how it must astonish and delight us, how it must overcome our spirits, and melt our hearts and put our whole soul into a flame![6]

Writing from the same century, Thomas Watson exclaimed, "When I believe God's love to me, this makes me weep that I should sin against so good a God."[7] Alexander Maclaren surfaced this same subject in the form of a question, "For is not man's sin blackest when seen against the bright background of God's fatherly love?"[8]

To John, the Lord's love was the one quality he treasured most! Of course this love came straight from the heart of the Father, in that Jesus said to see him is to see the Father (John 14:8).

Given how powerful the Father's love is as a motivation for holy living, we can easily anticipate the enemy's attempts to dissuade us of this glorious truth. A. B. Simpson warned of such attempts, saying, "He points to some mysterious trial or privation and he insinuates the subtle doubt of our Father's love ...."[9]

This tactic was also used against the children of Israel. The real reason for their failures in the wilderness was identified by Moses in Deuteronomy 1:27 when he said of the Jews, they murmured in their tents that God hated them. Well! Once that thought took root, the fruit of it was easily predictable. It was for this reason that A. B. Simpson declared, "The only safe place for faith is in absolute, unfaltering confidence, every moment, in the love of God."[10]

We should understand that the formidable challenges of life do not convey the Father's heart toward us, at least not in the way we sometimes think. But our response to these challenges may well reflect our heart toward God. Offering explanation, A. B. Simpson writes: "All the experiences of life come to us as tests; and as we meet them, our loving Father is watching, with intense and jealous love, to see us overcome; and if we fail, he is deeply disappointed, and our great adversary is filled with joy and triumph."[11]

In meditating on the fact God loves us, we would do well to see how Scripture distinguishes God's love from the love of this world. One distinctive quality is the fact God's love is an *enduring* love. Despite our weaknesses and the innumerable ways we needlessly disappoint him, God loves us—without any interruption or dissipation of affection—to the end!

Romans 15:5 reinforced this point when it called God the "God of patience," a perfect example of which was provided in the Old Testament. Toward the beginning of the book of Genesis, we learn what happened in this story.

Long before there was a Bible, or a church, or the gifts of the Holy Spirit, a man by the name of Enoch walked this earth, enjoying a close companionship with God for three centuries. Now Enoch lived in a day of much wickedness, a wickedness that had to be judged if repentance didn't occur.

So God spoke prophetically to his people by giving Enoch a son whose name declared a message. The son's name was Methuselah, which, literally translated, means "When he is gone, it will come." And this became Enoch's message to the world: "By the time my son dies—and who knows when that will be? It may come soon, it may come late—a great cataclysmic judgment will come upon the earth, *unless* you turn away from your sins and toward the God who loves you."

Well, as a testimony to God's enduring love, Methuselah lived longer than any man in history—for 969 years!

This, by the way, is the same patience Jeremiah saw at the potter's wheel that day. Whenever the potter dealt with recalcitrant clay, instead of throwing it away, as easily he could have done, he kept working it, shaping it, smoothing it, eventually bringing it to form. And this proved to be a gospel to Jeremiah—the gospel of the indomitable patience of God! A patience that every child of God has also experienced, because when failing and falling an exasperating number of times, they were able to return to a Father who never gave up on them.

Not only does the Lord's love endure, but according to Scripture it *enriches*. Romans 8:32 declares this: "He who did not spare his own Son, but delivered him up for us all, how shall he not with him freely give us all things?" What a marvelous verse this is! Certainly worthy of extended examination!

We often think of the suffering Jesus experienced but we scarcely contemplate the suffering the Father experienced—at Calvary, yes, but at other times, too: in Gethsemane, at the Roman whipping post. Such unspeakable agony! The Father didn't want that hideous heap of sin on the shoulders of his Beloved! How could he ever want fellowship with his Son cut off?

None of us will ever know—on this side of heaven, anyway—all the Father went through to secure our salvation. But this much we can know. The Father didn't do what he did in a cold, mechanical, let's-follow-the-program kind of spirit. The heart-piercing agony he endured produced an anguish too great for words to communicate! But having so suffered—when he said "no" to Jesus in order to say "yes" to us—do we actually think that if he, in that most difficult of all trials, gave us Jesus—the best gift, extracting the highest price—that he will now be reluctant to give us other blessings in life?

Gethsemane shows the Father's heart! He will "freely" give you, Scripture says—not reluctantly, grudgingly, sparingly—but freely give "all things": be it material or immaterial, whether it be things having to do with your circumstances or things having to do with your character.

And he does this—why? *Because that's his heart!* And it is that you should reckon on when you go to him in prayer. On this point A. B. Simpson writes,

> Beloved, there is not a promise in your catalogue of promises, there is not a thought of blessing in your inmost heart, there is not a purpose of victory in your soul which did not originate with him. You can depend upon his loyalty and love. His great heart is set upon blessing you ....[12]

Yes, there may be times when the Father seems to be denying you, just as Jesus appeared to be denying the Syrophonecian woman that day when she sought healing for her daughter. But in the end, she got what she sought. "It was then," A. B. Simpson said, "that the Lord revealed the deep, intense love that had been waiting all through this trial of her faith to give its great reward."[13] For a season love hid so its fuller expression could later manifest.

In addition to an enduring and an enriching love, the Father's love toward us is also an *elevating* love. Just how elevating this love is was made clear when Jesus said, "I am in my Father and you in me and I in you" (John 14:20). By speaking these words, Jesus skyrocketed our significance beyond the highest aspiration we ever had! For when Jesus declared the Father would love us like he loved Jesus (John 17:23), and that the Father would give us the kind of glory he gave Jesus (John 17:22), our significance soared even higher. Words like these, if believed and received, surpass every thought previously believed about self-worth!

We who were made of dust ... we whose lives are but a vapor ... we who are as grass ... we who have offended the Father with years of deliberate sin. How can God possibly take those who are so vile and wretched and come this close to putting them into the Trinity? Answer: It's because they are not vile and wretched anymore! If they sin, it is a contradiction of who they are and not a reflection of who they are. Their real identity is singularly rooted in divine life, about which the church knows little.

While we don't want a *seduction* of Christianity, triggered by ungrounded and ill-founded speculation, we also don't want a *reduction* of Christianity, brought about by a turning away from words that Jesus clearly spoke.

What at the very least we can agree on is that the Father has a destiny for us which, if we saw it even partially, would overwhelm us. In his book, *Jesus, Our Man in Glory*, A. W. Tozer said that "we do not comprehend the glory that will be ours in that future day when, leaning on the arms of our heavenly Bridegroom, we are led into the presence of the Father in heaven with exceeding joy."[14]

To finally see our real identity, our sure destiny as heaven holds it forth, has immense applications for this life. One application being this: Whenever we have those moments when others don't seem to appreciate us, or when life itself seems to have settled into ruts of routine, we can rally our hearts with the encouragement we are on a journey toward a glory so stupendous that, once revealed, all our biggest dreams will be dwarfed.

As we focus on Scripture's portrait of the Father, it continually amazes us he is excellent in every way—especially when we contemplate alternatives! For example, what if the Father only had love, but he wasn't too bright? Sort of a sweet and gentle Gomer Pyle—"Gaawly!" Or what if the Father had impressive power, but the lights were turned off upstairs, like one of those Sylvester Stallone characters? Or what if he had power and wisdom, but there was no hint of forthcoming love—a robotic god utterly remote from creature emotions? But to have all three—love, power, and wisdom—in such a perfect blend, irresistibly draws us toward him in an unstoppable way.

Making this point, Thomas Goodwin wrote: "Heaven and glory are the highest things we are comprehensive of; when he would set out how great a God, how glorious a Father he is, he calleth him heavenly Father, a Father of glory in distinction to all fatherhoods."[15] There is no Father like our Father!

So, yes, an enduring love, an enriching love, an elevating love, but let's make one point clear—it is not an unconditional love. Both the church and the world like to talk about unconditional love, but the fact is no such love exists! There *are* conditions—even to God's love! Always have been. Always will be. We sing about "God's infinite grace," as if grace extends that far, but Scripture never says that! Abounding grace, yes; infinite grace, no. God's grace isn't infinite any more than his love is unconditional.

By adding hyperbole to sentiment, we dishonor God. By mixing self-intoxicating emotions with thoughts contrary to his Word, we dishonor God. We may launch our souls into an orbit of transcendent delight, but if this flight has an off-course trajectory into delusion, that kind of worship never honors God.

Our delight must spring from the facts God revealed; we can't be making this up as we go along. According to biblical facts, there *are* conditions set forth for inheriting eternal life, just as there are conditions sets forth for accessing greater degrees of this life while on earth. To speak as if these conditions don't exist, when they do, is misleading.

For example, if we won't confess, and repent, and turn our life over to God in lordship, then—because love and grace do have limits, do have preconditions—we're going to experience the judgment of God! Jesus himself said the reason the Father didn't leave him is because "I always do those things which please him" (John 8:29). Hypothetically, had this condition not been met, the outcome would have been different.

Again, the Father will daily manifest himself, to whom? Not to rebellious sinners, and not to the stuck-in-carnality Christians, but to those who keep his commandments (John 14:21). Here, the condition essential for God's manifested presence is obedience. A. B. Simpson warned how the flip side of this dynamic occurs. According to Simpson, "when we disobey God, we shall soon want to leave his presence altogether."[16]

Another condition essential for receiving God's love is faith. Romans 5:2 says we have access to grace by faith, which is exactly what Ephesians 2:8 says, "For by grace are you saved through faith ...." But what if faith isn't functioning? Then grace will be out of reach! Hebrews 10:35 says we will gain great reward *if we continue in our faith.* The condition prerequisite for great rewards, then, is what? Endurance!

So, summing up this point we can say that multiple conditions are repeatedly set forth in Scripture if a believer would obtain from God. Perhaps greater clarity on this issue is achieved by saying: *Accessing* God's love is conditional, even though the *availing* of God's love is not.

It is commonly observed that God doesn't have favorites; and there is some truth to this observation, in that Scripture declares four times that God is "no respecter of persons." So, yes, God extends his love to all people, independent of personal merit. And, yes, God judges all people by the same standard, with the same impartiality. However, there is a sense God does have favorites.

True, this favor wasn't arbitrarily granted or capriciously bestowed. For God's greater favor was extended because a few people believed God, when others did not. They obeyed God, when others did not. They immersed themselves in his Word, when others did not. They stayed long in the closet of prayer, when others did not. They stood strong in the battle against evil, when others did not.

The sanctified lifestyles of these people brought God's favor, not unlike the favor Peter, James, and John received. This favor, so treasured and inspiring, came not because they were the lucky winners of a lottery, but because they allowed themselves to be loved by a love that produces a life of consistent obedience.

Certainly, as we contemplate this life of obedience, we do not have to be discouraged about all it requires; it is the joy of the Father's fellowship that will motivate and strengthen us to do as Jesus did and remain steadfast in our obedience. Moreover, that new nature he put in us has within it all the law demands (Hebrews 8:10). Therefore, the life God wants us to live, he already supplied in our new nature.

Just know that the love that began our obedience will also sustain it. So as we draw close to the Father and receive from the Father, our motive and ability to be like him will steadily increase.

What further incentivizes this drawing close is the fact Father doesn't just know best—he is the best! Thomas Watson spoke truly when he said, "Such as have God for their Father are the happiest persons on earth ...."[17] And they are! The hymn writer's words are true: "... there is no other way to be happy in Jesus but to trust and obey."

Have you discovered in your own life how obedience leads to happiness? If this truth is somewhat new to you, then put it to the test. Thomas Manton, the seventeenth-century Puritan writer said, "All sin is rooted in a love of pleasure more than of God."[18]

How ironic this deception, because the greatest pleasure, the greatest happiness, is to be found in God. So will you pursue the higher happiness through obedience, and do so, as Manton put it "not only by vow and purpose but when it comes to trial"?[19]

Yes, do it today. And do it again tomorrow. In fact, do it always—for the Father.

Reflection Questions

1. Of the various gifts from God discussed in this chapter, which one means the most to you? The focus of this question is not which gift is the most important, theologically, but which gift is the most important to *you*, given what is going on in your life right now.

2. Assuming the same context provided by the previous question, select one of the three dimensions of God's love discussed in this chapter and explain why it means the most to you.

3. How does the love Jesus had for the Father impact you?

4. Are you going through life feeling loved by God? Please explain.

Chapter 8

Divinity's Direction—Part I

One of the biggest mistakes a Christian can make is to attempt to get closer to God through prayer, worship, fellowship, and ministry while the Bible, the whole time, remains a closed book. To the degree sanctioned lapses from God's Word are permitted, Christians are going to find themselves less and less accessible to God and more and more vulnerable to encroachments of evil.

This particular outcome isn't recent, for even the Old Testament reports it. God said, in Jeremiah 4:22, "For my people are foolish ... They are wise to do evil, but to do good they have no knowledge." No knowledge? Foolish? A condition among God's people?

Yes, due to the nature we were born with, and the instincts and inclinations of that nature that are a part of our phantom self, the flesh, sinning is often more natural to us than virtue is. As it turns out, no one has to go to school to be trained in selfishness. And no one has to learn how to lie. Actually, sin and selfishness predate kindergarten by several years. However, doing good (as the Bible defines good) involves a "counterflow" effort that requires special training.

With respect to this training, the psalmist said, "Your word have I hid in my heart that I might not sin against you" (Psalm 119:11). The rationale prompting these words was simply this: Because the imprinting of sin in our lives results in near-automatic behaviors, we need our mental circuitry broken with thought stoppages that come straight from the Word of God. A biblically defined alternative already stored—not in our minds only, but also in our hearts—is a strong deterrent to temptation's appeals.

But if truth is only floating in the shallows of the mental, it won't be retrieved during the day of temptation. And even if it is retrieved, it will fare no better than kindling does in the presence of fire. Only the word treasured in our heart will exert the vehemence necessary for victory. G. D. Watson declared, "It is the living word touching our faculties, piercing our conscience, melting our hearts, moving our will, vitalizing our motives which prepare us for obedience."[1] The strength and strategy of *that* word will be effective for us, as it was for Jesus while tempted in the wilderness.

One might suppose that when it came to the most dramatic showdown ever—Jesus and the Devil, each representing a supernatural kingdom, each on a collision course with the other—that there would be a weaponry display far more sophisticated than mankind had ever seen before! Surprisingly, though, instead of seeing shrieking demons, invading angels, and miracles countering miracles in the sky, we simply see Jesus holding up the Word, almost as a soldier holds up a shield. True, while the temptations employed that day were extraordinarily subtle, the defense Scripture offered proved in every instance invincible.

One might ask if God's Word in the hands of an ordinary believer could achieve similar results. This question arises because notable achievements in other domains are better accounted for by the unique abilities of the one who succeeded and not by the particular instruments they used to succeed.

Beethoven, for example, could compose extraordinary music on an ordinary piano; but that's because of his genius and not because of the piano.

George Herman Ruth set records in baseball that exist to this day. But these records had little to do with the bat the "Great Bambino" swung or the ball the Babe pitched. It was his rare and unmatched talents that explain these records, not the equipment he used.

So might not the same be true of the Word in the hands of the Master? Not exactly. According to Jesus, the Word sufficient for him that day in the wilderness will also make *us* clean (John 15:3), will build *us* up (Acts 20:32), will make *us* grow (I Peter 2:2), will furnish *us* sufficiently for all things (II Timothy 3:16). However—and this is the key point—if our only exposure to the Word is limited to church attendance on Sunday, then, for us, the Word won't achieve any of these things. Occasional intakes of God's Word will leave us as anemic spiritually as would the same frequency of food intake leave us anemic physically.

This is why the Bible says we're to desire the Word in the same way a baby desires milk (I Peter 2:2). So will a baby forgo milk due to forgetfulness about time? No, that won't ever happen! Well, then, could busyness or preoccupying interest account for missed bottle feedings? No, that won't happen, either! A baby *has* to have milk—and no explanation on a parent's part will deter this desire! In fact, if milk isn't forthcoming soon, the baby will vocalize insistence, wailing away in red-face anger!

By contrast, most Christians today will forgo the milk of God's Word without a peep of protest. Moreover, this take-it-or-leave-it attitude they have often means they leave it. It doesn't bother them. It doesn't make them long for what it is lacking. They may even justify their neglect by pointing an accusing finger at their schedules. Commenting on this response, Miles J. Stanford said:

> It is often the case that hungry believers, needy as they know themselves to be, are more eager for experience than they are for revelation. They want a minimum of truth and study, with a maximum of results. But the more experienced-centered these believers become, the less truth-established they will be. The penalty of this emphasis is self-centeredness instead of Christ-centeredness.[2]

Thus this result: disobedience and not obedience! Deficient in truth, they couldn't fool a fool, but they do fool themselves—to the point their excuse-making will take on a ring of truth. Words they would have choked on before, if such words had ever attempted to escape their lips, will be uttered later without any embarrassment at all.

But what do you think would happen if one of these Christians suffered an injury that required one hour of physical therapy each day? Why, with instant discipline and total diligence he or she would undergo that therapy and never miss a session! But doesn't this change in schedule raise a question about how this hour, which they said they didn't have for God's Word, suddenly became available?

The answer is simple: When it comes to top priorities, *we find the time*! Priorities of lesser rank may get shuffled, if not squeezed out entirely, but the time for top priorities is always found. According Tozer, the paramount importance of Scripture warrants this high-priority status.

> Whatever keeps me from the Bible is my enemy, however harmless it may appear to be. Whatever engages my attention when I should be meditating on God and things eternal does injury to my soul. Let the cares of life crowd out the Scriptures from my mind and I have suffered loss where I can least afford it. Let me accept anything else instead of the Scriptures and I have been cheated and robbed to my eternal confusion.[3]

If we go even three days without meeting the Lord in the Word, we will shrivel inside as surely as a punctured balloon, although not quite as fast. So, yes, the Word is indispensable to our growth, but so is the Holy Spirit.

Mindful of his disciples' future need, Jesus said the Holy Spirit would be sent to "teach you all things and bring to your remembrance all things that I said to you" (John 14:26). To these disciples, the "teaching of all things" included certain things Jesus had not taught (because they couldn't bear them yet), such things as Paul later taught in the Book of Ephesians and in the Book of Romans.

Of course, it was under the collective remembrance of these men that the New Testament was written. In writing it, however, these men weren't reduced to passive stenographers, in that their words were never the robotic byproduct of some mystical trance. Nevertheless, the words they did write were so supernaturally superintended by the Holy Spirit they were totally of God, and weren't in any way diluted by the participation of men.

In the beginning, the early church gathered to study "the apostles' doctrine" (Acts 2:42). But because these apostles would soon give their lives for what they taught, it became necessary to preserve their teaching in what is now a part of the Bible. Thus, with Scripture clearly in view, Jesus stressed its importance for obedience that night he went to Gethsemane.

Prophecy had said these men would scatter as sheep, and they did. To keep this failure from being inevitable in the future, Jesus spoke words his disciples would later remember, and Scripture would later record. Included in these words was this emphasis on Scripture's role for facilitating obedience.

In assessing the relationship we all ought to have with the Bible, Sir Arthur Blackwell summed up this relationship with four words—admit, submit, commit, and transmit. Let's begin to explore this valuable insight as we consider in this chapter the first two words he suggested.

Admit

First, we must admit what kind of book the Bible is. II Timothy 3:16 asserts that "All Scripture is inspired by God ...." This means that *he* breathed it, that its contents are the product of *his* mind. Therefore, the Bible has an indefectible authority; so much so the words "it is written" is deemed sufficient to clinch an argument and foreclose all discussion.[4] A. B. Simpson declared, "There is no testimony that needs to be more emphatically pressed upon the hearts of men today than the inspiration and supreme authority of the Word of God."[5]

Even though the Bible was written by more than forty different authors over a period of more than fifteen hundred years (these authors having different temperaments, backgrounds, and social standings), the fact remains that its contents originated outside the rim of human genius. The Bible isn't a compilation of man's best thoughts; for no man could know much of what Scripture disclosed unless God revealed it.

For example, long before science confirmed it, or man even suspected it, the Bible told us the earth was a sphere suspended in space hanging on nothing. Now how could anyone living more than three thousand years ago possibly know that?

Little wonder, then, when contemplating the declarations of Genesis, that the nineteenth-century French physicist, Jean Baptiste Biot, remarked, "Either Moses was as profoundly instructed in the sciences as is our century, or he was inspired."[6]

Scripture further validates itself by what it says about God. One could search all the books in all the libraries of the world and never find anything close to the biblical portrayal of God. When checking out the mythologies of Rome and Greece, the postulates of sophisticated philosophers, or the representations of the more crude in culture, we find either impish, vindictive gods, having all the foibles of man, or some nonpersonal, nonhistorical force that exudes its supposed wisdom far from the investigative forays of man. What we do not find, ever, is a depiction of God that mirrors the God of the Bible.

The depiction of God conveyed in Scripture just isn't what men would have conceived! For who would have imagined God becoming a baby, or God dying like a criminal, or the Son of God leaving this life with the cry that he had been forsaken by the Father? And who would have imagined the Son of God doubted by his family, rejected by his nearest neighbors, and deemed immoral by the religious leaders of his country? Had humans written the Bible, thoughts like these would have been omitted.

Also, had humans likened God to some creature in the animal world, it wouldn't have been a cute little lamb. A tiger, maybe; a lion, perhaps; or maybe even an eagle—but not a child's pet—a cuddly, huggable, wool-giving wonder!

Moreover, had Scripture been of human origin it would have come to terms with eternity in the same way every other religion did: on the premise of good works rewarded and bad works punished. This, of course, is not what Scripture did.

What should be obvious—indeed, unmistakably and unambiguously obvious—is that the surmises of man and the declarations of God are not the same! So, in this regard, the prophet's assessment is totally correct: God's ways are not our ways and his thoughts are not our thoughts. What the Bible says about God, man, salvation, and virtually any daily-life problem is radically different from what people typically think.

Even those books written by the world's most brilliant of men come nowhere close—in the truths they present, in their power to minister—to the book God wrote. It was this fact that caused Tozer to observe "... one of Isaiah's eloquent chapters or David's inspired psalms contains more help for mankind than all the output of the finest minds of Greece during the centuries of her glory."[7]

So why would anybody think this Grand Canyon gap (between man's reason and God's revelation) has suddenly closed in our day? On what basis would they believe, as they make their journey through life with their Bibles closed and their televisions on, that they and the Lord are pretty much on the same page? Would not a thirty-minute conversation with these people prove precisely the opposite? And would not a review of their problem-solving also prove the same thing?

It should be more than apparent that everyone of us needs a word from outside the flux of time and space, a word confluently given (the product of two free agents, human and divine), but a word so supernaturally superintended Scripture is able to declare, as it does more than 3800 times, "Thus says the Lord."

Fully endorsing Scripture's authority, A. W. Tozer described what happens to those who withhold this endorsement.

> Let a man question the inspiration of the Scripture and a curious, even monstrous, inversion takes place: thereafter he judges the Word instead of letting the word judge him; he

determines what the Word should teach instead of permitting it to determine what he should believe; he edits, amends, strikes out, adds at his pleasure; but always he sits above the Word and makes it amenable to him instead of kneeling before God and becoming amenable to the Word.[8]

To admit what kind of book the Bible it is to acknowledge it is far better than any book of the month but is actually the book of the ages, the eternal Word of God that will never pass away.

A. B. Simpson said, "The Bible is the mirror of God." It shows us what God is like, which apart from a revelation straight out of heaven we would never know. Illustrating our clueless condition, Simpson, in one passage, described a mindless mouse.

The little mouse that enters the cathedral has no eyes for the beauty of the architecture, no ears for the harmonies of the music, and no soul for the inspiration of the message it hears. All it sees is the crumb which is to satisfy its hunger, and all the rest is lost upon it.[9]

A. B. Simpson then said:

The Bible is more than a mirror. It is a love letter with your name inscribed upon it, a bankbook by which you draw from your great deposit all that it promises. The only way to make the Bible interesting is to learn to read it with your own name in it and to see in every promise a direct message for you.[10]

Further expounding the relationship between the Bible and God, G. D. Watson wrote: "God's words are expressions of the attributes and qualities of God's person and character." To search the Scripture, therefore, is to see the heart of God. And as for our own hearts, those needs are met best when we receive from God's Word. For as Dr. Watson noted, "... every truth in God as uttered in his Word corresponds with the capabilities and the needs of our nature."[11]

Accordingly, there are two attributes of Scripture that must be included whenever we admit what kind of a book the Bible is: 1) disclosures of divinity, unique to this one book and superior to all other books, and 2) the ability to nurture the needs of the human heart, to the extent that heart becomes more than human but divine (II Peter 1:4). These revelations about both God and man are essential.

Submit

Once we've acknowledged the unprecedented credentials of the Bible, we must then submit to what the Bible has to say. This submitting involves both a tender heart and a teachable spirit, each totally yielded to the gripping and governing of God's Word. In this regard, Acts 17:11 talks about receiving the Word with all readiness of mind.

Studies show that it takes the person in the pew only a third of the time to understand what the preacher is attempting to say. The other two-thirds of that time the listener's mind is doing something else—either wandering off into distractible thoughts, or allowing the Holy Spirit to make important connections between the generalized principles of the Word and the specific areas of a person's life that need those principles the most.

But before we can activate a tender and teachable heart, the Bible says we're first going to have to lay down all uncleanness and wickedness (James 1:21), for only then will we have the requisite meekness needed to see the Word salvage our souls.

Protracted sin, welcomed sin, will stop the intended ministry of the Word, which includes delivering us from predicaments we can't solve and from hurts we can't remedy. John Bunyan said, "This book will keep you from sin, or sin will keep you from this book."

Submitting to the Bible's message *before* it is heard is therefore essential to heart purity. The premise for this conclusion being: God isn't going to give truth to the heart that doesn't want it.

If the evil that corrodes, the evil that ruins, doesn't trigger an alarm at this point, then evil hasn't just encroached, it has embedded. Those who permit such a thing are dreadfully naïve about the dangers of sin. Thomas Guthrie, Scotland's eloquent preacher, once asked about who ...

> smiles to deceive, sings to lure, kisses to betray and flings her arms around our neck to leap with us into perdition?—Sin! Who turns the soft and gentlest hearts to stone? Who hurls reason from her lofty throne and impels sinners, mad as Gadarene's swine, down the precipice, into a lake of fire?—Sin![12]

Don't you see? The life of holiness is not an option; it's an obligation. Therefore, urging a proper response to this obligation, A. B. Simpson insisted:

> You must refuse the evil. You must say no sin. You must give God the right to make you holy. You cannot make yourself holy, but you can consent that he shall. Are you sick enough of sin to do this? Are you ready to take the first step which the old soldier so well describes as "right about face"? That is what the word repentance really means. It is to look the other way, to think the other way and to change your attitude toward sin and God.[13]

Of course, to properly submit to the Word also involves the Holy Spirit. In setting the proper context for this affirmation you must understand: The Father originated the Word, Jesus articulated the Word, but it is the Holy Spirit who brings the Word to our understanding with life-giving impact.

The Word we see on Scripture's pages is God's revelation, but the Word that finds its place in our heart is God's illumination. And, really, the miracle of illumination is every bit as great as the miracle of revelation!

Illumination takes what would have been limp, lame, lifeless truth—what Scripture calls "letter and death" (II Corinthians 3:6)—and turns it into testimony-altering reality, what Scripture calls "spirit and life" (John 6:63).

Did you know the only time we hear a wren sing is when it sings bass, and the only time we hear a bullfrog croak is when it vocalizes in the tenor range? Due to our auditory limitations, everything else in the respective ranges of these creatures can't be heard by the human ear.

And in a parallel way, the same is true with our capacity to hear Scripture. Human brainpower, however commendable its genius may be, lacks the tracking range to discern the truths of God's Word. Therefore, we need the Holy Spirit to overcome what for us would have been an insurmountable deficit.

Now, if truth-pondering were relegated to philosophers and poets only, and even to them this was but an optional enrichment, then maybe the Word and the Spirit wouldn't be critical to us. But because the decisions we make will be based on the truth we know, we can't afford to make our decisions based on erroneous information.

F. F. Bosworth said, "Faith begins where the will of God is known."[14] Consequently, what we *don't* know will hurt us, a fact underscored by God's word to Hosea, "My people are destroyed by a lack of knowledge ...." (Hosea 4:6). Check out the context for this statement in Hosea and you will see what the real problem was. The verse I just quoted quotes God saying, "... because thou has rejected knowledge, I will also reject thee ...." So here we learn it was their failure to submit that cut them off from knowledge. The transferable principle for us? God isn't going to tell us what we don't want to know.

Discerning the truth is a highly challenged endeavor in our day, due to the devil's persistent attempts to obfuscate whenever possible. By manufacturing multiple versions of truth, each layer grayer than the other, Satan schemes to confuse even the elect. This prompted Tozer to write:

So skilled is error at imitating truth that the two are constantly being mistaken for each other. It is therefore critically important that the Christian take full advantage of every provision God has made to save him from delusion. These are prayer, faith, constant meditation on Scripture, obedience, humility, hard, serious thought, and the illumination of the Holy Spirit.[15]

The old-time preachers said it well: We must "function with unction"—this anointing of God that teaches the truths of God. Because without the Holy Spirit taking the blinders off so God's Word *can* shine undimmed, we are vulnerable to the spiritual darkness where many dangers lurk.

Like a blind man encircled by muggers, we, too, will be clueless and defenseless, the inevitable prey of a punishing malice. To avoid this peril, we need the Holy Spirit to open our eyes; which is the reason Thomas Watson urged, "Pray that the same Spirit that wrote the Word may assist you in reading it."[16] For without his indispensable assistance, your efforts will be doomed.

In some older versions of Scripture we see the word "hearken" uttered by God or prophets prior to an importance message. G. D. Watson pointed out: "The word 'hearken' is composed of two words, *hear* and *ken*; the one denotes the function of the ear, the other the function of the eye."[17]

Although God causes the ear to hear and the eye to see, there *is* a responsibility we have. G. D. Watson explained:

> He means for all our power of looking and listening, all our power for undistracted attention, shall be centered upon the information he is about to give us ... Divine truth enters into us in proportion to the strength and continuity of our attention to it.[18]

Further extolling this effort, Watson wrote:

> To hearken to God! What a serene, blessed attitude of soul! To leave every receptive capacity open to him—the ear listening, the eye seeing, the heart longing, for every step of his feet, every word of his lips, every touch of his Spirit.[19]

The information that flows from this kind of intimacy exceeds the expectations of the one who sought it. Indeed, so profound and practical is this information it elevates recipients to a life much higher than they ever thought possible. None of this can happen, however, in the heart of divided loyalties, the heart that willingly negotiates with sin. For the heart that welcomes sin, rejects revelation.

To close one's spirit through sin, and then open the Bible with your mind only, is as foolish as it is futile. Word-to-soul transactions failed in the Old Testament, and they will fail today. There was a reason God gave what those in the Old Testament didn't have, a born-again spirit. That spirit is essential for getting God's truth! But if an unyielding soul presents itself to God, nothing much can happen in that condition. Not until submission occurs, thus allowing the spirit to function.

Admit and submit—two preconditions, if the Bible is going to serve us well. Once we acknowledge the unsurpassable credentials of this book, we can then move to stage two by submitting our lives to the God who wrote it. The most preposterous proposition, though, one many Christians deem operable, involves admitting without submitting. For many Christians, honorific words come freely when talking about the supremacy of Scripture. But when a rebellious life turns its pages, is it any wonder why so little benefit is gained?

The word we need in the battle against sin simply won't work if we've already left the battlefield. To put the white flag up to Satan means the whiter whiteness of God's holiness will not manifest.

In the next chapter we will examine two other stages for processing God's Word. But both stages are off-limits, if the first two stages aren't locked down in sacred resolve.

So, is there some unfinished business you need to do with the Lord? Do you want the Bible to be to you what it has been to other people? Listen, the yawns and glassy eyes don't have to continue! The Scripture can come to life for you, too, *if* you'll let God minister it to a spirit no longer shut down by sin.

Reflection Questions

1. This chapter presents a contrast between the treasured word and the word floating in the shallows of the mental. In terms of an overall assessment, which of the two is more characteristic of you?

2. A. W. Tozer addresses the need to be saved from confusion and delusion by getting the truth from God's Word. Are you able to retrospectively identify an experience where you misread a situation and by so doing brought pain into your life? If so, share this account; and if possible, share those scriptures that could have redirected you and spared you all this pain. Perhaps the group can suggest some scriptures.

3. Does the predicament of "admitting but not submitting" currently describe you? Please explain.

Chapter 9

Divinity's Direction—Part II

No one serious about obeying God should pursue this goal while relying on common sense. Our mind is exalted too much if we think it can discern all the obstacles to disobedience. The obtuseness of the human mind, especially when spiritual realities confront it, prevent a person from devising effective strategies for obedience. The discerning and devising needed can never be expected from a spiritual-tracking source clouded by the murkiness of mystery.

Military leaders, well aware of the fog of war during the chaos of battle, certainly know that disorientation is sometimes inescapable. Well, in spiritual warfare this same phenomenon presents, especially to those unaware of the divine directions set forth in Scripture.

The disciples we see in Gethsemane were obviously confused men. And this confusion, exploited by the enemy, caused them to retreat in defeat. This didn't have to happen, though, because Jesus sought to prepare these men for what they would face.

So was the preparation offered inadequate? No, that wasn't the problem. Yet, despite the word they had received from Jesus, the result was disastrously disappointing. And just here you might insert yourself in this story and find much in common with these disciples. You've got God's Word, right? You know there's nothing defective with the Word, right? So why all the failure?

Is failure inevitable? Many Christians think it is. Worth noting, however, is that Jesus didn't finish his statement, "In this world there is much tribulation ...." with the observation "... and that that's just the way it is in this world. You might as well get used to it." No, what Jesus said was different: "... be of good cheer for I have overcome the world."

To ourselves we may think, "Well, I'm glad somebody made it, but what about the rest of us? Can we overcome?" Indeed, we can! And that's why Jesus said, "be of good cheer." Now, if he did but we can't, there's really not much to cheer about. Perhaps in the next world there is, once we get out of this world. But that is not the gospel message!

We are told that sin shall have no dominion over us (Romans 6:14). None! And that applies to this world! So to that end Jesus set forth ten principles for achieving sustained obedience. One of these principles, introduced in the preceding chapter, emphasizes the foundational role Scripture has. The unimpeachable Word of God eliminates confusion. So the reception of such reliable guidance is obviously important.

In the previous chapter we considered two words Sir Arthur Blackwell said describes a proper relationship to the Word, the words "admit" and "submit." In this chapter we will consider two other words he stipulated, beginning with the word, "commit."

Commit

We see the best example of this quality in Jesus, of whom Scripture says that when the ultimate sacrifice came, "... he steadfastly set his face to go to Jerusalem" (Luke 9:51). Scripture reports that every attempt to get him to turn back—from Peter, from Lucifer, from the crowd that day at Golgotha, failed. For his mission was set! His resolve was unshakable! Therefore, his purpose could not be deterred!

The commitment the Lord made was never one of a set jaw and a stiff spine. Remember, Peter attempted a commitment like that in the garden—and saw it overcome in mere moments! Something much more durable is required if our commitment to the Word is to remain unflinching, unwavering, undaunted.

To commit properly we must see with enlightened eyes. For any courage dependent on natural thinking is vulnerable to defeat, no matter how much huffing and puffing bravery is vowed, such as Peter did in the Upper Room. The Word by itself, though, isn't enough, though. For unless the Holy Spirit illumines the Word, there can be light without sight.

It was William Tyndale who first translated, printed, and published an English version of the Bible—but not without a persecution that caused him to move his family three times! On the very day Tyndale first set his type, invading vandals destroyed it.

Undeterred, this man of God resumed his task in another land, whereupon he hid these printed Bibles in sacks of flour and smuggled them back to England. As it turned out, these Bibles were discovered by those who didn't want the Bible made available to common people. So the manuscripts were confiscated, and William Tyndale was first strangled—then set on fire!

But before dying William Tyndale prayed this simple prayer, "Lord, open the King of England's eyes." History records that prayer made its way to heaven on October 6, 1536. And in 1611, this prayer was answered in the most astounding way with the publication of what came to be the most popular Bible of all time, the King James Bible.

Now, in the same way God opened the King of England's, God will open your eyes and mine, enabling words that have long been familiar to us to at last implode with revolutionary impact. It is *this* kind of seeing that spares us confusion and keeps us firm in our commitment. And not halfhearted commitment, either, but wholehearted commitment.

There is a difference between these two types of commitment, a difference known all too well by the enemy who seeks to reduce one to the other. Observing both types of commitment, A. B. Simpson wrote:

> There are some who believe the Bible,
> And some who believe a part;
> Some trust with a reservation,
> And some with all their heart.[1]

To trust the Bible with all our heart is certainly the goal. But prior to this *governing* by the Word, there must first be a *gripping* by the Word. Jessie Penn-Lewis explained how Heaven's holding occurs.

> ... if God gives you a message which he means you to take hold of, *he holds you* even when you appear to lose it. His message given to you, *lays hold of you.* That word has divine life and energy in it, and it can grip you, and hold you to it. God requires your co-operation, of course, and you must actively take the word by faith; but the power is in the word itself when God has spoken it to you.[2]

Having been gripped by the Word through our Spirit-taught minds, we will next be strengthened to hold onto it in the same way Jacob held onto the angel when he cried, "I will not let you go unless you bless me!"

Such a commitment to the Word was conveyed in the King James Version of Scripture by using the word "heed." More than once we are instructed to heed what God says. So, offering an explanation of this word, A. B. Simpson wrote:

> The word "heed" is derived from the word "head," and it means that we should give our most earnest and careful attention ... How little attention we give to his Word! Preoccupied by a thousand other things when we hear it, and distracted afterwards by the whirl of the world's cares, pleasures and temptations, it scarcely finds lodgment in our minds ....[3]

There finally came a time in Jacob's life when this was no longer so. For many years Jacob lived a self-absorbed life, seeking to engineer everyone into his debt. Regarding this stage in Jacob's life, Alexander Maclaren stacked these descriptors: "Cool, calculating, subtle, with a very keen eye to his own interests and not at all scrupulous as to the means by which he secured them; he had no generous impulses and few unselfish affections."4 The cheat, the conniver, knew what he wanted—and was determined to get it!

But then came that night when Jacob, quite alone and very afraid, found himself in a fight with an angel. During this fight the angel dislocated Jacob's thigh, which is the strongest part of the body. When that occurred, Jacob could have fallen to the ground, defenseless and defeated. But because Jacob continued to hold onto this angel (which was really God), the announcement went forth that Jacob was the winner.

The winner? Yes, it was a determined dependence that enabled God to release blessings into Jacob's life, and to do so with a freedom and fullness Jacob's obtuse thinking had long disallowed.

Just know there will come a time when God also tests us. G. D. Watson wrote:

> It is in these testings and these trials and these strange experiences you go through that you are driven to your Bibles. You search the Psalms and the Prophets to find a parallel case with your own, and you find one in the inspired Word of God. It is in these trials and troubles that people learn how to appreciate the Word of God in a way that young Christians know nothing on earth about.5

In such times, Watson wrote, "We are to keep the Word he commits to us, and he keeps the soul we commit to him."6

In fact, the greatest blessing this world has ever known came into being because someone agreed to the Word, despite the awful predicament this acceptance presented. You remember Scripture's account of another angel appearance, the angel Gabriel appearing to Mary. This unmarried, Palestinian girl thought she knew what her future was going to be. She would marry Joseph, a carpenter from Nazareth; and then, like her parents and their parents, she would devote her life to raising a family as a good Jewish wife and mother.

But then one day—and, oh, what a day!—the angel Gabriel appeared to tell this teenage girl that the Lord from on High had chosen her to become the mother of the Son of God.

So how was Mary going to explain this proposed pregnancy? She, an unmarried virgin, miraculously impregnated by God ... and now—wonder of wonders!—blessed with a child! A story like this would certainly set tongues wagging! And her husband-to-be wondering!

Of course, had Mary declined, and had other prospective mothers similarly declined, Jesus wouldn't have been born. And that's because—for Mary then, and for us today—the Word by itself can't produce the desired result—not without a commitment from the human heart. In fact, it wasn't until Mary spoke those crucial words, "Be it unto me according to your Word," that the angel could then depart and the miracle could then occur.

What followed Bethlehem came to be known as "the hidden years," the years that saw baby Jesus grow up to be a man. There was, we know, an appearance of the boy Jesus at the temple, but other than that not much is known about those growing-up years. Except for a few family members, no one knew that the Messiah was in their midst.

Finally, the time came for Jesus to declare himself. You know the story. While attending a wedding at Cana of Galilee, Mary discovered that her very dear friends had run out of wine—and this represented a monumental embarrassment in that day! The wedding feast was such a highlight in Jewish life that families would scrimp and save for years to assure abundance. But since these wedding feasts often lasted for a week or longer, calculating and providing the needs for them was no easy task. In this instance, the dreaded shortage occurred; so Mary went to Jesus.

In hearing what Mary had to say, Jesus was immediately faced with a quandary: What was he supposed to do—to perform a miracle? But why would Mary think this was an option? Jesus had never performed a miracle! Yet it was clear that was what Mary was asking! This implied request posed a major problem for Jesus, because he knew that if he did what Mary was asking, his days of quiet ministry were over.

Knowing that Mary was expecting a miracle, Jesus reminded her, tenderly, that his hour hadn't come yet; meaning, of course, the appointed time for this new ministry phase to begin had not arrived. Undeterred, Mary released her faith by speaking words to the servants so reminiscent of the words she had spoken more than three decades earlier, "Whatever he says to you, do it" (John 2:5).

Wasn't this how Mary responded to that word from the Lord many years before—God spoke, she complied, and a miracle occurred? Well, as Mary found herself facing the impossible again, she knew exactly what was needed—a word, and then obedience to that word, and a complete trust in God. Hence, this little lady walked away from Jesus with complete confidence. She didn't know what Jesus would do, nor how he would do it, but the important point is—*she did not withdraw her request*! To the contrary, her faith *expected* a miracle that day, or she wouldn't have said anything to the servants. Instead, she would have apologized for this intrusion on the divine timetable and returned to her friends with feeble words of comfort.

Do you see how exalted this transaction was? Here we find an intersecting of the human and the divine! At the outset, God approaches Mary with a request that put her in a dilemma. And now Mary was approaching God with a request that put him in a dilemma. When Jesus went to the wedding party that day, he had no idea his ministry was about to be launched to another level. Having laid omniscience aside to become a man, Jesus was totally dependent, always, on knowledge flowing from the Father—*and the Father hadn't said anything to Jesus about this*!

But when Mary came to Jesus with this request, this Jewish mother who wasn't easily going to be denied, *that request moved God*! And suddenly—what do you know?—Jesus got a word he hadn't received before!

The result wasn't just a miracle (although Israel hadn't seen one of these for centuries), but a miracle of a higher order, what theologians call a nature miracle. For in order to turn water into wine, the whole process of grapes being planted, nurtured, plucked, aged, squeezed, and distilled had to be completely bypassed. Instead, water became what water could not become. The transformation, obviously, wasn't natural; it was supernatural.

When evaluating Scripture's reports of miracles, A. B. Simpson noted how "the devil is trying to get the supernatural out of the Bible, out of the church, and out of our individual Christian lives ...."[7] Yet, myriad, magnificent miracles were prominent throughout Jesus' ministry, and all had their beginning that day in Cana.

The impossible happened all because someone sought a word, got a word, and obeyed that word. And doesn't this speak a much-needed encouragement for your life? Perhaps you find yourself in a situation that seems to have impossibility written all over it. So what should you do—accept what reason is telling you and respond to the situation with a sweet smile and utter futility? Or should you do as Mary did and move both the heart and hand of God with an expectancy rooted in the Word, an expectancy that refuses to be deterred by the testimonies of sense and sight?

"Do whatever he says to you." These words from Mother Mary speak of *complete* commitment, do they not? Yet, many restrict their commitment by doing only that part of Scripture they agree with, or that part that isn't inconvenient, or that part that isn't hard. The selective obedience that edits God keeps self on the throne, thereby preventing awesome answers from God.

Transmit

There can be no doubt that great blessings come whenever the Word of God is believed and activated. But because God doesn't want us to keep the blessings of his Word to ourselves, we are often instructed to pass these on. Sir Arthur Blackwell said, "Don't be a pool; be a stream. Don't hoard you riches; share the bounties of the Lord's table with another. Make every truth tenfold your own by passing it on."

Isn't it interesting that when the Bible says we're to let the Word dwell in us richly, it then tell us we're to teach others (Colossians 3:16)? We may think, "But I don't have the gift of teaching! No one has ever asked me to teach—and for good reason!"

Maybe so, but whenever the Word translates you—that is, whenever you prove a Bible principle in your life, and experience the fulfillment of a Bible promise—you are to share what happened to you with others. People are fascinated to hear what God has done in another believer's life. Truth couched in personal testimony is doubly irresistible in its appeal.

For this precise reason, before God instructed parents to diligently teach their children, he first declared "... these words which I command you shall be on *your* heart ...." (Deuteronomy 6:6, 7). Piety by proxy wasn't an option. Alexander Maclaren wrote, "The Jewish father was not to send his child to some Levite or other to get his question answered, but was to answer it himself."[8] And the same holds true for today.

Parents are to regularly and systematically teach their children God's Word. This is not a transferable responsibility that can be shuffled off to the pastor, youth leader, or Sunday School teacher. However, for that word to be taught effectively, it must first be on the parent's hearts. Because if it is not on their hearts, the kids will know it is not, and rebellion will likely rise in their hearts.

So if all is not well between you and the Lord, do as David did in Psalm 51 and return to the Lord with both an honest confession and radical repentance. Having finally come to the Lord in this way, after serious sin and stout stonewalling, what did David say? "Then will I teach transgressors their ways and sinners will be converted."

Notice the time sequence implied here. First comes confession, repentance, and its resulting forgiveness and joy, and *then* comes the teaching. This makes a lot of sense, because to teach beyond our experience, or contrary to our experience, is to perpetuate a fraud bound to be discovered.

Maybe you are like other Christians, in that you don't have much to say about the Bible? Could it be that the real reason for this isn't your lack of giftedness, as you have said, nor your lack of eloquence, as you have also said, but because there isn't enough of a good news story in you that motivates you to speak up? The word muted in our own lives isn't likely to motivate anyone else.

Here's the deal. If the teachings of God's Word never become testimonies for you, and the principles of his Word never get proven in your life, you won't be able to teach what you don't know, nor give what you don't have. Vance Havner said it well: "We have neither learned nor taught a Bible truth until we observed it, put it into practice."[9]

Make no mistake: God does want you to teach! But this isn't going to happen—with his sponsorship, anyway—until first you *admit* what kind of book the Bible is; and then with a tender and teachable heart *submit* to what it has to say, and next *commit* to its ongoing authority in your life. For only then will you be able to *transmit* to others what God has energized in you.

Again, it is sheer illusion for anyone to think a person can get close to the Lord while the Bible remains a closed book. And really—even if the Bible is opened, studied, memorized, and taught, that still won't provide an effective deterrent to sin. Not by itself, anyway. But what *will* get the job done is the revealed Word hidden with purpose in our hearts.

This hiding of the Word in our hearts is like stashing a treasure, such as was done during those pirate days of old. A special place is always going to be found for treasure: a place that provides easy enough access but also top-notch protection.

So why is this head-to-heart transition so seldom made by Bible readers? One reason, according to Spurgeon, is that "much apparent Bible reading is not reading at all. The verses passes under the eye, and the sentences glide over the mind, but there is no true Bible reading."[10] Failing to achieve focus assures minimal understanding and no spiritual gain.

In his book, *Helps to Holiness*, Samuel Brengle wrote:

> If you want to hold the truth fast and not let it slip, you must read and read and re-read the Bible. You must constantly refresh your minds with its truths ... John Wesley, in his old age, having read and read and re-read the Bible, said of himself—"I am *homo unius libri*—a man of one book."[11]

If only we could make such a claim and have it be true, right? But be aware that a noble aspiration like this will not go unchallenged. Ever alert to this fact, Lilias Trotter wrote, "... Satan knows well the power of concentration. If a soul is likely to get under the sway of inspiration, 'this one thing I do,' he will turn all his energies to bring in side interests that will shatter the gathering intensity."[12]

A single-minded devotion to Scripture will energize the commitment of those who make it and help them see each distraction for what it really is, a sad and sorry substitute for the God of the Word.

God is in his Word; and therefore if we really want to meet him, we must meet him there. Remember, the Bible seldom consulted predicts a spiritual growth constantly stagnated. So the only way to avoid sin and obey God is to stay in his Word—heeding, hearkening, and harvesting until no distractions or substitutes remain.

The rally cry of Thomas Watson is worth adopting, "Let us lead Scripture lives."[13] Let the Word become flesh again, as we incarnate its truths in a visible testimony worthy of God's name.

The authentic Christian life *can* be transmitted with appeal. Instead of being hid under a bushel of hindering sin, the light will shine, the fruit will show, the glory will manifest. Therefore, that which could have remained on a shelf, some dusty book seldom opened, is now seen by eyes that need this revelation.

So let the Bible translate you! And let Satan, who lost his campaign against Jesus in the wilderness, experience another defeat—with sin repeatedly resisted by you, and the righteousness of God continually displayed in you.

Reflection Questions

1. How has this chapter influenced your decision to meet the Lord in the Word daily?

2. Describe a recent experience in which the Holy Spirit made a scripture come alive for you.

3. Is there a seemingly impossible situation you're facing right now? If so, how does the story of Mary relate to this situation?

4. Do you share testimonies of how God's Word has worked in your life? Assess why your answer is what it is.

Chapter 10

Peace's Protection—Part I

It is the most natural thing in the world to prefer safety to danger and security to risk. So strong is this desire that there's no need cataloguing all the dangers that promote it or all the contingencies that compel it. People wanting job security, for example, will seek tenure, no-cut contracts, or union protection (if they can get it); and those wanting psychological security will seek people who exhibit positive emotions, shared values, and common interests.

Wanting security isn't wrong. But we must be careful not to go looking for it in all the wrong places, or lunge for what may turn out to be a sham security.

What all of us would much prefer is a trouble-free life where contentment comes easily and frustration doesn't come at all. Yet, to our chagrin, Scripture tells us neither the devil, nor God, wants us to have this kind of life. That the devil would agitate and frustrate we can well understand, but why wouldn't God sanction the trouble-free life?

Many years ago a passenger was looking out an airplane window when he noticed some curious looking devices attached to the underside of the wings. He asked the stewardess what they were. Not knowing the answer, the stewardess visited the cockpit and soon returned with this explanation. Those devices, she said, were called vortex generators. Their main function was to roughen up the air. This particular plane flew better, aeronautical engineers discovered, if there were some turbulence underneath the plane.

And might not the same thing be said about our journey through life? Often, it is during the smooth times, the times when all is going well and we haven't a care in the world that our heads get turned, our hearts get divided, and our spiritual muscles become soft. It is instructive, in this regard, to note that when Paul listed the things that might separate us from the love of God, he didn't just list the more ominous realities like death, depths, demons, and devils. But he included "life," "heights," and "things present," realizing the desirable and the seemingly safe pose their threats, too (Romans 8:38, 39).

It must again be acknowledged that many of our troubles were never sponsored by God, actively or passively, and therefore, if the proper theology were in place, these problems should have been resisted and not accepted. Nevertheless, while not wanting to eulogize trouble, there needs to be recognition that one of the reasons God wants turbulence in our lives is because of its character-building benefits. In his book, *Living and Enjoying the Fruit of the Spirit*, Ian Barclay gives the following account:

> A young man once went to his pastor, George Mueller, with a spiritual problem. He said, "Mr. Mueller, my Christian life lacks patience. I wonder if you could show me how to find it?"
>
> George Mueller told the young man that his problem was not too difficult to solve, and suggested that they both kneel in prayer. The pastor prayed, "Lord, I want you to give this young man some tribulation in his life. Give him weeks of tribulation; make that the experience of every moment of every day."
>
> The young man got up and pulled George Mueller to his feet. "I am sorry, I think you must have misunderstood me—it is patience that I want and not tribulation."

"Indeed," said the pastor. "The Bible quite clearly says that 'tribulation worketh patience,' so you won't find it in any other way." [1]

Among the benefits tribulation offers us is this propensity to turn us so completely toward the Lord that he becomes plan A and there won't even be a plan B. The Bible says that patience—which is the decision to keep faith on the job—will make us perfect, entire, lacking nothing (James 1:4). Of course, life on Easy Street won't achieve this; and neither will hibernating in a place of supposed safety. The only way this benefit can be produced is through the vortex generators of tribulation.

The fifth chapter of Hebrews speaks words on this topic which at first seem puzzling. Attempting to sort this out in his book, *Tribulation Worketh*, G. D. Watson wrote:

We are taught here that Jesus learned obedience by the things which he suffered, and we are also taught that by his sufferings and obedience he was also made perfect; and that being made perfect, he was fitted to be the Author of salvation to all who obey him.

The question comes: Was not Christ divine and perfect and complete from the beginning? Did he need suffering in order to teach him obedience? Did he need obedience in order to make him perfect? There seems to be implied in this language that Jesus was very imperfect, and that there was a liability in him to disobedience, etc. [2]

Erasing all such doubts from the mind, Watson asserted:

Jesus brought into this world with him the essence, the spirit of perfect obedience. The trend and drift and constitution and bias of his own will and heart was in the line of obedience. There was never one atom of rebellion, there was never one scintilla of disobedience, in the outward or in the inner life. He never did one single thing, and he never had the disposition to do a single thing to displease God. Every breath he drew and every act he performed and every outgoing of his heart pleased God.[3]

So in what sense, then, did Jesus learn obedience and complete his perfection? Watson answered this question, saying, "You must remember that the principle of obedience is one thing—that lies in the heart—but the application of that principle is something else."[4] Though nothing was ever added to the heart (there was never a need for that), what was added were manifestations from the heart.

Commenting on this verse about Jesus learning obedience through suffering, Watson acknowledged:

Many have stumbled over this scripture. Jesus had in him the principles of perfect obedience from his birth, and he never once disobeyed the Father in thought, word, or act. But that perfect spirit of obedience had to be brought out in a thousand various applications and directions ....[5]

The Bible tells us this obedience was exercised during the most trying of circumstances. And this is where we will pick up our story.

As Jesus and the remaining eleven disciples were talking in the Upper Room, the impression was clearly reinforced that there was danger in the air. Earlier, Jesus had announced to the disciples that the time was at hand for him to be delivered up as a sacrifice. Therefore, realizing the relationship between danger and disobedience, Jesus said, "Peace I leave with you, my peace give I unto you, not as the world gives do I give you. Let not your heart be troubled, neither let it be afraid" (John 14:27).

This peace provision was made (for the disciples then and for us today) because once fear muscles into one's life, it tends to totally take over, replacing one's capacity to reason and, more concerning still, replacing the rightful role that God's Word should have in daily decision-making.

The resulting discombobulating within will become a perfect setup for sin. Because once a believer has been pried loose from his faith, he'll accept almost anything that will relieve his pain, or at least diminish the pressure being exerted against him. For the disciples, this meant denying Jesus and scattering in wild fright like a bunch of sheep.

Given the fact that fear is the main way the enemy accesses our lives, it is important that we understand how this tactic works. Paul said we are not ignorant of Satan's devices (II Corinthians 2:11). Which is to say, we know his tricks, we know his traps, we know how he operates. But, while Paul and others mature in the faith possess this knowledge, most people do not. Knowing how Satan operates—especially when it comes to utilizing his most destructive device, fear—remains a mystery to them.

The Alarm of Adverse Circumstances

There are at least three factors that account for the sudden and destructive impact of fear. First, there is an adverse circumstance. When learning that something foreboding is about to occur, it is common for the mind to go out of gear and for conclusions to be drawn that aren't true at all. This, then, may activate what psychologists call dichotomized thinking, an eclipsing of the vast middle by lapsing into extreme either/or thinking. This "all good" or "all bad" mindset can swiftly swing to "all bad." And should that occur, emotions will then freeze this picture so that in this fixed and static state it feels as if it is the only perspective that could be true, although it is not.

An example of dichotomized thinking is found in the Old Testament story of Jacob receiving news that young Benjamin must return to Egypt. His older brother Simeon was being held in prison there, and now, the brothers said, Benjamin was being summoned to report to the official who put him there.

Almost at once Jacob sinks into despair, saying, "Joseph is dead. Simeon is gone. Benjamin is now being taken away. All things are against me" (Genesis 42:36). But was this true? To one who saw only the bad it certainly seemed that way.

Having insight into this despairing perspective, Dr. J. H. Jowett wrote:

Sometimes the darkness settles down upon our life, and we think that all is over, and the blessedness is spent. There is a grave somewhere—maybe it is the grave of a loved one, or the grave of some fair, cherished hope, or of some fond and promising ambition. And that grave seems to be as big as the world.[6]

Jowett continues: "In how many millions of lives the sunshine has fled, and all the birds are hushed, and it seems as though the final night has fallen, and as if there will be spring no more!"[7]

Likewise, F. B. Meyer observed:

We are often tempted to judge hastily, and by appearances; by our own despondent, sorrowful hearts; or by the reports of others. We may say that certain things are against us, when, if we would only look beyond appearances and circumstances to God, we should find that he had been working, and was working, mightily on our behalf—that all was for our lasting good.[8]

Dichotomized thinking distorts reality. As it turned out, Joseph *wasn't* dead, Simeon *wasn't* going to be kept in prison. And Benjamin *wasn't* going to prison. In reality, God was at work behind the scenes, rescuing Jacob's family from famine, and elevating every single one of them to a place of plenty and prosperity for many years to come.

Yet, the dichotomous mindset can be so invested in what it thinks, it gives God no credit, gives faith no possibility to work, and then refuses to believe good news even when it arrives.

Scripture reports that when Jacob was later informed that his son Joseph was not only alive but was now the governor of Egypt, Jacob refused to believe it (Genesis

45:26). This is typical of dichotomous thinking. Accordingly, F. B. Meyer declared:

> Blind unbelief is sure to err,
> And scan his work in vain,
> God is his own interpreter,
> And He will make it plain.[9]

Yet even when made plain, dichotomized thinking can be slow to see what's true.

There is another erroneous perspective that often gets dragged into this, something psychologists call catastrophic thinking. Catastrophic thinking doesn't calibrate, and therefore a problem that really may be a "two" in its severity gets interpreted as an "eight." This is simply fear doing what it typically does, exaggerating. Jacob's brother, Esau, is an example of this.

One day Esau returned home from one of us game-hunting expeditions, weak from hunger and perhaps from the journey itself. Ah, but an aroma greeted him that led straight to the stew Jacob was cooking in the kitchen!

Upon seeing his big harry brother, Jacob squinted his calculating eyes and decided to strike a bargain: "My stew for your birthright," Jacob proposed.

On the face of it, this proposition was totally absurd—you mean so much for so little? But notice how Esau responded. With much drama in his voice, his knees buckle in supposed feinting, as his eyelids flutter in supposed exhaustion. Our sufferer then exclaimed, with heaved sighs and a cracking voice, "I'm at the point of death! What good is the birthright going to do me?" (Genesis 25:32).

Really? This man had only a few minutes to live? I don't think so! A *real* starvation victim couldn't stand, couldn't talk, and could barely remain conscious. So do you think there was some catastrophic thinking going on?

Apparently so, because in mere moments this guy turned around and "woofed" down a big plate of stew—something a real starvation victim could never do! Here we see the erratic Esau exaggerating his problem—and that ended up in deep regret and a major loss!

The person gripped by catastrophic thinking (and it may be a very intelligent person) is fixated in his conclusions, totally convinced that the outcome is as inevitable as he or she has projected it to be. This, then, creates a great upheaval inside that may result in a foolish attempt to defense a wrongly perceived problem.

By yielding to impulse and not reason, Esau sold his birthright—a family fortune that could have blessed him for years! This transaction—on its surface and in its details—was nothing short of preposterous! As might be expected, Esau later rued the day he made this decision. The consequence of catastrophic thinking, lamentable loss, is actually common to this mindset, yet uncommon in its pain.

Another consequence of fear is this: Fear in its ascendancy can cut a Christian off from Jesus, which is exactly what happened in the garden that night. When the disciples saw Jesus led away by the soldiers, something happened to them that has happened to many believers since. The Bible says these disciples followed Jesus from "a far." Yes, they were going in the same direction Jesus was going, but now they weren't as close to him as they had been before. The distance between Jesus and these disciples became greater and greater, until eventually they turned to go in one direction, while Jesus went in another.

Isn't that what fear does to us, too? It wedges between us and the Lord, and then it creates an increasing distance between us and the Lord! Fear will cause the Lord to get smaller in our eyes as the fellowship distance from him becomes greater. Then, eventually, fear will cause us to go in a different direction than where the Lord is going. In this way, fear fractures our fellowship with the Lord, thereby separating us from the ultimate source of overcoming strength.

The opposite dynamic was recommended by A. W. Tozer in his book, *The Warfare of the Spirit.*

True faith delivers from fear by consciously interposing God between it and the object that would make it afraid. The soul that lives in God is surrounded by the divine Presence so that no enemy can approach it without first disposing of God, a palpable impossibility.[10]

The disciples were stunned beyond words that Jesus let himself to be led away from the garden like that! But why were they stunned? For one solid week Jesus had told them *in detail* everything that was going to happen—so this was hardly a surprise attack!

The real reason they were stunned was due to denial (one form of fixated thinking), which had blocked out everything Jesus said. This is the kind of denial that is much in evidence in our hearts when we think, "Why should anything bad happen to me now that Jesus is in my life? Speak to me about good things—the blessings, the promises, the glory of his kingdom! Tell me how God will make my life abundant! Tell me about the destiny he has mapped for me and all the good things about heaven!"

A sense of entitlement soon becomes operational in our lives, wherein presumptuous thinking is wrongly deduced from God's promises. Also operational in our lives is a grid that permits access to parts of Scripture and blocks access to other parts of Scripture.

These adverse circumstances that come our way always carry a message, a Goliath-like taunt meant to send us into cowardice. For the disciples, the arrest of Jesus and his subsequent execution meant he must not have been God. This premise, once accepted, then compelled the conclusion: All the hopes they had attached to him weren't coming true!

Just know that fear always slanders God and that it always tempts us with some form of dichotomized, catastrophic thinking. In this state of mind, we won't check to see what the Word of God has to say about our fear. Instead, we'll uncritically accept the message from the enemy as true—when, considering the source, it has to be false!

Not wanting to fall into this pattern, the psalmist took himself in hand and asked the question straight out, "Why are you cast down, O my soul? And why are you disquieted in me?" (Psalm 42:5). This step, so important for recovery, refuses to let unidentified feelings ramble around in the basement of our soul. Instead, the mind gets focused, a problem-solving mindset gets activated until, soon enough, a diagnosis is made, which then commences a search for a solution. As John Henry Jowett pointed out, the welfare of our peace need not be vulnerable to circumstances, for "the peace of Jesus is evidently not synonymous with the quietness of settled circumstance ... It can coexist with turbulence."[11]

The Sabotaging of a Low Self-Image

A second factor conducive to a fear-attack is a low self-image. At times, fear can almost bludgeon our sensibilities with its devastating threats. It can reduce us to near insignificance so fast that even a cowardly crawl is more elevated than where we have been cast! In our minds, defeat is certain; so, for us, the only question that remains is, where can we hide?

Did the disciples see how they could stand strong in the midst of Roman soldiers, a hostile government, and the almost hysterical vengeance of an angry mob? No, with the exception of Thomas' resignation of doom and Peter's ill-advised attempt at bravery, courage among this group was nowhere to be found.

Someone has painted a picture entitled, "Silent Saturday." It is a picture of these disciples sitting behind bolted doors with the most forlorn expressions on their faces. With their heads in their hands, time painfully passes with no altering of pose. No one says anything. No one does anything. Because, as Alexander Maclaren observed, the conclusion these men drew about the cross was along these lines: "His death seems to demonstrate his claims to be madness, his hope to be futile, his promises to be wind."[12] Hence, the reason for this stillness, this silence, is clear: With all hope gone, what was there to say?

For many people today, this dreaded silence has become a much longer season. Feeling overwhelmed, bitter, hollow, and empty, they too have no motivation to go on. Much like the Gethsemane-exiting disciples, fear has marched in and stomped their hopes into near oblivion. And just as ruthlessly, fear has remained on the scene in regiment, ready to move against any semblance of restored hope. So, whether they know it, fear has actually converted them into false worshippers, as they now believe and bow down to what was never from God.

Perhaps you'll recall from the Old Testament how Gideon felt totally overmatched by the surrounding Midianite army. Knowing how fear finds fertile soil in the mud of low self-esteem, God addressed this farmer who had never had a single day of military service in his life as a "mighty man of valor." The reason God spoke that way was this: He knew that Gideon would never stand up to fear as long as he retained the image he had of himself. That image, therefore, had to be changed!

Because we are all born inferior (in that babies can't do what big people do), this sense of inferiority can gain a huge advantage over us long before adult years. We may try to beat it back by impressive overachievement, but studies show inferiority feelings can't be cured that way. For despite the respect we have earned—or, in more unusual cases, the adulation that we have received—festering underneath this puff of positives are all these "not okay" feelings that have been with us for as long as we can remember.

The Accuser knows exactly where the target is; so he launches his accusations against our inadequacies, not just because he is mean, but for more tactical reasons. The devil knows that if he can remind us of our sorry and sinful past, he can then drive a wedge between us and the Lord that will effectively shut down the one bridge essential for God's provisions to cross, the bridge of faith.

Then, once our faith bridge is in collapse, we can be tempted to utilize a foolish defense the devil can easily defeat.

The Illusions of Imagination

A third factor conducive to a fear attack is one's own imagination. What an awesome couple these two make, fear and imagination, as they dance wildly into the night! Satan knows if he can get his fear pictures onto our mental screen, he will win. It doesn't matter how much of God's Word we know, these fear pictures can neutralize all that. So, as far as Satan is concerned, let the dance begin!

The Bible alerts us to how fear brings torment (I John 4:18). Before adverse circumstances do what they do, fear will first cause us to suffer its consequences a hundred times before it happens, and often a hundred times worse than what actually happens. Each flashing of fear onto our mental screen represents a deeper cutting into our hearts and an ever widening division in our minds. In this regard, it is interesting to learn the etymology of the word "worry." John Haggai informs us:

> The word "worry" comes from the Greek word *merimnao* which is a combination of two words: *merizo* meaning "to divide" and *nous* meaning "mind" (including the faculties of perceiving, understanding, feeling, judging, determining).[13]

By contrast, the Greek word for "peace," the word *eirene*, literally means to bind together. Obviously, God doesn't want us coming apart; rather, in the vernacular of the day, he wants us to have it "all together."

It sometimes seems that the ones more vulnerable to fear-attacks are those who, being more emotionally inclined, live soulishly. In his book, *The Spiritual Man*, Watchman Nee referred to these Christians as "Bohemians" who function, he says, in this fashion.

> On a windy morning or a moonlit night, for example, they are apt to be pouring out their souls in sentimental songs. They frequently bemoan their lives, shedding many tears of self-pity. These individuals love literature, and are simply ravished by its beauty. They also enjoy humming a few lyric poems, for this gives them a transcendent feeling. They visit mountains, lakes, and streams, for this brings them closer to nature. Upon seeing the declining course of this world, they begin to entertain thoughts of leading a detached existence. How ascendant, how pure they are! Not like other believers who appear to be so materialistic, so pedestrian, so enmeshed.

> These Christians deem themselves most spiritual,
> not recognizing how incredibly soulish they are.
> Such carnality presents the greatest obstacle to
> their entering a wholly spiritual realm because
> they are governed so completely by their
> emotions.[14]

Indeed, the overly emotional, the overly imaginative, present a big target for Satan's fiery darts!

When informed by Scripture that we are to cast down those imaginations in conflict with the Word of God, we may wonder out loud how we're supposed to do this. Actually, we are to do this by reexamining, in the light of God's Word, what we've just discussed: our view of the circumstances, our view of ourself, and our view of some fear-engendered image.

The circumstances, if we view it with natural eyes and carnal minds, may very well be intimidating. However, that intimidation will substantially shrink, if we'll focus on the promised resources of God and on the very character of God that assures these resources will be released in a timely way.

As for that low self-image that frequently plagues us, it too will become a nonfactor once the Lord's exalted and elevated assessment of us becomes a revelation to us. Since the Lord has given us his heart, his life, and his nature, there is no way these feelings of inferiority are accurate. We are seated in heavenly places, not on some stool for a fool.

True enough, the Accuser may send destructive feelings our way. But, remember, we can send these feelings right back to the pit from which they came!

What should always prevail in our minds is that God's assessment of us is far truer than what the devil would have us believe! So instead of uncritically accepting his images as accurate representations of the truth, we can experience the spell of every one of them being broken by the sweet assurances of God. In the same way a parent will comfort a child afraid of menacing shadows in the closet, and suspected movements under the bed, God will settle our rapidly beating hearts with reminders that these fears are imagined after all, no more true today than what our little minds conjured up when we were young and afraid in our beds at night.

There is one other way that our imagination can help us gain what may seem an elusive victory. The Bible tells us God wants to break the power of the present over our lives and learn to live under the power of the world to come. But how can this be achieved? A. B. Simpson explains.

> The Holy Spirit alone can make this real. He can paint upon the chambers of imagination the picture of the celestial city, the inviting crown, the unending day, the life where death and sin and sorrow shall come no more, the thrones and principalities we have conquered, and the realization of all the hopes, longings and outreachings which the things of time have only mocked and which must often find their satisfaction there.[15]

To the extent eternity envelopes time, intersects time, and looms larger than time, the things of this world shrink.

The good news is this. Once we understand how fear operates, and then scrutinize it with the truth that sets free, our minds *won't* go out of gear like they did before; and, too, we *won't* be lunging in this direction and that in a vain and often sinful attempt to protect ourselves. What God has given the believer is a peace that doesn't vanish when rumors start flying and when malice starts scheming our ruin.

In his book, *Apostolic Testimony*, A. B. Simpson writes:

> One of the sweetest comforts of the Christian is the thought that he is saved both from his past and future. The promise of the Lord is, "The Lord will go before you and the God of Jacob shall be your rearguard." That is, God will take care of your future and your past. But the ungodly have no such overshadowing Presence. The past remains in all its grim reality and fraught with all its future fruition, and, before, there is

foreboding, fear and the thousand anxieties that all the world's philosophy is unable to still.[16]

To go through life with both our past and future protected, and with our present imbued with God's precious, life-lifting presence, is an uncommon blessing for which we should be continually thankful.

Yes, there's a connection between danger and disobedience—a connection that the enemy is skilled to exploit! For this reason, precisely, a prevailing peace is needed—especially if you and I are going to maintain the God-glorifying obedience so essential to our welfare.

Reflection Questions

1. Of the three factors discussed in this chapter that set up fear, which one works more frequently in your life? Please explain.

2. This chapter speaks of certain cognitive errors— denial, fixated thinking, dichotomous thinking, and catastrophic thinking. Can you think of a recent example where one of these mindsets hindered you?

3. Given the principle that danger tempts disobedience by first robbing you of your peace, check out your past to see how this principle has worked in your life. Please discuss.

Chapter 11

Peace's Protection—Part II

Nearly every nation has experienced the scourge of drugs. In many nations, in fact, entire neighborhoods have been taken over by this addiction. So why do so many pill-popping, needle-sharing, powder-snorting people turn to drugs in the first place?

Many causes, obviously, contribute to the drug war. Yet, we wouldn't be oversimplifying in the slightest by surfacing this one underlying motive: It has to do with "the peace of God that passes all understanding." People want that! And they also want what the Bible calls "fullness of joy." So drug users, internally ravaged by destructive emotions, resort to almost anything that offers relief—if not a temporary, artificial high. But what they get is a counterfeit of God's peace.

Due to the elusiveness of peace (and its counterpart, joy), drug users will take insane risks to get their "fix." While no one wants to be victimized, especially when it destroys respect and proves injurious to others, these consequences are nevertheless blocked from contemplation by an insatiable desire to elevate emotions. Not for the thrill of it, mind you, but for the way it sedates pain, thereby giving an illusion that life is better than it is.

Significantly, it isn't just the pathetic "down and outer" who abuses drugs but also some of the most revered people around—lawyers, doctors, and suburban housewives. How tragic these addictions! Especially when the experience these people seek can be obtained in a nondestructive way. Scripture clearly tells us how this longed-for peace can be found—and kept!

So instead of trusting the world's solution for a lack of peace (which obviously doesn't work), we must ask ourselves: What does God say about obtaining the "real deal," a peace within that leaves one more tranquil than any drug could ever do? We ask this question aware that the absence of peace in our lives predicts disobedience; whereas the presence of God's peace predicts a triumph over temptation.

Having identified in the previous chapter the main ways fear comes into our lives, we will now, in this chapter, strategize for peace by offering three contrasts. Each contrast offered will juxtaposes a function of fear with a function of faith. And by putting it this way, those more astute in their thinking just learned a biblical principle—*the opposite of fear isn't peace, it's faith.*

This is such an important point to understand, because whenever fear comes thundering our way, many start scurrying here, there, and yonder trying to find peace. When in fact peace isn't really what we should be looking for—faith is!

So as we stand at the intersection of trouble and fear looking for the road marked peace, we won't find peace—not there anyway. And this may make us all the more upset! "Peace! Peace! Where is peace?" But peace can't be found at this intersection. First we must go down the road called faith; for it is only there, as we walk that road, that we will find our desired destination, peace.

Circumstance Versus Inner Stance

The first contrast we'll consider in this faith/fear juxtaposition is between circumstances and "inner stances." Do understand that fear wants us so mesmerized by the circumstances there will be a rush to judgment.

Upon hearing the circumstances speak—wherein the facts seem obvious and the conclusions compelling—the resolution all too quickly urged is that this is an open-and-shut case. There's no need to hear one more word! So let the verdict be rendered!

But wait! There *is* another side to this, if we'll just let the Word of God speak. For example, when David said, "Yea, though I walk through the valley of death," he was being honest about the circumstances. Like a predator, death was casting its foreboding shadows, making all seem dreary and dark. But that wasn't *all* that could be said, because David went on to say, "I will fear no evil." Why, David? Because you're so macho brave?

No, the real reason David said, "I will fear no evil" is because of his confidence in God. "You are with me," he said. "Your rod and your staff, they comfort me." So, recognizing how everything was ultimately in *God's* control and not in the control of the enemy, David made the decision to refuse fear. This was his "inner stance."

In another Davidic psalm, Psalm 27:3, we see this same contrast. "Though an army encamp against me ... though war may rise against me ..."—which, given the situation, was a very real and scary prospect! In setting forth this scenario, David talks about the wicked coming to eat his flesh! So what David was facing was greater than what most of us will ever face! *Nevertheless*, David said, "My heart shall not fear."

But that's crazy, David! Anyone about to go into hand-to-hand combat would fear! No, David insisted, "... in this will I be confident."

Do you see how David was exercising his will by not allowing feelings to take over and rule? David was making a determined decision that disallowed the participation of feelings in any way. Muzzling emotions' voice, rejecting emotions' message, judging what it wanted to say before it could even say it, David passed over emotions' desires with complete disdain, affirming instead, "The Lord is my life and my salvation; whom shall I fear?"

Isn't that good? For David, this was the *only* testimony he would consider. End of testimony! Case closed! Verdict rendered! Again, this was his "inner stance."

In taking this stance, it was not that David had an extra measure of bravery bestowed upon him. No, David was simply thinking this fear issue through. For when considering the puny powers of the enemy alongside the awesome powers of God, David concluded *fear made no sense*! This was a perspective reinforced many years later when Peter declared, "The Lord knows how to deliver the godly ...." (II Peter 2:9). Our deliverance, whatever circumstances we are in, poses no problem at all for him! And no Bible-taught soul should ever doubt this!

As the Lord thinks about the problems you and I are facing, he isn't perplexed. He knows exactly what will work to turn our situation around! But the one thing that will prevent him from doing so is the presence of fear activated in our lives. Fear is a form of unbelief, and since unbelief sidelines God, our first assignment is to refuse fear. This must be our inner stance!

Panic Versus Praise

The next contrast that will help us strategize against fear is the contrast between panic and praise. When Jesus said, "Let not your heart be troubled, neither let it be afraid," he wasn't making a suggestion. These words, written in the imperative mood, actually take the form of a command. Indeed, so important is this command Jesus gave it in other contexts as well (Matthew 24:4; Mark 13:7).

What, then, are we supposed to feel once fear has been successfully dispatched from our life? Jesus answered this question while on his way to Gethsemane, "Be of good cheer" (John 16:33). Ever aware that actions flow from attitudes, Jesus knew these disciples needed to get their attitude right *first*. This didn't exactly happen, Scripture reports; nevertheless, this is a principle more than once addressed in Scripture.

Do you recall the first instruction James gives to those who fall into various trials (James 1:2-8)? To "count it all joy"! And what was the first step that Paul cited when he laid out God's prescription for peace (Philippians 4:4-9)? To "rejoice in the Lord always, and again I say rejoice."

Rejoicing puts our focus on the Lord and on his solutions. Through rejoicing and praise we become more "promise-conscious"; whereas panic helps us be more "problem-conscious." Since we can't be looking one way and at the same time effectively walking another, we must look only to the Lord, confident of his great love for us.

Yet, how often the child of God loses the battle precisely here. God's love seems too far away—more theory than fact, a sentiment *not* certain. Hence, intimacy with God is damaged. We then feel orphaned and abandoned, especially when intimidating circumstances pressure us.

This gross misperception was rightly taken to task by John Owen, the great Puritan writer of the seventeenth-century, when he wrote, "The greatest sorrow and burden you can lay on the Father, the greatest unkindness you can do to him is not to believe he loves you."[1] Allow yourself to lapse into that confusion and you offend the God who is your present help while at the same time blocking the entrance of his peace into your soul. This cause-and-effect principle is not complicated, nor obscure. What it comes down to is this: To doubt his love is to forfeit his peace.

Although Scripture declares that "perfect love casts out fear," C. S. Lewis cautions:

> But so do several things—ignorance, alcohol, passion, presumption, and stupidity. It is very desirable that we should advance to that perfection of love in which we shall fear no longer; but it is very undesirable until we have reached that stage that we should allow any inferior agent to cast out our fear.[2]

Almost always, these inferior agents were enlisted by a panic all too willing to buy whatever Satan was selling. Were we to believe the truth about God's love, though, that belief would effectively dislodge our fear. We would not need anything else to do it.

Many Christians—never taking this step, never releasing their faith—are defeated almost at once; and then they have to scramble like crazy just to get back to the starting line! The psalmist said, "My heart is steadfast, O God, my heart is steadfast: I will sing and give praise" (Psalm 57:7). In these words, the psalmist was riveting his attention on the Lord, refusing to allow any diversion of focus. He did this because he knew that in the day of trouble God is best found in the passion of heart-filled praise.

Do you recall what Paul and Silas did after they were beaten, thrown in jail, and put in stocks? They sang praises to God until midnight! These two evangelists were really more "in the Spirit" than they were "in jail"! Moreover, because of this ongoing praise, God did his own little "Jailhouse Rock" number, flinging wide the doors of that prison and setting these prisoners free.

Pressure Versus Principle

A third contrast that distinguishes the right from the wrong approach to fear is the contrast between pressure and principle. Principle is found in the realm of the spiritual; pressure manifests in the realm of sense and sight. Now notice how both of these approaches are seen in Psalm 46. The psalmist begins, "God is our refuge and strength, a very present help in trouble. Therefore we will not fear" (vss.1, 2). This is a very important principle of God's Word, asserted in extended faith. According to this principle: No matter how severe the problem, there is always, for the believer, a place of protection.

The psalmist next contemplates the reality factor of pressure when he says, "Even though the earth be removed, and though the mountains be carried into the midst of the sea; though the waters roar and be troubled, though the mountains shake with its swelling" (vss.2, 3)—in other words, even if the metabolism of this universe goes nuts and the most cataclysmic manifestations occur, for me, principle *will* prevail over pressure, "I will not fear."

Hannah Whitall Smith, who spoke to audiences as large as ten-thousand people in nineteenth-century Europe, commented on this verse, saying, "The man who wavers in his faith is upset by the smallest trifles, yet the man who is steadfast in his faith can look on calmly at the ruin of all his universe."[3] The reason for this resolute refusal of fear stems from Scripture's assertion: God is a present help—not a late arrival to the scene, and not a mere spectator upon arrival. God offers refuge to those who will simply and singularly believe him for it.

There is a painting by a German artist that depicts a gathering storm. The clouds—thick, black and ominous—swirl angrily in the heavens. Trees are bending before the wind. Lightening is sizzling in the sky. Farm animals are running toward the barn. One can almost hear the crash of thunder as the storm's prelude announces the fury about to be unleashed. Appropriately, the one word title of this painting is "Refuge."

The day may come (and for some may already be here) when the clouds will hang black and low over your life. In such a time, what will you do? Be terrorized by the circumstances? Panic? Give in to pressure? Or will you voice the faith of the psalmist, "I will say of the Lord, 'He is my refuge and my fortress; my God, in him I will trust'" (Psalm 91:2).

Hannah Whitall Smith, whose books sold in the millions, wrote: "One cannot imagine any sensible refugee running into a fortress one day, and the next day running out among the enemy again. We should think that such a person had suddenly lost all his senses."[4] Yet, there are those in the church who do precisely this.

Many people, Christian people, can't bring themselves to claim this immediate and supernatural protection. They attempt to make their own defense instead—trying this, trying that—in order to secure some damage control, if not to bring this nightmare of a problem to a speedy conclusion. But the Bible says we won't have to be our own deliverer (and thus be stuck with inferior results), if we'll just believe God and stop all this double-mindedness. "He will deliver you," the psalmist declared (vs.3); because you have made the Lord your refuge (instead of some plan you engineered), no evil will befall you (vss. 9, 10).

Do make this distinction, though. Although the Lord's protection will be immediate, the Lord's deliverance may take longer. And if it does, don't make the mistake—in a vain attempt to take matters into your own hands—of running from your protection straight into the teeth of danger.

In our impatience, we will sometimes wonder out loud, "Where is God? Why isn't he doing more than he's doing?" But if these are the thoughts entertained in our minds, it is a clear indication that something is already wrong. For if we had been receiving his peace-preserving protection, we would have been experiencing him firsthand—and thus there wouldn't be this question, where is God? In the place of a sense of absence, there would be this experience of his presence.

In his book, *The Secret of Guidance*, F. B. Meyer counseled:

> We often make a great mistake, thinking that God is not guiding us at all, because we cannot see God far in front. But this is not his method. He only undertakes that the steps of a good man should be ordered by the Lord. Not next year, but tomorrow. Not the next mile, but the next yard. Not the whole pattern, but the next stitch in the canvas. If you expect more than this, you will be disappointed and get back into the dark.[5]

Remember, through it all, God isn't just solving your problem, but, more important to him, he is working a nobler character in you. It is in this respect that you must come to understand that his agenda is bigger than yours. What you want is for the problem to go away, but what God wants is for his bride-to-be to be brought into greater glory! Therefore, by getting your problem solved through dependence on the Word and the sacrifices of praise, you are learning to receive from God, to have intimacy with God, and to grow into the kind of maturity that refuses panic.

You should always be careful to see if underneath your desire for the problem to go away is the hidden desire for God himself to go away. We need to be honest about this, because our addiction to independent living prefers more distancing between God and ourselves than what we are willing to admit. Though we're willing for God to help at those times we call upon him to do so, we don't want those times determined by him instead of by us.

In his book, *Flee, Follow, Fight*, Bruce Wideman offered an encouraging perspective on the seeming lack of evidence for God being at work when it seems he isn't there.

Imagine yourself in a theater watching a play. The first act comes to an end and the curtain is drawn. You cannot see anything going on behind the curtain, and so as far as you know, there is not anything going on. But presently the curtain is opened. All the furniture has been arranged, and new scenery settings are in the background. Something was happening, but you were just not aware of it.

It is like that in the theater of our lives. The curtain is drawn and God won't let us see behind the curtain. So far as we know, nothing is taking place. We can't see any changes. We can't see any improvement in our situation, and sometimes we conclude that God isn't doing anything. But presently he opens the curtain and we see that he was busy all the time.[6]

Jesus was busy protecting the disciples, too. But even though it was happening right in front of their eyes, these disciples—amazingly! incomprehensibly!—still didn't see it. Today there are others who don't see God at work in their lives.

With this fact in mind, let's revisit the garden to see, in a way maybe you've never seen before, the Lord protecting his own.

The Lord's Protection Plan

Jesus previously determined that his arrest must take place out of town when everyone else was asleep. If it took place in town, a volatile crowd reaction (which was likely) risked the deaths of the disciples.

Jesus also determined that the disciples needed to be with him when the arrest occurred. Because if they heard about the arrest later, having never been present when it happened, their faith-collapse might have resulted in irreversible despair, if not immediate suicide. Apparently, then, there was something these disciples needed to see in Jesus' arrest that would later steady their faith.

What was it? Of paramount importance, they needed to see for themselves that Jesus was no victim.

John's Gospel tells of how Jesus orchestrated all that occurred in the garden with a calmness and mastery that showed him to be in complete control. Accompanying Judas to the garden that night was a Roman cohort. This would mean somewhere between 500 and 600 troops. But if there were auxiliary soldiers accompanying them, which typically would be the case, then there would be as many as a thousand soldiers—240 cavalry, and 760 infantry—a very sizable military contingent!

But why would so many soldiers be sent to arrest a preacher at midnight? This appears not to make sense. Jesus never had an army, or even a small band of security guards. Besides, the garden where Jesus was to be found—not just that night, but on many nights—wasn't open to the public; it was a small private garden. The point being: Such a scene was not one to accommodate a vast gathering of rebel insurrectionists. So why were so many soldiers sent to arrest Jesus?

The answer to this question is insane, but here's the reason: Jesus had performed so many miracles the religious authorities had to consider the possibility he might indeed be God. And if it turned out that he was, the decision they made was to fight him! Therefore, they all came to the garden that night armed to the teeth!

One may well wonder, how can anyone think they can fight God and win? I don't know. Ask Satan that question, because that's where this idea began. What's more, in the millennial reign of the Lord on earth, there will be another group who will rise and rebel against him who they *know* to be God.

Now, the fact that the soldiers brought lanterns and torches is also intriguing, because at that time of the year (the first week in April), the moon was in full phase, shedding so much light, historians report, it almost seemed like day. So why the torches? This is so ironic—men in need of torches in order to find the Light of the world!

The reason for all these torches was simply this: The authorities thought Jesus might be hiding in some cave. And if so, with the aid of these torches and lanterns, they were going to find him!

Since Jesus knew how dangerous this scenario would be for the disciples, he and they weren't hiding in a cave. Instead, when the soldiers entered the garden that night, Jesus strode masterfully across the garden to meet them.

According to Scripture, it was Jesus who initiated the encounter by asking, "Whom are you seeking?" In reply, they no doubt read their orders when they said, "Jesus of Nazareth"—and perhaps that last word "Nazareth" brought the intonations of a slur.

In response to this slur, what happened next was nothing short of awesome! Because when Jesus responded, "I am he" (actually "he" is italicized, meaning it isn't a part of the original text), every soldier there was knocked down flat.

So what happened? Was this some sort of domino effect—one soldier fell, so they all fell? Such a suggestion (which is all the anti-miracle crowd is left with) is patently absurd, because it gives these superbly trained soldiers no credit.

What actually occurred was this: When Jesus said "I am"—an expression divine in both form and content: the virtual equivalency for Jehovah, the great I AM—Jesus was briefly and partially transformed into the blinding light of his pre-incarnate glory, just as he had been on the mountain top only a few days before with Peter, James, and John. And this light knocked Rome's finest flat!

Subdued in this way, an opportunity presented itself for Jesus and his disciples to exit the garden quickly and, by so doing, escape the judgment of unjust men. But, no, Jesus wasn't looking for an escape. He was purposing to lay his life down for the sheep! Indeed, more than once the Bible makes it clear that no man or men could ever *take* his life, whatever their number may be, and whatever cache of weapons they might have with them. The idea that Jesus was first surprised, then surrounded, and then, by coercion, surrendered, is completely refuted by the biblical narrative.

Now the disciples needed to see that, just as they also needed to see the miracle Jesus performed in the garden that night when he supernaturally reattached the ear of Malchus (one of the soldiers), that Peter had cut off with the sword. This presence of the supernatural, which never would have been reported by the soldiers (or by the religious authorities) had not the disciples seen it for themselves, cast this arrest scene in an entirely different light than what these disciples might have imagined had the arrest taken place in their absence.

This moment of glory should have helped at least three of the apostles—Peter, James, and John—better process what was happening. For these men had just seen the Lord transfigured on the mountain. There, they saw Jesus' glory displayed even stronger. So this experience should have helped them conclude that no army could take Jesus' life, since he had already shown that he could avoid death if he wanted to. In his commentary about this mountaintop event, Ray Stedman observed:

> ... our Lord did not have to die. That is one of the meanings of the transfiguration; he had no reason to pass through death. He could step back across the boundary of time into eternity without passing through death.[7]

Given this already demonstrated ability, these apostles should have known that Jesus was never overpowered by Roman soldiers. *He* possessed the ability to step into eternity whenever he wanted to! Therefore, it was his love, and not his weakness, that kept him in the garden that night.

What an amazing scene—soldiers lying everywhere, hundreds of them, while Jesus waits for them to regain full consciousness so they can arrest him!

When the moment of glory passed and the soldiers returned to their feet (still not exactly sure what had happened), Jesus asked them a second time, "Whom are you seeking?" (John 18:7). Jesus did this, no doubt, to get them to read their orders twice, thus firmly establishing in their minds the parameters of their mission.

After having them repeating their orders, Jesus then asked the soldiers to let his disciples go—which the soldiers were bound by protocol and law to do.

Do you see how Jesus was protecting these disciples? When it came to the moment of crisis, his concern was for them and not at all for himself. He did all this, John tells us, "that the saying might be fulfilled which he spoke, 'Of those whom you gave me I have lost none'" (John 18:9), implying that if these disciples had been captured, they wouldn't have made it. This would have been the end, not just of their lives but of their salvation.

But how can that be? Doesn't the Bible say we can't lose our salvation? Yes it does, but if it weren't for the protecting care of God, we could lose our salvation.

If there were total, unrestricted access to the believer, hell could overwhelm the convert at the moment he or she was making the decision to accept Jesus. Everything could then be eternally lost. "But God is faithful," I Corinthians 10:13 declares, "... who will not allow you to be tempted above what you are able ...." Isn't that good? Ours is a shepherd who will stop the wolves before they get to the lambs!

A Rejection of the Lord's Protection

Despite the Lord's protecting hand, and *despite* the miracles in the garden, and *despite* that calmness of soul so marvelously exhibited by the Lord, the disciples still suffered a near collapse of their faith that night. Why? Because they succumbed to the same error many of us make—dichotomized thinking—in that they saw only the bad and not the good. Oh, they knew the good had happened. Jesus had shown himself to be God in a way no mere mortal could ever do. Nevertheless, emotionally they were totally invested in the bad; and therefore the good, while witnessed and acknowledged, remained a lifeless, powerless fact in their lives. And this is exactly what fear will do to us.

These disciples suffered this near collapse of their faith also because of catastrophic thinking. Focusing only on the arrest and the terrible crucifixion that followed, they were sure of the worst—that their faith was in vain and that Jesus wasn't the Messiah after all!

By employing faulty if/then thinking (what logicians call an enthymeme), these disciples concluded that on the basis of this and this and this, that such and such an outcome had to be the result. But, as it turned out, what they thought *wasn't* the result. What they at the time regarded as the very worst day in their lives is now revered worldwide as "Good Friday."

So be careful of these cognitive errors. Start doubting your doubts! If dichotomized thinking is on the scene, ask yourself: What's wrong with this picture? What factors are either missing, or being minimized, or being discounted? And if catastrophic thinking is on the scene, ask yourself: What facts might shrink this problem to different proportions than what seems to be the case? And if faulty if/then thinking is on the scene, ask yourself: What other outcomes might fit this same set of facts?

In making this assessment, don't let the enemy of your soul short-circuit your thinking by pushing an interpretation that is neat, logical, plausible—and entirely wrong! So, when executing thought management, keep in mind how the Lord's responded to those travelers on the Road to Emmaus. Instead of commending them for their love and giving them sympathy for their depression, Jesus called them fools.

Fools, for looking at the picture the way the enemy framed it, and fools for blocking what God previously said. Apparently, even lovers of the Lord can succumb to contaminated thinking.

While calamity and confusion often go together, we must break these two up by purposing to *think*—not our thoughts, of course, for that will never do, but the thoughts of him who has the panoramic view of our entire situation. Since the Word always works, we need the Holy Spirit (and perhaps a friend or well-trained scriptural counselor) to minister it to us! But we must never accept what the Word already told us did not come from God, a spirit of fear (II Timothy 1:7).

I love the way Isaiah 41:10 puts this. It says "fear not," a straight-out command to be taken every bit as seriously as all the other commands God gives. "Fear not," God says, "for I am with you." Now, if God were a distant deity, his attention and resources focused elsewhere in the universe, then maybe fear would be understandable. But the most frequent promise in Scripture cites God being at hand, totally tuned in, ever ready to help. Therefore, there is absolutely no reason to fear!

This verse in Isaiah continues by saying, "Be not dismayed, for I am your God." Now the Hebrew word for "dismayed" is the same word used to describe the Jewish army when Goliath was coming out day and night to taunt them. To Israel's army at that point, the problem seemed impossible. For as this giant of a man raged against them, boasting of what he would do and declaring how their defeat was certain, they bought in to all that, causing their confidence to completely unravel!

Well, if you and I didn't have God, or maybe we had another god, this unraveling would make total sense. But with him who has all might at our side (this is why he is called God Almighty), this unraveling makes no sense at all. The prophet Zephaniah offered the assurance, "The Lord thy God in the midst of thee is mighty; he will save ...." (Zephaniah 3:17). There can be no question about that!

In the Isaiah passage, God then says—and as I quote it, will you receive it personally as God's word to you?—"I *will* strengthen you. Yes, I *will* help you. Yes, I *will* uphold you with my righteousness right hand." God's three "I wills," passionately promised so we will refuse fear!

This means that even if an intimidating problem comes our way—as happened to the disciples with the encircling soldiers, the subsequent mockery, and then the killing of their God—we can still be in perfect peace throughout the problem—beginning, middle, and end. Moreover, because Jesus had offered his peace to them *before* the problem came, the disciples could have gone through this ordeal completely protected in their emotions.

By not letting the Lord's peace work in their lives, however, they went through a needlessly horrible experience, sinning all the while as they did it.

Is this what we've been doing? Have we been allowing the same cognitive errors that worked against them to work against us? We don't have to go through life with fear in control, because the Lord has a peace for us far better than what any psychologist can give. But we're going to have to *take* this peace with disciplined thinking if we want this peace to take us into the kind of tranquil living God intends for us to enjoy. Instead of allowing our brain to go out of gear and a flood of emotions to dictate our behavior, we must seal off the inroads of unbelief by refusing to succumb to the cognitive errors that have defeated us so often in the past.

To summarize, these cognitive errors include: 1) dichotomized thinking (the situation is all white or all black); 2) catastrophic thinking (where calibration breaks down and a mild or moderate problem is seen to be severe); 3) fixated thinking (where reasoning is refused and conclusions too quickly cement); 4) blocked thinking (when factors that should be taken into account are discounted, instinctively and stubbornly); 5) if/then thinking (when a conclusion is uncritically accepted as the necessary outcome of a given premise); 6) and "this is that" thinking (when a similar experience of the past is erroneously imposed on the present, fostering the false conclusion that the bad thing that happened then is about to happen again).

What happened to the disciples in the garden that night has happened to many others since. Some people, it seems, are particularly vulnerable to these cognitive errors—to the extent almost every one of them will occur at the same time! For these people, the compounded misery that results is so severe, so traumatic, it is difficult to describe. *But* new ways of thinking can stop all this—and rather quickly, too!

Critical to this turnaround is an early recognition of wrong thinking. This recognition will allow you to draw from Scripture the counter-thinking that will successfully challenge cognitive errors. It may take a big dose of Spirit-energized willpower at first, especially when old fears reassert themselves in almost paralyzing proportions. But don't be overcome by this onslaught of destructive emotions.

These emotions are normal, especially for those who have become highly developed in their fears. However, by verbalizing God's promises in praise, wherein you thank the Lord for the victory he will give, all these vicious attacks on your emotions, and against your faith, will lose their powers. At which point a stabilizing reassurance will enable better decisions.

The goal? Consistent obedience defining your life so God's release of treasured and unmeasured blessings are unhindered.

Our response? Hopefully, it is one that settles on a workable, biblical strategy, instead of one that faces the next trial as clueless as the ones before.

Reflection Questions

1. If you were to act like David and disallow fear to speak, what fear messages would you shut down? And what faith messages would you replace them with?

2. This chapter presents three contrasts between the right and wrong way to approach fear. Of the three, which one speaks the most to you? Please explain.

3. Identify one of the strategies discussed in this chapter that addresses a particular cognitive error and make some connections with your life. In doing so, share how obedience is helped and disobedience is hindered.

Chapter 12

Gratitude's Goal

Success doesn't just happen; certain factors promote it while other factors sabotage it. No matter what the endeavor—be it in academics, business, sports, or entertainment—there will be identifiable criteria in each which, if met, predict success; and if not met, predict failure.

In some cases success is still possible if one aspect of performance can compensate for other deficiencies. This is rare. Usually there is one factor for which there can be no compensation, one factor that will decisively determine the outcome.

Those analyzing the swing of, say, a golfer or a baseball player will study videotape for hours, looking for that one point in the process where the de-compensating begins. They do this because they know from that point on there can be no recovery. One particular mistake, by setting up every other mistake, assures failure.

So what might be the one flaw in the Christian life that predicts success or failure? To answer this question, we will direct our attention to the first chapter of Paul's letter to the Romans, where, toward the end of that chapter, we find a detailed autopsy of reprobate ruin. Here Paul provides a sequential breakdown of all that went wrong before God gave up on these people. Significantly, this twelve verse profile begins with an assertion easily overlooked, "neither were they thankful" (Romans 1:21).

Don't you see? That flung the door open! That gave the enemy access! Indeed, once *that* factor manifested, everything else unraveled.

If our gratitude toward the Lord begins to decline, and if our thankfulness for who he is and for what he has done recedes far into the background, then it may be axiomatically predicted that sin is about to prevail. Consider your own life. When reviewing spiritual patterns of the past, isn't it true that for you the doorway to defeat swung open once gratitude left the room?

To preoccupy yourself with what *you* want, or to wallow in bitterness about what *you* didn't get, is to walk straight toward the buzz saw of inevitable defeat.

The journey from the Upper Room to the garden, and then from the garden to the cross, saw the Lord making this precise point. Speaking to his disciples, Jesus said, "You have heard me say to you, 'I am going away and coming back to you.' If you loved me, you would rejoice because I said 'I am going to the Father,' for My Father is greater than I'" (John 14:28).

Rejoice? Why, these disciples were on the other end of the attitudinal spectrum! They were utterly perplexed! Totally discouraged! To the man, they were dispirited, disheartened, dismayed, dejected! The impact of this impending trauma was doing its worst. So instead of a spirit of rejoicing rising within, it was a spirit of heaviness descending upon.

For several weeks these disciples had been experiencing what to them was a horrible nightmare. They couldn't imagine why Jesus had to die! Perceiving their distress, Jesus made this telling observation: If you had my interest at heart, he said, your faith and feelings wouldn't be where they are right now. For by looking at the problem with the sole agenda of determining its effect on you, you have set yourselves up for needless anguish.

Jesus hit the bulls-eye with a laser beam, didn't he? The difference between the troubled heart of verse 27 and the rejoicing heart of verse 28 is the difference between an ultimate concern for self and an ultimate concern for God. If the focus shifts, the problems begin.

This is a truth many have discovered. Whenever there is a shrinking of self and, in tandem, the elevating of some higher priority, that effectively stops the harm the enemy purposes to administer. This approach enables disciples to see God, hear God, and eventually please God—which is gratitude's ultimate goal.

The decision for Jesus to leave heaven and come to earth incurred a sacrifice too great for the disciples to comprehend. Nevertheless, the understanding they did have was enough to appreciate why Jesus wanted to go back to heaven. It wasn't just the angels, the throne, or the streets of gold that motivated. What most motivated Jesus' desire was his reunion with the Father, about which George MacDonald wrote, "The joy of the Lord's life, that which made it life to him, was the Father. Of him, Jesus was always thinking, to him Jesus was always turning."[1]

Constantly Jesus talked about the Father! The purpose and passion of Jesus' life began and ended with him! So, having clearly known this as the disciples did, couldn't this thought have entered *somewhere* into their thinking? Couldn't they have framed their perspective of the Lord's death a little more broadly than they did?

The Lack of Thanksgiving

It would be encouraging if the thankful spirit absent in the garden was later recovered and now thrives in the church. But such is not the case. Frederick W. Faber wrote, "If we had to name any one thing which seems unaccountably to fallen out of most men's practical religion altogether, it would be the duty of thanksgiving. It would not be easy to exaggerate the neglect of this duty."[2]

Someone has said that if you want to find gratitude, you're going to have to look it up in a dictionary—because gratitude can't be found anywhere else! This is an overstatement, perhaps. Nevertheless, there is this tendency to take what we have for granted—always looking for more, intensifying our desire for more, before mobilizing our resources to get more. More, more, more! But if this is the theme song of our life, we can be certain that many sour notes will ruin it.

One such sour note was recorded in the Old Testament. Commenting on I Kings, chapter 9, and the sour note of ingratitude discussed in this passage, A. B. Simpson wrote:

> This is a little chapter from the story of Solomon and Hiram; it is also a chapter from the story of many a Christian life. Solomon had given to his friend 20 cities in the land of Galilee in recognition of his kindness in supplying timber and other material for the magnificent temple which had just been erected; but when Hiram went to view the cities he was terribly displeased with them and bitterly disappointed with the gift of his friend, so he called them Cabul, which means displeasing.
>
> There are a good many people still who live in the Land of Cabul—the country of discontent—the clime where the sun rarely shines and the birds never sing.[3]

And this is not a good place to live! James S. Stewart, Scotland's great preacher of the twentieth-century, writes: "Oh, why are we so dull and thankless often, grudging our gratitude? I am sure the saints in heaven must sometimes be nonplussed at the stinginess of our Hosannas here on earth."[4] As Thomas Watson observed, "Many have tears in their eyes and complaints in their mouths, but few have harps in their hands and are blessing and praising the name of God."[5]

For an outcome to fall short of one's expectation is an obvious trigger for ingratitude, but the problem of ingratitude goes deeper than this. So perverse is the human heart, ingratitude may exhibit even if expectations are fully met. We see an example of that in the New Testament.

In the seventeenth chapter of Luke's Gospel, we are told of ten lepers who positioned themselves by the side of the road hoping to gain the Lord's attention. In doing so, these lepers kept their distance from other nearby travelers by shouting, "Unclean! Unclean!"

Can you just imagine the humiliation these lepers felt? The natural instinct for all of us is to mask our faults, not to advertise them! We don't want people to know about our defects! These verbalized warnings were necessary, however, for two reasons: first, because of the contagion of their disease; and second, because the law specifically required such notification.

In one respect, this scene was a common occurrence; the dreaded disease of leprosy had made outcasts of many people. But in another respect this gathering of lepers *wasn't* a common occurrence—for who would want all this humiliation? The looks of pity .... the gasps of horror ... mothers covering the eyes of their children ... fathers herding the family away with accelerated pace .... Who would want to be the cause of that?

Far preferable to these lepers was that they remained huddled in yonder cave with those having the same affliction. But needs must! So, pursuing what they perceived to be their "last-chance" hope, these lepers were on a mission that day, intent that the miracle worker would hear their cry.

While the shock of seeing these grossly disfigured people triggered an almost automatic instinct to turn away, also repulsive when it occurred was the shrill in their cries and the sheer anguish in their voices.

Refusing to be repelled, though, Jesus instead was compelled: It seems the release of his compassion for these lepers could not be stopped! Yet, Jesus released this compassion in a most unusual way when he declared, "Go to go to the High Priest to have your healing certified."

Certified? But they weren't healed yet! *Certified?* Whatever did this Galilean mean?

The lepers' first reaction to Jesus' reply, even if it never found voice, was the disturbing thought: Are we being mocked? Is this some sort of a joke? Are we being played for fools?

The answer to these unasked questions was simply this: Front-loading faith was essential for the miracle they wanted. These men had to act with anticipation that their need was going to be met. A "wait and see" attitude was out of the question. So Jesus was giving them a faith assignment.

Such a strategy wasn't new, really. For what did Jesus say to the lame man beside the pool? "Take up your bed and walk." Think of it: this man who hadn't taken a single step for thirty-eight years! These words from Jesus seemed absurd! And what Jesus said to the lepers seemed equally absurd. For they knew what everyone else knew: Their disease was permanent! There was no known cure!

Another obstacle had to be overcome by these lepers, one they were very well aware of, namely this: It was illegal for lepers to go anywhere in public! Therefore, if these lepers went to the High Priest *in this condition*, there would be a swift reprisal against them, from which they would never recover! So, upon hearing Jesus' words, the lepers had to wonder: Was this rabbi of reputation setting them up?

If you don't know by now, you need to know: The way of faith often surfaces doubts about God. This is statistically normal, and if processed correctly, it is useful. Why? Because doubt brings focus to key issues: Is God good? And are his words reliable?

However, doubt does have to be resolved, because the only way faith makes sense is if the character of God can be trusted. Indeed—for the lepers then, and for us today—there can be no advance in the spiritual life and no obtaining from God unless the goodness of God is affirmed.

The dynamics of faith, once undertaken, will also call into question not only the integrity of God but also the sanity of self. Talk about certified! It seemed certifiably crazy to act as these lepers were being called on to do contrary to the clear evidence of sight. To better grasp this fact, let's break the daring of this deed down just a bit.

For lepers to slip away from understood boundaries at the edge of town would have been bad enough. But for lepers to walk openly into Jerusalem would have been far worse! Yet, what Jesus was asking them to do was even worse! Because to enter the temple still contagious, would be nothing short of outrageous! And if they proceeded to seek out the High Priest—oh, my! That would been a scandal of epoch proportions, especially if they managed to infect him!

And how would Jesus then be regarded, the one who told these ten contagious lepers to find the High Priest?

As we examine what Jesus proposed that day and peel back each layer of its implications, we find ourselves stunned. To any objective observer, this mission was more than daring, worse than brazen, more extreme than audacious; it was nothing short of spectacularly stupid! Who in their right mind would do such a thing!

One also has to wonder how stupefied the High Priest later was when all these lepers approached him. Why, his eyes must have glazed over! As he consulted the dusty archives of his thinking, he was trying to determine what he was supposed to do.

Certification for leprosy healing? Um, no one in the history of Israel had ever been healed of leprosy! Miriam, the sister of Moses, had been healed of leprosy one week after its onset. But the sudden appearance and spread of that leprosy was a judgment from God. Moreover, the leprosy disappeared as suddenly as it came, once she learned her lesson. Accordingly, the Levitical laws for her healing were never invoked.

The only person healed of leprosy was Naaman—and he was a Syrian, not a Jew! Moreover, that miracle occurred hundreds of years ago! So what, pray tell, is *this* all about—now we have *ten* lepers who have been healed, all on the same day?

Everything about this episode defied not only natural thinking but centuries of documented history! Are you beginning to see now how encompassing faith is? It requires us to come to terms, first, with who God is: Can we trust him? Is his word worthy of our confidence? But also looming large are the questions: Are we willing to follow the Word and not the world? Will we come under the authority of Jesus even if it appears that in so doing our well-being may be threatened?

These are major issues that have to be decided. Well, as these lepers departed that day, suddenly it happened! The lesions healed! The sores fell away! Their skin became perfectly and wonderfully normal! Yet, the jubilation experienced by these lepers ended not as we could have wished; for, yes, they did get healed—every deformity in every man! But the ending of this story comes with this lament from the lips of our Lord. Because when only one of these lepers came back to thank him, Jesus said, "Were there not ten cleansed? But where are the other nine?"

There it stands on the pages of Scripture forever ... what God thinks of our failure to give him thanks. P. T. Forsythe once said, "We have churches of the nicest, kindest people who have nothing apostolic and missionary, who never the soul's despair or its breathless gratitude."[6] Obviously unaware of both the depths of despair and the trajectory of joy, gratitude is scarce; and when given seems hollow.

Toots Shore, the famous New York nightclub owner, used to say, "I owe it all to the Man upstairs!" Well, he may have had a lump of something in his throat whenever he said that, but did he actually think that it was God setting up those drinks, and that it was God bringing on the next act?

In the movie *Shenandoah*, Jimmy Stewart plays a farmer not wanting to get involved in the Civil War. With tension mounting and armies invading, this father sits with his large family around the dinner table and offers these words of thanks. "Lord," he said, acknowledging divine presence before referring to the food on the table. "It came from our land. *We* plowed it! *We* planted it! *We* harvested it! And *we* prepared it!" Then, having made each of these points with emphasis, the father's voice trailed off as he hurried up the conclusion of this prayer with no enthusiasm at all, "But thank you just the same. Amen!"

Well, that prayer is not too far removed from what most people think. To them, God isn't all that involved; he just lets us do for ourselves. Actually, this type of thinking is only one step away from dropping the blessing altogether.

One day Harry Ironside, the well-known Bible teacher, went into a restaurant to eat and, as was his custom, bowed his head to give thanks. Seeing this silent observance, a somewhat snooty man said, "I never give thanks for my food!"

An awkward silence followed as discernible tension injected the atmosphere. Upon completing his prayer, Dr. Ironside lifted his head, and then one eyebrow, to say, "And neither does my dog!" And with that, everyone sitting at nearby tables began to laugh. One person not laughing was God.

To Thank or Not To Thank

Not giving thanks to the Lord is hardly a laughing matter, though, because Scripture tells us not to forget all his benefits (Psalm 103:2). Since the alternative to forgetting is focusing, let's do that for a few moments.

Is it not true that there are medicine bottles in your cabinets and mine that we don't use nowadays? And is it not also true that there are pillows on our beds that once witnessed the tortured turning of fevered foreheads—but not so today? And isn't just as true that there are classifieds we once read in a desperate search for a job—but that day has passed?

There is ample evidence in most homes to testify of needs met, desires fulfilled, and good plans accomplished. So if we were to give any thought at all to what has already occurred, the instinct of gratitude would automatically trigger. A thinking person is a thanking person!

Be aware, however, that by not thinking and thanking, which was true of those people in Romans 1, a consequence of great irony begins its onset: *the inability to think at all*! The Bible tells us what happened to these people who weren't thankful: their foolish heart was darkened; and further: claiming to be wise, they became fools (Romans 1:21, 22).

Some of these people may have been highly esteemed intellectuals in the academic community. They may have gained coveted esteem for credentials earned and skills mastered. Yet, they became dumb and dumber when it came to understanding life. This is the inevitable consequence of persistent ingratitude.

As we continue to engage this proposed enterprise of thinking, let's try this thought on for size: Have you ever stopped to think what it would be like if these thankless people were right? What if no benefits came from God? What if God had never promised anything to anybody? Why, if that were the case, we, without the promises of God, would have to assume we're on our own. With each problem presenting, and each evil encroaching, we would have to scramble like crazy and just do the best we can.

Such isn't the case for the believer, though, because God has given 7,487 promises addressing every need in life. Moreover, through these promises God is actually giving himself away. He is pledging to give—out of the full array of his vast resources—all that is needed for our well-being and success. So surely this fact is sufficient cause for an upgrade in gratitude: that is, from perfunctory, obligated praise to effusive, heartfelt praise for these amazing resources of God!

The Book of Ephesians, sometimes called "the treasure book of the Bible," uses the word "inheritance" four times, the word "riches" five times, the words "fullness" or "filled" seven times; and then speaks of "the unsearchable riches of Christ"—unsearchable not in the sense these riches can't be located, but in the sense that when found there seems to be no end!

According to Ephesians, Father has blessed us with *every* spiritual blessing (Ephesians 1:3). Now the word "has" means it's an accomplished fact. The word "every" means nothing has been left out. The word "spiritual" describes its location; for even if these blessings are material in nature, they are in the spirit realm, in the extended hands of God. And there these blessings will remain until claimed by faith!

As it now stands, ever since the curse was reversed at Calvary, every known blessing possible on this side of heaven is available to the commonwealth of God's people—which is reason enough to generate unceasing thanks!

A "Thanksliving" Lifestyle

The call to thanksgiving isn't reserved for meal times, gift-giving occasions, or annual holidays only. Words of thanksgiving are expected on these occasions, and too often are nearly ruined, either by the conscripted person who mumbles thanks with embarrassment, or by the eager volunteer who stages supposed thanks, while obviously in love with the sound of his voice.

Of course, thanksgiving should extend beyond holidays and become a lifestyle. Ephesians 5:20 says we're to be "giving thanks always"—that is, before the problem, in the middle of the problem, and after the problem has been solved. But you say, "I can't turn my emotions on and off like that." Maybe not, but thanksgiving isn't dependent on certain biorhythms cycling through at peak levels of the month. Nor is it dependent on certain fortuitous circumstances that suddenly jack up emotions. This is why I Thessalonians 5:18 declares, "In everything give thanks; for this is the will of Christ Jesus concerning you."

Did you get that? The appeal is to the will; for it is one's will—and not one's emotions—that should trigger thanksgiving. Let it be understood that all Christians, as an act of the will in obedience to the Lord, are to give thanks. But for the bad things that occur? No, not for that, but for the way the Lord will enable us to face these bad things. James S. Stewart observed that "one of the functions of religion is to make us thankful, not in proportion to favorable circumstances—no atom of credit for that—it is precisely to help us to keep thanking the Lord in the face of the most testing circumstances."[7]

There is a functional benefit attached to this command, and it is this: Through thanks we can tap into the omnipotence of God. Giving thanks extends faith; and faith, it must be remembered, is the one bridge that connects us to grace, to the sufficient supply of God, so asked prayer will be answered prayer (Romans 4:16; 5:2).

Talk about a lifestyle! On four different occasions the Bible said we are to *live* by faith. This means that every domain in daily living must be encountered and engaged through faith transactions with God.

The summons for our thanks to be continual and not intermittent is repeated in Scripture. When we worship, for example, we are told to "come before his presence with thanksgiving" (Psalm 95:2). When we pray, we are told to make our requests known unto God "with thanksgiving" (Philippians 4:6). When we live out our lives, we are told, "... whatever you do in word or deed, do all in the name of the Lord Jesus, giving thanks ...." (Colossians 3:17).

Accordingly, all of life is to be seen through the prism of praise and is to be measured by the thermometer of thanks.

So why is it that some Christians are more occasional than habitual in their giving of thanks? The fact that life has been hard on them, or that they have a more reserved temperament, hardly accounts for their scarcity of thanks. The real reason for this paucity of praise is pinpointed by the Spirit of God's words found in Colossians 2:7, where the believer is instructed to be "rooted and built up in him and established in the faith, as you have been taught, abounding in it with thanksgiving."

In a mixing of metaphors, two images are presented in this verse—the image of a tree and the image of a building. The tree, we know, has roots, through which the entire organism receives nourishment so that the trunk, branches, and leaves can steadily grow. But if for some reason the roots aren't functioning properly, deterioration and death will soon set in, causing that once sturdy tree to fall.

Is this your problem? Are you not "processing" in any regular, ongoing way the needed nourishment from God's Word? Could it be that *your* roots not tapping into the presence of God? If so, the budding and bloom of thanksgiving will be missing.

To "build up," as Colossians says, implies—at least in the construction industry—that one story is going to be added to another. So, with this goal in mind, the poet exhorted himself, saying, "Build thee more stately mansions, O my soul." To speak metaphorically, the poet's goal wasn't just a modest little house. Something more marvelous was in mind—an edifice that advertises God is the architect!

Coalescing these two metaphors we can say: If there's no evidence of growth in our lives—if the foundation got laid at the time of our conversion but little more happened afterward—then, because the Christian life isn't working for us, we may be thin in our thanks and grounded in our gratitude.

Gratitude and Obedience

The relationship between gratitude and obedience is more important than we know. To further assess this fact consider what is occurring in those people who *are* engaged in a season of praise. Because their focus is on the Lord and not on self, their self-life is effectively set aside. This release from self enables, through praise, the soul's transport into the spirit realm where God is so near and sin is so far away. Moreover, this shrinking of self also removes the very target Satan must hit if he is going to entice believers to sin. The self greedy for more will get more—from Satan!

But as our spirit soars during praise, we will feel the presence of God. This will also draw us away from competing desires. The stunning beauty of the Lord's life—the love he has for us, the love he extends to us—will make these competing desires detestable, and the Lord's will far preferable.

Even God's Word will become more real to us, once praise ushers us into God's presence. Consequently, what had long languished in the lowlands of sterile facts will rise to impart a witness that can transform these facts into truth. Perhaps, by personal experience, you already understand how this works. On this point, Tozer offered welcomed insight.

> The essence of my belief is that there is a difference, a vast difference, between fact and truth. Truth in the Scriptures is more than a fact. A fact may be detached, impersonal, cold and totally disassociated from life. Truth, on the other hand, is warm, living and spiritual. A theological fact may be held in the mind for a lifetime without having any positive effect upon the moral character; but truth is creative, saving, transforming, and it always changes the one who receives it into a humbler and holier man. At what point, then, does a theological fact become for the one that holds it a life-giving truth? At the point where obedience begins.[8]

This, when you think about it, is a circle that life should go in, where the praise that leads to obedience is reinforced by an obedience that extends praise.

One of the reasons praise is seen as a spiritual weapon is because praise drives the enemy away. Lucifer lost his place in heaven over praise (since he wanted to start receiving what he had been giving). Then he lost the title deed of earth over this same issue, when Jesus refused to bow to him in the wilderness. So, having suffered such shattering defeats, Satan doesn't want to be anywhere around during a season of passionate praise.

Praise sends Satan AWOL from the battle! And by vacating the premises, the child of God gains a huge advantage. Paul Billheimer observed, "Satan is allergic to praise, so where there is massive, triumphant praise, Satan is paralyzed, bound, and banished."9 Elaborating further, Billheimer wrote:

> Since praise produces the atmosphere in which the Divine Presence resides, it is the most effective shield against Satan and satanic attack. Because praise is anathema to him, it is the most powerful defense, the most devastating weapon in conflict with him.10

However, should increased vulnerability later envelope the believer, causing strength of soul to dissipate, the disobedience had Satan planned for may yet be thwarted if the believer will give God what the Bible calls "the sacrifice of praise." Again, this is where the will is important. If we exercise our will, determined to praise the Lord even when we don't feel like it, our emotions will change soon enough. And it is most important they do! For if the devil can discourage us, he can then defeat us.

As a matter of strategy, therefore, the Bible tells us to put on the garment of praise instead of the spirit of heaviness (Isaiah 61:3). We can praise our way out of depression! And, by activating faith through praise, we can also avoid the defeat the devil wants to send.

There's a story in the Old Testament that links gratitude to obedience. When Joseph was serving his Egyptian master, Potiphar, Potiphar's wife, with more cunning than charm, attempted to force herself on Joseph. But her plot was foiled, the Bible tells us, when Joseph fled the premises, saying, "How can I do this great wickedness and sin against God?" (Genesis 39:7). In reflecting on Joseph's response, the sense of shock he experienced becomes apparent, a factor that deserves further reflection.

Unlike people today, totally desensitized by sin, Joseph's sensitivity flared up immediately—*and that served to protect him*! Cardinal Newman once said, "It is one great security against sin, to be shocked at it."

True, nothing seems to shock people today. But for those who do cultivate a sweet relationship with the Lord and do welcome his presence throughout the day, shock will sound an alarm, so they spot sin as the intruder it is—and a most unwelcomed intruder at that!

The victory Joseph experienced was also helped by the way Joseph framed the issue. To Joseph, the choice was between God and sin. And since God had been so good to him, Joseph couldn't imagine choosing sin. One wonders, though, if this thought would have surfaced had not gratitude previously made its deep imprinting. The grateful heart is always tender toward God.

Occasional, halfhearted gratitude won't make an imprinting like this, though. Instead, when temptation comes knocking, it is self that will answer the door. A self that listens with an agenda of wanting to know what's in it for me? What pleasure can I experience, what advantage can I gain?

Such a contemptuous, calculating self would never frame the issue like Joseph did. And that's why the temptation will last longer, and get stronger, whenever self participates. Conversely, the question Joseph asked cut this struggle off before it gained any momentum.

It was Joseph's gratitude that led to victory. Victory, you inquire? Being thrown into prison isn't much of a victory! Well, the path to victory was surer and shorter from prison than it was from Potiphar's house. Chrysostom wisely pointed out that Joseph was better off in prison than he would have been had he remained in a setting where these temptations would have increased.

A key principle is this: For a person to sin, he or she must first become oblivious to God's goodness! Spiritual blindness, personal forgetfulness, a dissociative state of mind—something like that must first set in. If, however, the opposite occurs, as it did with Joseph—if this person focuses on all the ways that God had blessed him, had suffered for him, had been patient with him, and had forgiven him—such a flood of memories will provide the necessary cold shower that alters the plans of lust.

Karl Bath's assertion that "all sin is simply ingratitude" fits somewhere in this picture. At minimum, a good gush of gratitude is sufficient to stop sin before redirecting the energy it wanted to exploit toward some higher, holier purpose.

There is yet another way gratitude leads to obedience. You see, a gratitude for God's greatest display of love (what was accomplished on the cross) will inspire a love willing to take up the cross *that nails self.* Watchman Nee observed that "the three qualifications in God's selection of overcomers are: 1) they must be wholly for the glory of God; 2) they must be fearful of nothing; and 3) they must allow the cross to deal with self."[11]

It should be pointed out that whenever self is nailed to the cross, Satan has no target. Moreover, when self stays on the cross, the sin in others is better overcome, too. In his book, *Forever Triumphant*, F. J. Huegel illustrated how this can occur.

> A sergeant of the British forces over in Egypt, manifesting a fine Christian spirit in his dealings with the men, was called before his chaplain who said, "Sergeant, tell me how you were converted." "It is very simple," replied the sergeant, "we were back at camp where we were having great sport with a Christian soldier, the only Christian in the regiment. He was the butt of jokes, jeered and mocked, and at night when he would kneel beside his cot to pray, boots would fly from every quarter aimed at his head. One night I took my boots and cracked him on the head as he knelt beside me in prayer. He said nothing. In the morning, Chaplain, I found my boots beside my bed all shined up and ready for me to get into. In this

way I was paid by the one I had so cruelly wronged. Chaplain, it was too much. It broke my heart. I couldn't resist such a testimony. I surrendered to Christ."

Victory in its sublimest manifestation is nothing more or less than the Spirit of Christ, which is love and a willingness to die for others, revealing itself under circumstances which ordinarily call forth anger, impatience, hatred and revenge.[12]

To that one who loves God enough to let him do the crucifying, sin is more easily overcome; and its victory is more likely extended to others.

Yet how many people, even people in the church, can give testimony after testimony of a life so self-absorbed that the cause of Christ is nowhere to be seen! This was apparently true of the disciples shortly before the Lord's death. Being more concerned for themselves than they were for him, an opening appeared which the devil was quick to see; and in storming through this opening, the rout was on! The most devastating defeat, which never had to happen, swiftly overcame them.

What could have stopped all this? Gratitude! A gratitude that was looking at the problem from the perspective of what would bless Jesus.

Had gratitude been present in the garden that night, an entirely different way of thinking, and feeling, and doing would have produced an entirely different outcome—one much more God-glorifying than what the biblical record was compelled to report.

Reflection Questions

1. How would you rate your faithfulness to give thanks? Please explain.

2. Do you tend to view life by how it impacts you, or by how it impacts the Lord?

3. Have you had experiences where a spirit of thanksgiving helped you to overcome temptation? Please share a recent example.

4. By acting in ways that aren't at all normal, the crucified life offers a strong testimony which impacts others. Has your gratitude to the Lord extended this far, wherein self is on the cross and showing God's love to others is more important?

Chapter 13

The Problem's Proportions—Part I

We could all wish that life was problem-free: that there were no money problems, health problems, relationship problems, or any other problem that would sap our energy and sabotage our peace. But ever since we were toddlers we have been confronted by the fact life has very serious problems.

One might think that children's stories would focus only on cute little animals and all the nice times enjoyed at grandmother's house. Children stories, however, hold nothing back when it comes to the darker side of life. Their depictions of the big bad wolf, menacing giants, rampaging tigers, and the Wicked Witch of the East are presented with vivid and frightening detail. Then again—these are just children stories.

When picking up the Bible—this gospel of goodness, grace, gladness, and God—we might expect caroling angels, happy miracles, and visions of heaven. What we discover, though, are kings who burn babies, devils who possess children, men who massacre women, and a God who drowns nearly everyone in sight. Other ominous realities—such as the ravages of war, the destructions of nature, the torture of mental illnesses, and man's inhumanity to man have made it quite clear we live in a very scary world.

When taking into account all these plaguing problems, the Lord's announcement, "In this world you will have tribulation," seems to have been the least insightful thing he ever said. Yet, these words were really more of a revelation than we know. I say that because the Jews had long believed that once the Messiah came, the shackles of foreign powers would be thrown off and, due to the might of David's greater Son, Israel would be restored to the bounty of worldwide supremacy. Just as the Messiah's visitation was about to end, though, Jesus set this optimistic notion aside by projecting, of all things, an *increase* of problems and not their virtual elimination, as the Jews had hoped.

This vision of trouble-free living where swords are beaten into plowshares and lions lie down by the lambs enticed the Jews of yesterday in a way far greater than the "South Seas island" fantasy entices some people today. Oh, to be able to get away from it all, to lay spread eagle on the beach as gentle breezes and warm sunshine caress all our worries away! Such utopian pleasures were not at hand, Jesus said, for trials of ego-shattering, history-shaking proportions were about to be encountered.

The Resistance

Before examining the resistance that comes because of evil, we must first examine the resistance that comes from God. And by that I mean God's resistance to the smooth and easy way. Concerned about this resistance, St. Theresa, a nun from fifteenth-century Spain, wrote in her diary, "Lord, when wilt Thou cease to strew our path with obstacles?"

The Lord answered her, "Murmur not, for it is thus that I treat my friends." Teresa sighed and replied, "Ah, dear, Lord, and that is why Thou hast so few."[1]

Perhaps so, but the easy life will hide our weaknesses so that not even we discover them. Moreover, it will prevent us from developing strengths that can only be developed during a trial.

The theology of trials, or we might call it the theology of tests, needs to be taught today or God's people are going to misread their circumstances; and by doing so, they will misconstrue the heart of God.

Confusion on the battlefield often leads to defeat. Therefore, purposing to prevent such confusion—so we can better understand what's coming from where—we will focus next on God's role in some of this, because he does have one. God is hardly a bystander when trouble comes. His role is prominent and, if all goes as planned, beneficial. But to see that, we need extraordinary vision, what may well be classified as 50/20 vision.

Genesis 50:20 records Joseph's words to his brothers after the long ordeal he endured in Egypt. The brothers intended him evil, but God was at work, superseding all they did to bring about good. You should know that in the midst of every trial, there is a test. Yes, evil may set out to do its worst—and God sanctions none of that today. But in the middle of the trial, none of which may have come from God, there is a test that did come from God.

To make some distinctions between a trial and a test we can say this. A trial has designs to make life worse; a test has designs to make life better. A trial involves destructive pressures; a test involves constructive principles. A trial is that which comes against you; a test is how you respond. It's important to understand the differences between the two.

If you respond in the right way, God will use what was designed for your harm and "work all things together for good" (Romans 8:26). Those with 50/20 vision will see this.

It would have been easy for Joseph to view his circumstances on the horizontal level only—the brutal brothers, the evil Egyptians, the despicable woman. And had he done so, he would have become bitter. And by leaving God out of the picture, he would have also made a monumental mistake! But because God was precious to Joseph, the Lord was never out of view!

Therefore, there was a happy ending in this story, but maybe not the ending you have in mind: where Joseph becomes a great leader in Egypt and all his family are reunited. No, the best outcome of this story is not that. The most impressive outcome, recognized by many Bible commentators, is that Joseph became the most Christlike figure in the Old Testament. What an amazing accomplishment! What a treasured tribute!

But would such splendid character have emerged if Joseph didn't pass the tests God had administered for his eternal benefit? There is a very real sense in which these tests were more important than the trials. And that's what we must see, too: the test *in* the trial, for there is one.

In every trial there is a test which, if passed, can advance our character (the Christlike life). Yet, how few there are who focus on character when the trials of life come. People are more focused on getting what they want: that is, for the trial to end, for a happy outcome to occur, for improved circumstances to manifest. And, yes, God wants those things, too. But not more than he wants our character developed!

Just know that as with Joseph so also with us, tests reveal character, and in some sense congeal character. Reflecting on this point, John Henry Jowett wrote:

> Character is more surely revealed, and most certainly impoverished or enriched, in which seem to be the little occasions of life than in those which seem to be great. It is likely that the real test comes not in the crisis of some single crashing event, but in the long-drawn-out process of wearisome and smaller events.[2]

How we respond to these tests is an indicator of character, if not a progress report on what needs to be improved.

The greater the tests, in number and difficulty, the more advanced our spiritual growth. Reflecting on this fact, C. S Lewis wrote, "If we were stronger, we might be less tenderly treated. If we were braver, we might be sent with far less help to defend far more desperate posts in the great battle."[3]

Tests develop the believer, and are therefore essential to spiritual growth. So if you have failed a lot of tests, perhaps as much as a hundred of them. Guess what? Test 101 is on its way! To understood this as you should, would make you grateful. For if all testing ceased, that would mean you could never advance.

Imagine the teacher saying, "Time's up! Test over! The results are locked in!" Is that good news? Not always. There comes a time when the teacher knows it's useless to give or take the test again. As C. S. Lewis put it, "Finality must come sometime, and it does not require a very robust faith to believe that omniscience knows when."[4]

So, again, whatever the downside of test-taking, the alternative is considerably worse. It means we've reached the end, and that may not include graduation, or even retention, but instead a permanent demotion.

Faith-testing, the record shows, wasn't limited to the first heralds of the gospel; it continues today, thus eliciting this commentary from A. B. Simpson:

> There is a prevalent idea that the power of God in a human life should lift us above all trials, conflicts and struggles. The fact is, the power of God always brings a conflict and a struggle. One would have thought that on his great missionary journey to Rome, Paul would have been carried by some mighty providence above the power of storms and tempests and enemies. But, on the contrary, it was one long hard fight with the persecuting Jews, with wild tempests, with venomous vipers and all the powers of earth and hell; and at last he was saved, as it seemed by the narrowest margin and had to swim ashore at Malta on a piece of wreckage and barely escape a watery grave.
>
> Was that like a God of infinite power? Yes, just like him![5]

G. D. Watson, called the "apostle of sanctification," also understood the necessity of God's tests. In his book, *Love Abounding*, Watson wrote, "The higher men rise toward God, the more God will test their faith."[6] In his book, *Pure Gold*, Watson said believers "are led through processes of severe trials, hot furnace-testings, which put to thorough proof every virtue and every grace of their hearts."[7]

Further addressing this theme in his book, *Soul Food*, G. D. Watson described the intended results of God's test when he wrote: "It withers our cleverness, cauterizes our smartness, teaches us true humiliation and self-abasement. It clips the rattling talkativeness from our tongue ... and shows us our demerit in a strong light."[8] For without this knowledge, we would never make needed changes.

But should these intended results not manifest as they should, then a demotion may be in order. Dealing quite frankly with this demotion, G. D. Watson—in his book, *Tribulation Worketh*—wrote these words: "Some who desire to be saints of the larger magnitudes, when the testing adequate to those magnitudes are brought to bear upon them, fail, and dwindle down to lesser ranks."[9]

In his book, *The Secret of Spiritual Power*, G. D. Watson explained why this need not happen. Speaking of God, Watson said, "He often tests our faith, but at the last moment, in the worst extremity, his train of infinite mercy and provision has arrived on scheduled time."[10] These tests don't have to end in failure; they *can* end in welcomed joy.

It is doubtful anyone the test itself. During the throes of a severe testing, we may find ourselves, in the words of Amy Carmichael, "discontent with the ways of God."[11] It was during the great trial of his life, remember, that Job expressed this very sentiment. In her book, *The Story of Job*, Jessie Penn-Lewis, reported this all-too-human fact.

"Let me alone," he cries to God. Why should you magnify frail man by setting your heart upon him, visiting him and testing him every moment? Oh that you would turn your eyes from me (7:17-19)! "If I have sinned, what can I do unto Thee, O Thou watcher of men?"[12]

In this soulful complaint, Job envisioned the big eye of heaven always watching him, God always testing him. But was this complaint true? No, it was not. The trial of Job lasted about nine months; and after that, he lived another one hundred forty years with no testing like this ever again.

Another verbalization of Job's "discontent with the ways of God" is seen in chapter 23, where Job complained about a silent heaven. This is a complaint, seen multiple times in the Old Testament, that has been given voice by many of us.

Offering commentary about this complaint, Jessie-Penn Lewis wrote:

> Job is obliged to confess that he has no word from God during his deep trial. Whichever way he moves—forward, backward, to the left or to the right—he cannot perceive a trace of his workings or his presence.
>
> This hiding of God gives the bitterest pain of all, but it is useless trying to find him when he withdraws himself from the consciousness; no agonizing in prayer or writhing in self-effort can compel him to unveil his face when he hides himself in thick darkness.[13]

Besides, all this silence isn't as mysterious as we sometimes suppose; for isn't it true that silence is always required during a test?

We may vent discontent about the ways of God, but we would never do this if we understood the positive purposes of these test. Contrary to some of our unexamined assumptions, the Lord's testing will strengthen our faith. On this point, F. B. Meyer, in his biography of Jeremiah, writes:

> God graduates the trials of our life; he allows the lesser to precede the greater. He gives us the opportunity to learn to trust him in slighter difficulties, that faith may become muscular and strong, and that we may be able to walk to him during the surge of the ocean. Be sure that whatever your trials and troubles are this hour, God has allowed them to come to afford you an opportunity of preparation for future days.[14]

The trials we face are never random and ruthless, capricious in the way they come and cruel in the way they operate—at least not singularly so. Those with malice in their hearts may have targeted us, but the One who has only love in his heart has a far better outcome in mind.

You should know, ever and always, that these trials weren't sent because the mood of God suddenly turned sour. G. D. Watson observed, "The history of piety will show that thousands who seemed to suffer most directly from the hand of God have been the very ones that loved God with a surpassing flame of devotion."[15]

Again, the God who administers these tests has nothing but love in his heart when he does so.

Imperative also for us to know is that during these tests we must take refuge in the Lord's wisdom—for the Good Shepherd knows where he is taking us! *We* may be bewildered—at times, unable to make sense of it all—but the Lord has *already* made sense of it all! Divine providence comprehends all, and masters all.

In his book, *Our Own God*, G. D. Watson used a vivid metaphor to describe Sovereignty at work:

> God's providence—there is nothing in all the world like it; so mysterious, so multiplied, so exact, so vigilant, so minute, so intricate. It is like an immense loom, with millions of threads and flying shuttles, that may seem to be moving in opposite directions and tangled in every way, yet forever weaving out a pattern of God's ways with every figure and color in the right place, sufficient to thrill the intellects of saints and angels.[16]

That we are sometimes confused is understandable enough, given our knothole perspective on life. Yet, there is much value in Robert Louis Stevenson's observation: "If I from my spy-hole, looking upon a fraction of the universe, yet perceive some broken evidences of a plan, shall I be so mad as to complain that all cannot be desciphered?"[17]

All is *not* random and meaningless! The purposes of God, disclosed in Scripture already, are hardly hidden to the child of God. As A. B. Simpson summarily put it: "God is testing us now that he may shake out of us the things that are transient and temporal, and that we may be established in the things which cannot be shaken and which shall remain. This is the meaning of all the tests and trials of life."[18]

As for the confusion that sometimes puts us in a quandary: this *confusion* is exactly why we shouldn't draw any *conclusion*—especially conclusions that slander God. You and I simply don't know enough to prosecute that case! But we do know enough not to take it!

Unassailably true, unalterably true, is the Bible's revelation of the character of Christ. And what the Bible reveals is more than sufficient for our trust. This is why, in the midst of perplexity and pain, "Faith knows that there is a loving purpose running through every trial, and that the Great Refiner has a meaning for every degree of heat to which the furnace is raised ...."[19] So wrote F. B. Meyer in his book, *Christ in Isaiah*.

A major part of this meaning relates to the new strength it gives us once the trial has been mastered. J. H. Jowett stressed, "We cannot affirm this to ourselves too often and too confidently: conquered perils become allies: in every victory there is a transfer of dynamics."[20] For what threatened to overcome us will be put in reverse, triggering a new confidence—in the words of Scripture, "Experience produces hope" (Romans 5:5).

It was precisely because of these trials that Samuel Rutherford cried, "Oh, what I owe to the file, and the hammer and the furnace of the Lord Jesus!" Martin Luther exclaimed, "My temptations have been my masters in divinity." And Hannah Whitall Smith declared, "Temptation is plainly one of the instruments used by God to complete our perfection ...."[21] Disassociating such experiences from the plan of God may result in missing his plan.

All who are in the faith will be tested; that much is assured. As the Puritan writer Thomas Manton put it, "Never a Christian went out of this world, but, one time or other, God tried him in some eminent point of self-denial ....[22] Thus, Peter counsels, "Think it not strange concerning the fiery trial .... (I Peter 4:19). Because, given Scripture's testimony, there's nothing strange or unusual about it! Trials taking our measure in order to increase our stature will come. Taking note of this fact, James S. Stewart wrote:

It is immensely significant that all the great masters of the spiritual life—St. Augustine, a' Kempis, St. Theresa—warn us repeatedly that we must reckon for the day when helpers fail and comforts flee and God seems to withdraw his face, and the wilderness clamps down upon our souls.[23]

When such a time comes, we must remember that profound wisdom and hidden love are embedded in each test. In his book, *Coals of Fire*, G. D. Watson declared, "God will select the test with infinite skill, and have it so applied to us to prove our heart loyalty to him at the very core."[24] Furnishing this proof puts the finishing touches on faith.

The tests God selects often targets what we want most. Thomas Goodwin wrote, "... as God tried Abraham in his Isaac, so God will the sons of Abraham in what is dearest to them ...."[25] The design if these tests in not to deprive but to help us deploy. Testing is done so we can succeed, or so we can see where we need to be strengthened in order to succeed.

Testing brings the good out. It allows God to promote us. It launches us into a new season of our life. At issue, though, is this: How will we respond to these tests? Will we falter and fail? Or will we press in closer and closer to the Lord in order to obtain his overcoming power?

One form of testing that scarcely gets noticed is the testing of many gray days when nothing eventful happens. During such a season, the road to the horizon is flat, with nothing appealing or foreboding drawing attention. There is neither sunshine nor rain, as each day seems like the last. Faceless people and dull routine occupy both center and circumference. Prayers drained of inspiration are greeted, seemingly, by a locked door and a thrown-away key. We may think we're talking to a throne, but it feels like we're talking to a wall.

John Henry Jowett described the result of this daily perception when he wrote, "Perhaps the test of monotony is more severe than the test of an emergency. Perhaps the long pull tends more to exhaustion than some tremendous but momentary strain."[26] And perhaps, too, God is checking the gravitation of soul when all props and prompts are withdrawn.

In testing's more graduated form, we may find ourself in circumstances where no one can help us. Consequently, a loneliness of soul will set in, during which, as G. D. Watson put it, "We seem to pace the boundless shore of our solitary island, waiting for any sort of a change to break upon our experience."[27]

Our first reaction to such isolation—even if it is more spiritual than geographic—may be panic. Commenting on this experience, Watson described the feeling of "being caged in, hampered, and tied in an inexplicable manner. Providence seems to go off and leave us to the heartlessness of a thousand petty demons who pervade every little circumstance."[28] And should this panic be indulged, we will have completely misunderstood God's purpose!

His deeper purpose relates to this truth: If our faith is dependent on others for its survival, then God may have to orchestrate circumstances, for our eternal good, where these substitutes for God are removed for a season. Offering additional insight, A. B. Simpson wrote:

> The tests will come to all such souls; they will find these favorable influences withdrawn, and these helpful surroundings changed, and they will be compelled to fall back on their own resources and their own direct knowledge of God and his sustaining grace. And when no longer pressed forward by stronger spirits and upheld by helpful hands, but met by opposition, misunderstanding, uncongenial associations, and, perhaps, direct persecution, they will soon find whether their purpose is rooted in God, and their spirit united to the living Christ and whether they are abiding in him as the source of their strength and service.[29]

No doubt, the most severe test is like that which the apostles endured, about which the Apostle Paul wrote, "We have been made a spectacle" (II Corinthians 4:9). The Greek word for "spectacle" means theater. This reference perhaps anticipated the violence on display against Christians in Roman amphitheaters. There, the crowd became a mob, moved to frenzy by the violence. With bright eyes and black hearts, onlookers savored every ghastly wound with euphoric glee.

Talk about a test! This was much more than a test—this was the final exam!

Yet, as A. B. Simpson asserted, "There is no situation so trying and difficult but God can sustain us in it ...."[30] Richard Sibbes, the seventeenth-century Puritan writer, encouraged those doubting this fact, saying, "... we lament, `I shall never get through such a trial.' But if God brings us into the trial he will be with us in the trial, and at length bring us out, more refined."[31]

To experience the faithfulness of God during a trial inflicted by the meanest of men may well amplify one's testimony from continent to continent and put us in company with the truly great from every age. G. D. Watson observed:

> If our religious life should be an uninterrupted season of summer days, it would debar us from knowing the large portion of the moral experiences with the world; it would exclude us from the inner and sublime fellowship of the martyrs and the white-robed company who have gone up through great tribulation.[32]

So are these trials perpetual? No, God doesn't perpetually test us, for well before our arrival in heaven, there will be relief and repose on earth. Acknowledging this fact, John Henry Jowett wrote, "There are softer seasons among the years, times when the springs in the life are unsealed, and lovely purposes come to birth."[33] From the pen of G. D Watson we see a similar sentiment expressed:

> It is generally true of the sanctified life that after the soul has gone through various testings and

spiritual conflicts, there comes a time when it experiences a greater enjoyment, a serener vision and firmer establishment than it knew in the first stage of heart cleansing.[34]

Until that day comes, however, we must be open to adversity developing character. Emerging from the crucible of suffering, if all goes as God purposed, will be a purer, nobler, stronger soul. And is this not an outcome you desire?

In his book, *Tried by Fire*, F. B. Meyer discussed this outcome.

There is utility in every trial. It is intended to reveal the secrets of our hearts; to humble us and prove us; to winnow us as corn is shaken in a sieve; to detach us from the earthly and visible; to create in us an eager desire for the realities which can alone quench our cravings and endure forever.[35]

When writing about the benefits of such trials, G. D. Watson added realism to his optimism when he explained:

It is almost impossible for us to see any benefits of being tempted while we are passing through them; the sensibilities are so pierced by fiery darts, the mind is so distracted by evil suggestions, the will is so upset with opposite motives, the rattle of spiritual musketry and smoke of battles obscures the vision from seeing any blessing likely to come from it. Nevertheless, afterwards it yieldeth the peaceable fruit of righteousness to them who are properly exercised thereby.[36]

True, not all problems have this potential for good. Those problems that come because of our foolishness, or because of our sinfulness, are hardly to be compared with the problems resulting from our commitment to do the Lord's work. George Mueller, for example, didn't have to have all the problems he had. It was only because he sponsored four orphanages and more than ten thousand orphans that his problems piled up.

Perhaps each Christian would do well to ask if his or her problems are attributable to a kingdom-extending, devil-resisting labor; or if these are the kind of problems—self-inflicted and Satan-inspired—that keep one back at the fort instead of being out there on the frontlines?

Everyone has problems. But the critical question is, how many have problems incurred from a committed life? Problems like this are in a distinctly different category! Stories about solving problems ... we all love to hear them. But when those problems relate to advancing the cause of God, these stories have increased inspiration.

So of interest to us at this point—for purposes of instruction and inspiration—is to see how Jesus handled such problems.

The Resources

As Jesus approached the biggest problem he would ever face, it is instructive that he didn't split from the disciples and face it by himself. He instead focused on the disciples, teaching *them* how to stand strong in the day of trouble. By itself, this factor says something about how to best handle our problems. The transferable principle is this: To succeed with our own problems, we would do well to help others with theirs.

In certain places in Africa, it is customary for women to carry food, clothes, or some other needed supply in a bundle tied to the end of a stick. Before draping this stick over their shoulders, these women first fastened a rock to the other end of the stick. In doing so they discovered this added weight made their own burden easier to carry. Similarly, the Lord's devotion to the apostles, manifested when his own burden was the greatest, illustrates this principle.

Addressing his impending death, Jesus told the apostles, "And now I have told you before it comes, that when it does come to pass, you may believe. I will no longer talk much with you, for the ruler of the world is coming, and he has nothing in me" (John 14:29, 30). What is particularly striking about these words is the sequence in which they appear. Instead of talking about the devil and death first, Jesus initially focused on the disciples' resources—the Spirit's strength, Heaven's hope, the Father's fellowship, and Divinity's direction. This sequence provided a more accurate framing of the picture.

Almost always, you should know, the devil will attempt to put a smaller frame on the picture in order to highlight every intimidating aspect of the problem. If the devil can get us to be "problem-conscious," our defeat will be made more certain. But if the Lord can get us to be "promise-conscious," our victory will be more certain. Once we become aware of God's resources and rewards, the shoddy counterfeits Satan dazzles before our eyes will not have much appeal. To the contrary! Instead of a mind of mush, we will be fully alert. And instead of letting our backbone become a squirmy noodle, it will be steeled with determination.

This principle of "framing" is so important to our obedience it must not be overlooked. Therefore, before drawing any conclusion about any problem, we must first inquire about the picture we are seeing—what's in it, what's not in it, and how is this picture being framed? Are we seeing *only* the problem? If so, we should go no further in our examination of it! Because if we do, we are likely to fall for one of Satan's most successful tricks—deception through framing. The better course is to go to the Lord and ask him how he would frame this picture.

In doing this, be aware: The Lord won't skew the picture to make us feel better, since minimizing solves nothing! This is why Jesus didn't romanticize his death as merely "passing over to the other side." And it is also why he didn't speak of the devil as a toothless, clawless lion that couldn't do any harm. Instead, Jesus made it clear that what was about to happen was *the* climactic battle in his life, more fierce and far-reaching than any other battle he had ever fought.

In this way, Jesus was neither the eagle nor the ostrich; for he neither kept his head in the clouds of breathless piety, nor buried it in the sands of willful ignorance. Jesus saw exactly what was coming—and faced it head-on!

Just know that we aren't ever alone during the trials we face, unless we choose to be. At our side and at our disposal are all the resources of God sufficient for our victory. Aware of this truth, one saint of God said that "whenever God tests me, I test him."

Now, there was no insolence intended by this remark, only a readiness to respond to God's invitation in Malachi, "Test me, try me, prove me." For as we do this, we will experience the faithfulness of God in every trial, so that the triumphs God meant for us to experience will lift our life from a nondescript testimony that impresses no one to a life that illustrates that wonderful praise: "To God be the glory, great works he has done."

Reflection Questions

1. Give an example of how you previously framed a problem the wrong way (recent or current examples are preferable).

2. List two principles about "tests" and "trials" most relevant to your current experience.

3. How might a Christian misread what is occurring during a trial if the two principles which you listed were not understood.

Chapter 14

The Problem's Proportions—Part II

There is no question about the fact that life is hard. No one is ever exempted from life's trials, even those who have Jesus in their lives. The first disciples had Jesus with them—literally, physically—yet their trials increased. And had they not followed Jesus, they may have led a relatively quiet life, drawing no attention from the Roman army, the Jewish government, and he that is the great antagonist of God, Satan. But by being close to Jesus the disciples got close to danger. So Ray Stedman was right when he said, "To be in Christ is to be in trouble."

When the disciples left the Upper Room that night, there was for them no calmness of soul after "a quiet time" with the Lord, for these men were in the middle of a life-and-death conflict. Yes, they then went to a garden, but not to enjoy its serenity.

One could wish life could be defined by idyllic sentiments of romantic poetry—the flower, the butterfly, the puffy cloud, the gentle breeze. However, more than a century after the soldiers invaded Gethsemane, the Roman emperor Marcus Aurelius declared, "The art of living is more like that of wrestling than of dancing, the main thing is to stand firm and be ready for an unseen attack."

Scripture says we wrestle not against flesh and blood but against powers and principalities and other such forces that hold rank in Satan's evil empire. For the disciples then, and for us today, these forces are not entirely unknown. Scripture reveals enough about them so we won't be caught by surprise.

The ultimate goal in this battle for our souls is not just safety or episodic victory but what the Puritan preacher Thomas Goodwin called "habitual dispositions to good." The Bible summons us to consistent obedience with full expectation of compliance.[1] Similarly, A. W. Pink pointed out: "... that it should need no long and laborious argument to demonstrate that God must require obedience, full and hearty obedience ...."[2]

To that end, Jesus' discourse in the Upper Room is being examined in these pages in order to gather the clues he provided, and learn the lessons he taught, for obeying him always.

Any attempt to obey God will encounter problems; there's no use denying that. We viewed some of these problems more broadly in the previous chapter as we reflected on the trials Satan sends and the tests God sends. We learned there that Satan's trials and God's tests have different agendas. The believer is at risk if he focuses only on what Satan sent (the trial) and fails to focus on what God sent (the test). Unless we rivet our attention on God and view each trial from his perspective, we may fail his test and suffer the demotion that comes from having done so.

In this chapter we want to narrow our focus as we zoom in on the problem to get a more detailed view. Of course, no problem can be solved unless the problem is first defined. In attempting to define, we lay it down at the outset that the wispy sentiments of a romantic poet can't be trusted, and neither can the abstract conceptions of some secluded philosopher. Each see what they see in a more limited and distorted way, but it is the vertical verdict of eternity that is required.

A supreme wisdom, one that knows every strategy of evil, must be forthcoming. And this wisdom comes best not from those who succumbed to evil and must now give their dreadful testimony, but from the only man who left the Upper Room that night and didn't fail. Accordingly, with Jesus as our teacher and Scripture as our guide we want to gain his assessment of the problem. He who was never deceived, never overcome, deserves our full attention.

The Reality

The reality of the problem as Jesus defined it included two major components—what is true about Satan, and what is true about self. Let's briefly examine each component.

C. S. Lewis observed, "The New Testament has a good deal more to say about dark superhuman powers than about the fall of Adam."[3] Adam's fall brought consequences that were severe and lasting. But to assess this event, little is gained by studying Adam; much more is gained by studying Satan. Satan is not a mythological theme invented for symbolic purposes to discuss the phenomenon of evil. German theologian Erich Sauer declared:

> The fact is that the devil is a spiritual being, gifted with the highest intelligence, and though fallen, exceedingly powerful, whose existence cannot in any way be assailed by philosophy nor natural science. Since it is just in our world and in the universe immediately surrounding it that we observe disharmony, death and destruction, even a purely speculative contemplation of nature forces on us the conclusion that this world, and presumably the solar system connected with it, are the domain of this world-ruler and potentate.[4]

Jesus said Satan became the ruler of this world. Of course, he wasn't always the ruler of the world; originally, Adam had that role. But when Adam bent his knee to the Shining One, Satan grabbed the fallen scepter and claimed the dominion God gave Adam. This dominion remained with Satan until Jesus came and took it back. Commenting on the regaining of this false ruler's crown and the price that had to be paid, E. M. Bounds wrote:

> The Son of God remained silent at the devil's approach. The cross, its deep humiliation, bitter agony, its defeat and despair—it took all these to

lift the crown from Satan's brow and bring his throne down to dust and ashes. The adorable Son of God saw "the travail of his soul" and was satisfied (Isaiah 53:11).[5]

Before this toppling of Satan's throne, the enemy ruled ruthlessly in the earth. The ruin and wreckage he caused testified not only of Satan's malevolent character but also of his ability to be highly organized. In his book, *Victory over the Devil*, Jack R. Taylor observed:

> Satan's system is such that every responsibility in the diabolical plan to overthrow the power of God is understood. This responsibility level extends to every city, village, and hamlet. It continues until every institution, government house, home, and person is under the jurisdiction of some evil spirit's responsibility.[6]

Mapping the whole habitable earth like a general, Satan plotted our ruination with precision and detail. So, while we may not be thinking too much about the devil and his demons, it is quite sobering to realize that each has given considerable thought about us!

We know how Satan operates in the unseemly world of gangs, drugs, and prostitution. We even know how far his influence extends—from the greedy takeover artist of some business conglomerate to the power-hungry dictator of some banana republic; from the suburban housewife who is cheating on her husband to that respectable looking accountant who gets "creative" with the books; from the bully in the schoolyard who attacks a defenseless nerd to the computer monopolist who, by sheer brilliance, crushes his competitor.

Satan shoots the entire gamut—from the socially smug to the deadly thug! And he even makes his presence known at church by replacing the systematic teaching of God's Word with beautiful rituals, entertaining stories, leave-them-rolling-in-the-aisles-humor, or "dry as dust" why-did-we-bother-to-come lectures. Satan will replace godly leaders with toothy, master-of-ceremonies type pastors, business administrator type boards, manipulative-defend-their-turf staff, and heavy-handed, autocratic supervisors. He may not be listed in the bulletin, but Lucifer is on staff.

Not even the well-meaning Christian attempting to have his quiet time with the Lord is off-limits to Satan! In his book, *Winning the Invisible World*, E. M. Bounds said of Satan: "He is the destroyer of the seeds of good. Satan is so powerful that the incorruptible and eternal Word of God is prevented from accomplishing its saving efforts because of his vigilance and influence over the mind."[7] If Satan can sneak his suggestions in, those suggestions, like time bombs used to kill insects, will lay inconspicuously in some corner of our mind until the appointed time when they suddenly explode.

His ideas, revered at the university and disseminated to the nursery school, are brilliant in their ability to deceive. His pleasures, welcomed by the entertainment world and distributed to the nations, are seductive in their ability to control. His powers, sought by the darker element and loosed on the unsuspecting, are chilling in their ability to destroy. It really doesn't matter what the environment, Satan, who seems more the chameleon than the snake, blends right in—and in time rises to unrivaled prominence!

Upon cataloging the targets and strategies of Satan, we are impressed how no one has been overlooked and no weapon has gone unused. Visit any continent and every island and the evidence is plentiful that, no matter how idyllic the scene and flourishing the culture, Satan is there.

Check out the institutions man constructed, and all the ideologies man invented, and Satan's successes will be on prominent display. This formidable foe, intent on destruction in any way he can achieve it, will infiltrate the mind, decimate the heart, eradicate the will, attacking both body and soul, both family and church, because Satan is anti-God, anti-Christ, and anti-you!

Therefore, when facing temptation, reality requires recognition of the external enemy, Satan! To dismiss him as a myth, is to be "myth-taken"! What utter folly, Bill Gillham wrote, to "be matching wits with someone who has an IQ of

20,000."[8] This intellectual brilliance, evil to the core, is not to be taken lightly!

Yet, some balance must be brought to this discussion. To underestimate Satan secures no advantage, certainly; however to overestimate him is equally destructive. The Bible has more to say about self than it does about Satan, so our inspection of self must also be thorough.

Unless we can say what Jesus said, Satan has nothing in us, something in us *is* a big part of the problem. In many people the force of an unholy habit is so strong ominous outcomes are almost automatic. But this was not true of Jesus. The Bible declared, "In him is light and there is no darkness at all." None! Jesus was in every way pure, and was not in any way blemished.

In reviewing the record, J. N. D. Anderson could say of the Lord:

> There is in all his talk no trace of regret or hint of compunction, or suggestion of sorrow for shortcoming, or slightest vestige of remorse. He taught other men to think of themselves as sinners, he asserted plainly the human heart is evil, he told his disciples that every time they prayed they were to pray to be forgiven, but he never acts or speaks as though he himself has the slightest consciousness of having ever done anything other than what was pleasing to God.[9]

This absence of sin in the Lord's life meant that Satan didn't have a toe-hold from which he could gain a stronghold. Hence, without sin's encroachment, there could be no enlargement of sin's influence, and no encampment of sin's control. As far as Jesus was concerned, Satan had been completely shut out. Our record, unfortunately, isn't nearly this commendable. Good and evil in us may be so intertwined it is difficult to separate one from the other. Some think there's no domain in our life free from sin, and no deed in our life free from the intrusions of self.

Pondering this dilemma, the Russian writer, Alexander Solzhenitsyn, hypothesized:

If only there were evil people somewhere insidiously committing evil deeds, and it were necessary only to separate them from the rest of us to destroy them. But the line dividing good and evil cuts through the heart of every human being. And who is willing to destroy a piece of his own heart?[10]

Little wonder, then, that Goethe could say, "I have never heard of a sin being committed without knowing full well that I had the seed of it within myself."[11]

Even among the dedicated and consecrated this evil lurks, and for a while may not be discerned. One man who had a keener eye than most in this regard was A. W. Tozer whose prophetic editorials scorched the modern church with truths that weren't always well received. For example, in his book, *The Root of the Righteous*, Tozer insisted:

Christians, and especially very active ones, should take time out frequently to search their souls to be sure of their motives. Many a solo is sung to show off; many a sermon is preached as an exhibition of talent; many a church is founded as a slap at some other church. Even missionary activity may become competitive, and soul-winning may degenerate into a brush-salesman project to satisfy the flesh. Do not forget, the Pharisees were great missionaries and would compass sea and land to make a convert.[12]

In another book, *Leaning into the Wind*, Tozer elaborated on this same topic as he explored the way *inferior* motives may actually be *ulterior* motives hiding in the *interiors* of prayer.

Self turns what would otherwise be a pure and powerful prayer into a weak and ineffective one ... self, all bold and shameless, follows me to the altar, kneels with me in prayer, and destroys my prayer before it is uttered. It is possible to want the walls of Jerusalem rebuilt, but to want to be known as the Nehemiah who rebuilt them. It is possible to want the prophets of Baal defeated, but to dream of being the Elijah who stands dramatically on the mount to call down the fire for all the world to see. My strong desire for a reformation within the church may be rendered void by my secret desire to be known as another Luther.[13]

How subtle self can be! Even in the loftiest prayers and in the most noble goals, self can be camouflaged with disguises so effective not even the one in whom it is hiding may suspect its presence. Stephen Charnock, the London Puritan preacher, touched a raw nerve when he wrote, "Satan is never troubled to be pretendedly hated and really obeyed."[14] What we say with our lips may be contradicted by our lives.

Sinister Satan and subtle self—these are the two realities that must be addressed if the journey to our Gethsemane is going to end in victory.

The Readiness

The confidence and courage of the Gethsemane-bound Christ are traceable to the resources previously identified in this book, and to this fact also: that Satan had nothing in him. Likewise, if we want to stand strong in the day of temptation, we too must get to that place where Satan has nothing in us.

But, we ask, is this even possible? In a very real sense it is. Of course, unlike Jesus, we've already sinned, so our track record will never be like his. Nevertheless, at this stage in our walk with the Lord, there is a way to be free from the encroachments of sin—and free not just in the sense of forgiveness, but also free in the sense of a literal absence.

Paul Billheimer addressed this point when he wrote: "The only people who have genuine authority over Satan are those who choose to stay on the cross, allowing it to deliver them from all self-seeking, self-serving, and self-promotion."[15]

Many people, inside and outside the church, are willing to battle sin, but the war they wage and the sacrifice they make are not exactly what Scripture calls for. Uncovering this error with accuracy, Abraham Kuyper noted that:

> In his Word we do not read of "resignation," or "submission," or of reconciling oneself to one's lot. Such ideas come from the Stoics of ancient Greece and from the fatalistic Mohammedan's creed.[16]

But our battle must be fought differently! Seeing how many of the enemy's javelins we can catch was never God's way. For being on the recipient end of evil's attacks, and learning how to accept what he dishes out, is not the kind of strength God wants us to have.

Another detour from God's way of victory is reducing the battle by seeking, ever and always, to escape temptation. This will never work. In his book, *The Mystery of Iniquity*, F. J. Huegel explained why temptation is essential.

> There is nothing quite so human as temptation. It is the very quintessence of our humanity. The animal kingdom has much in common with man. But a horse or a tiger or a monkey cannot be tempted, and here lies the difference. Since man was made in the image of God, endowed as he is with a moral nature capable of choice between the good and the bad, obedience to God or disobedience, he can be tempted. And inasmuch as this moral nature of man does not really function save as he is tempted, he must be tempted.[17]

William James declared, "No man has matriculated in the university of life until he has been well tempted."[18] So any idea of escaping temptation by perpetual avoidance should be dislodged from our minds.

With an avoidance agenda that lacks biblical support, some Christians have attempted to escape temptation by escaping the world. There were those during the third century who reacted to the revelry in Rome and the excesses of a lascivious lifestyle by fleeing the city and seeking refuge in monasteries. Did that work? Not really, and Andrew Murray explained why:

> It is quite possible for a man to have made much progress in forsaking the world while the self-life retains full dominion within him. You see this fact illustrated in the case of the disciples. Peter could say with truth: "Lo, we have left all and followed Thee." Yet how manifestly did the selfish ego, with its self-pleasing and its self-confidence, still retain its full sway over him.[19]

Although the world with its temptations represents a rival god, it isn't the only rival god. Within our heart, self can be sitting with smugness on a throne that belongs only to God. And while self may make pronouncements that the one true God would affirm, the great offense, which can never be overlooked, is that self doesn't belong on that throne!

True enough, the external gods are bad, but they're not as entrenched as that one internal god, self. Thomas Watson exclaimed, "People are for the most part eaten up with self-love; they love their ease, the worldly profit, their lusts, but they do not have a drop of love to God."[20]

In a vain attempt to maintain its enthronement, self is willing to do all God wants it to do—study the Bible, sacrificially give, systematically eliminate evil habits, serve the Lord and his church with diligence. Nevertheless, all these efforts of the enthroned self are considerably lacking in resources and woefully lacking in outcome.

Noting this lack, and warning of its substitute, Ruth Paxson observed:

> We may have cut ourselves loose from every form of worldliness but in so doing have become critical and self-righteous. We may be loyal defenders of the faith, ready to lay down our lives for it and in so doing become bitter and unlovely. We may be faithful in the fulfilling of every

obligation to God and have given ourselves in self-sacrificing devotion to his cause and yet have no warm glow of love in our hearts, no spring of joy in our souls, no fervency of spirit in our communion with the Lord Jesus himself.[21]

What causes this marring of a seemingly otherwise splendid jewel? The enthroned self! The self willing to do anything the Bible instructs it to do—*except die*! This refusal to get off the throne and on the cross not only spoils the good intentions self may have, but exposes the corruption of its core.

What the sincere, steadfast, sacrificing self most needs to hear is this point articulated by Miles J. Stanford: "Only those 'alive from the dead'—that is, having appropriated their likeness with him in death—are bidden to present their instruments unto God. Crucifixion comes before consecration."[21] Not seeing this truth as they should have, those fleeing the city to the monastery created a different set of problems, more difficult to discern and therefore more difficult to overcome.

While self can be obedient in many observable ways, if it refuses the cross, it is rejecting the judgment God has made against it. And in doing this, disobedience is thriving at the core of so-called consecration. Perhaps the primary reason the cross is avoided is the unexamined perception that self is doing quite well "as is" and therefore the cross isn't necessary. Elaborating on this folly, Ray Stedman explained:

> We tend to think of ourselves as much more mature than we really are. Our power of self-deceit is almost incredible. Even in those times when we are trying to be ruthless and brutally honest about ourselves we can detect a self-esteem that is frightening. We may say, "I'm a stubborn, foolish, selfish person," but let someone agree with us at that point and we immediately bristle and say, "What do you mean? Why do you say that?"[23]

Unless we get beyond a surface acknowledgement of problems with our self-life, and unless we accept God's judgment about its utter futility, the cross will seem totally unnecessary to us. So we'll continue offering the Lord what he doesn't want: the consecrated self instead of the crucified self.

There can be no compromising here; because self, the enemy within, is altogether incapable of divine life. At best, it can only imitate but it can never generate the graces unique to this life. The very fact that self is still on the scene means the flow of divine life has been arrested. Just as long as one's self-life is being protected, consulted, and trusted, the Lord's life within will not, and cannot, be released.

It is only when self consents to the cross that the target Satan has been aiming at will suddenly disappear—and that brings revival! Roy Hession said: True revival is not the top blowing off, but the bottom dropping out.[24] For once self is brought all the way down to death, the life of God within our spirit arises and releases. Moreover, it is only in this state that we are then able to say what Jesus was able to say, the Evil One has nothing in us.

Satan can still be Satan—vicious, vindictive, and villainous. But not to be missed is the fact: If he has no target, he has no target! His fiery darts can fill the sky in a coming attack, yet every one of these missiles—destructive in design and deadly upon impact—are going to fall harmlessly to the ground. Beezlebub can huff and puff and, like the children's story puts it, threaten to "blow your house down." But your house isn't going anywhere! And the reason it isn't is because the same life that defeated him on the cross will defeat him again, once *you* are on the cross. Remember, the victory won at Calvary's cross is reinforced on our cross.

Yes, we have many resources—the Spirit's strength, Heaven's hope, the Father's fellowship, and Divinity's direction. And we may even have a clear recognition of reality—the outer enemy, Satan; and the inner enemy, self. Nevertheless, we won't have the victory we need until we can say what Jesus said, Satan "has nothing in me." A statement that can only be made when self is on the cross and Jesus is on the throne.

Reflection Questions

1. Is there currently a jurisdiction of the devil intact in your life? If so, name it so in prayer you can deal with it.

2. What tendency in your self-life do you most want eliminated?

3. Do you now understand the problem discussed in this chapter: substituting the consecrated life for the crucified life? In a sentence or two, define this problem. Then discuss its impact on you.

Chapter 15

Example's Encouragement

There will be times in your life and mine when the difference between obedience and disobedience may very well hinge on somebody's example. While principles are good, and promises are great, and the workings of the Holy Spirit are indispensable, still, there are those times when a flesh-and-blood example can mean so much.

In his book, *Humanity and God*, Samuel Chadwick tells of a time when a courageous influence worked its wonders.

> In the American Civil War Sheridan's army was attacked in his absence. The camp was routed. Men threw down their arms and fled like scared sheep. Suddenly they stopped, formed, turned, and drove back their foes and captured the artillery. What had happened to turn frightened sheep into conquering warriors, and a disgraceful rout into a glorious victory? General Sheridan had suddenly ridden into their midst, and, immediately, his conquering presence passed into their midst and they were changed.[1]

To see someone we know—a person who is both venerable and vulnerable—rise to meet a challenge that could have resulted in defeat is inspiring. And just to know that courage didn't die when the Apostle Paul did, and that love didn't expire when the Apostle John passed away, is very encouraging, especially when we see these virtues lived out in a believer we know.

How much steadier our growth would be today if we were under the wing of a more mature Christian, someone who knows what the Word of God has to say about every major doctrine and every major area of life. What a tremendous benefit could be ours if we could draw close to someone who doesn't have to be propped up or wound up, because the Spirit of God is renewing this person day after day (II Corinthians 4:16).

This benefit would be of greater value if this person didn't relate to us in a sentimental way (love without truth) or in a legalistic way (truth without love), but in a biblical way—speaking the truth in love (Ephesians 4:15).

The disciples had Jesus, Timothy had Paul—so who do you have? Is there someone Spirit-led and Word-bred tuned in to your needs, someone who will furnish needed nudges and private promptings whenever you begin to fall, or to fall away? How important such a person can be to the kind of obedience worthy of the Lord's name! Yet so few Christians have benefited from such an example—a fact sadly contrary to the divine design for church.

On the night of Jesus' arrest in the garden, the Lord concluded his comments in the Upper Room by telling the disciples, "But that the world may know that I love the Father, and as the Father gave me commandment, so I do ...." (John 14:31). Here, Jesus volunteered himself as an example of love-motivated obedience. And in retrospect we can see that Jesus exhibited what he exhorted—a willingness to obey, no matter how great the cost!

Significantly, the key to Jesus' success, identified again in this verse, was not his steeled determination or his devotion to truth, but the love Jesus had for the Father. This makes sense the more we think about it; for while rules and standards do have their place, a single blast from the fires of hell can completely obliterate them!

Andrew Murray wrote, "... it is not the code of laws, however clear and good, with its rewards or threats, that secures true obedience ..." and this is why "the expression 'obeying the commandments' is very seldom used in Scripture; it is almost always 'obeying me' ...."[2] For by connecting a command to a person and not to a code of ethics, a different dynamic emerges: one that brings a vibrant personality onto the scene, thus infusing through inspiration the strength to obey. It was at this point in redemption's drama, as was true always before, that Jesus' love for the Father kept him faithful to his calling.

It may surprise you to learn that Jesus did what he did because he was commanded to. We have often viewed his sacrifice as a voluntary act; which in one sense it was, but more precisely put it was a voluntary response to a command. The Father told Jesus what he must do; and Jesus, despite a struggle of soul unknown to man, chose to obey him.

When reflecting on the Father's command and Jesus' complete obedience, we find ourselves contemplating dynamics too incomprehensible to fathom. Yet, G. D. Watson was on safe grounds when he observed, "The Father is never commanded, is never sent on a mission, is never humiliated like the Son."[3]

Also a surprise for us to learn is that Jesus' death on the cross was motivated more by his love for the Father than it was by his love for us (John 17:4-9). Although we get the benefit of the overflow, Jesus made it clear that it was his love for the Father that sustained him through so ultimate a sacrifice.

What a wonderful example *this* is for the world to see!

Competent Caring in the Church

The search for models and mentors, people who could serve as examples to us, should reasonably begin in the church, and especially with that group who have had many years to learn and live. In undertaking this search, attempting to discern who can help us and who can't, we should be mindful of three classifications of Christians— children, young men, and fathers (I John 2:11-14). All in God's family are in one of these three categories, each defined by Scripture.

Obviously, we all begin the Christian life as a babe in Christ. It doesn't matter how intelligent or accomplished we were before we were born-again, we will not skip this stage. By definition, babies know very little, and therefore need help. This is where fathers come in. A spiritual father must draw close to the one he is caring for, offering provisions for anticipated needs—the milk of God's Word, the exercise of faith, and the walk of love. For without a nurturing such as this, spiritual growth becomes less likely.

As these spiritual children in the Lord begin to grow, the spiritual father will need to progress beyond the "goo goos" of the gospel, what the Book of Hebrews refers to as "the elementary doctrines," and begin to offer some meat. But this is precisely what many churches fail to do. Instead, week in and week out, the menu calls for more of the same—pabulum preaching. Offering a little bit of Scripture and a lot of stories, these churches systematically stunt their people into carnality. Unfortunately, "gospel-lite" churches are littering the landscape today, and the damage they do is not easily calculated.

When I was a young boy growing up in Florida, I attended annual family reunions where there was an abundance of food and people. My grandmother on this side of the family was one of thirteen children, so we often had triple digit attendance. But the one member of my extended family that I most remember is Cousin Harold.

Cousin Harold's parents would cut his food for him, put a spoon in his hands and promise him a nice automobile ride after lunch if he ate all his dinner. Should this promise not secure the desired response soon enough, they would proceed to feed Cousin Harold, urging him to open his mouth big and wide so the spoon (now an airplane) could safely land. This Harold, with something of a chuckle, would then do; and pretty soon he would make the "airplane" land in his own mouth, a feat we cousins were obliged to admire.

All this probably wouldn't have been that memorable to me were it not for the fact Harold was forty years old! In fact, the only thing wrong with Harold were his parents—they just wouldn't let their little boy grow up! Finally, Harold lashed out in rage at his parents and attempted to kill them. In thinking about this sad situation, I sometimes wonder if something similar is going on in the church. Leaders with little more sense than that possessed by Harold's parents are unwilling to do what it takes to achieve spiritual growth. They offer nothing different this year than all the years before. Apparently, the view from the bottom rung of the ladder is fine to them!

Significantly, the "Great Commission" uses the word "go" once and the word "teach" twice. This implies the need to devote an increased effort to those who have become Christians. Many in the church call this effort discipleship.

Back in the late 1970s and the early 1980s, discipleship became a popular movement in the evangelical church. In the September, 1979, issue of *Eternity* magazine David Waterman declared:

> Afoot in many different evangelical camps, irrespective of their different brand names, is a quiet, but persistently growing, revolution in interpersonal relationships called "discipleship" ... You are either a "discipler" or "disciplee," depending on your "age" and maturity in Christ and where you stand in relationship to someone else.[4]

Of concern to some people, though, was the model this movement was pursuing. Following A. B. Bruce's classic, *The Training of the Twelve*, it was assumed that Jesus' relationship with the twelve disciples should be the model employed today. But should it?

In contemplating this question, we should be reminded that the twelve left their families to follow Jesus. So are we going to require that of today's "disciplee"? According to Leroy Eims, Jesus spent about 13,000 hours with the twelve. To duplicate this effort would take, even with the more stringent discipleship programs, approximately 36 years. So are we going to require that of today's "discipler"?

The critics are right: The model for discipleship isn't to be found in the Gospels but comes from the book of Acts. In his book, *The Cost of Discipleship*, Dietrich Bonhoeffer contended, "It would be a false exegesis if we tried to behave as though we were the immediate contemporaries of the men whom Jesus called."[5]

Given the discrepancies between the perfections of Jesus and what is true about even the best discipler today, and the discrepancies between the time Jesus spent with his disciples and the time allotted to "disciplees" today, it is obvious that our discipleship efforts do not, nor should not, parallel what is seen in the Gospels. Furthermore, the fact we have the indwelling Spirit, which the twelve (while they were being trained) did not have, is also a variable not sufficiently contemplated by discipleship enthusiasts.

If a more accurate hermeneutic requires that our discipleship model should come from the Book of Acts, does that then mean that if a church is evangelizing, baptizing, and teaching people, this constitutes discipleship? No, it doesn't mean that at all. The commonsense concern that must not be overlooked is—are church members getting trained? The fact the church cranks out whatever it cranks out doesn't answer this question. Many studies show that impressive curriculum and excellent teachers do not by themselves produce effective results. Therefore, we must claim a liberty—allowed by Scripture, if consistent with Scripture—to do what must be done to secure better results.

The fact is we don't have an exhaustive knowledge of what the first Christians did to disciple converts in those little house churches. We do know that to become a Christian in those days represented both a scandal and a danger, a factor that greatly reduced nominal churchgoers.

In his book, *Christ the Eternal Son*, Tozer gave an example of the price people paid when they identified themselves as Christians. The man who came to Jesus in broad daylight and threw himself at the Master's feet is further identified by Tozer.

> Some scholars believe that this Nicodemus was Nicodemus Ben Gorian, a brother of the celebrated Jewish historian, Flavius Josephus. This Nicodemus was said to be one of the three richest men in Jerusalem at that time.

Whether history or legend, the story passed down through the centuries tells us that the daughter of Nicodemus Ben Gorian was reduced to picking up grain or corn off the streets of Jerusalem, where it had been thrown from the feed bags of horses as they traveled down the street. She picked up what she could in order to roast it and have something to eat.

Why was the daughter of one of Jerusalem's most wealthy men reduced to such a state of hunger?

The historians suggest at least that when Nicodemus finally threw in his lot with Jesus the Christ, he was stripped by the ruling society of all that he had. His property was confiscated and he was turned out as if he was the scum of the earth.[6]

From the first day the church came into existence, this attack by the world was immediate and harsh—hence, hundreds of people were rendered homeless on the day of Pentecost! Such intense persecution had a way of preventing nominal Christianity—for what person would pay such a high price for a faith not taken seriously?

By contrast, studies show how the nominal has become normal in today's churches. Although challenges and even failures did exist in the early church, the danger factor associated with identifying with the church predicted a more motivated gathering than that typically found in the average church today. The point being: Methods for the motivated may not be as effective with the non-motivated. Consequently, the church must think through whatever adjustments are needed for discipleship to take hold. In this sense Professor A. B. Bruce prayed correctly when he said, "Lord, give us a fearless inventiveness in thy service."[7]

The highly individualized attention Paul gave to the church at Ephesus (Acts 20:31) and to the church at Colossae (Colossians 1:28) does seem to indicate some one-to-one encounters. Additionally, all the "one another" verses (there are 58 of them) strongly suggest individual care received from small groups. Even in the Book of Acts it appears that the didactic part of discipleship must have involved more than attending a worship service.

The lost-in-anonymity routine so prevalent in the modern church must be overcome if discipleship is to begin. We do ourselves much harm if we incubate in self-chosen isolation, resisting the healing touch of others. Samuel Chadwick, the English pastor and professor, illustrated this point by telling the story of a musician who visited the Cathedral at Fribourg. When this musician heard the great organ, he went into the organ loft and asked to play it.

> The old organist in jealousy for his instrument at first refused, but was at length prevailed upon, and allowed the stranger to try what was claimed to be the greatest organ in Europe. After standing by in an ecstasy of delight and amazement, he suddenly laid his hands on the inspired musician and exclaimed, "Who are you? What is your name?" "Mendelssohn," replied the player; and with tears in his eyes the old man exclaimed, "And can it be that I had so nearly refused to let Mendelssohn to touch this organ?"[8]

Many have disallowed the touch from those who could bless their lives. This must not be if discipleship is going to occur in the church.

Equally imperative for leadership is to develop a strategy that connects those in need of discipleship with the spiritual fathers who can provide it. Of course, there must be spiritual mothers, too—if such a ministry is provided to those of the same gender, similar to the model discussed in Titus, chapter two.

Since discipleship involves the transference of a life, and not just the transference of principles, what is of utmost importance is that the "disciple" consistently exhibits the released life of the Lord. Dullness of spirit disqualifies.

In his commentary on the Book of Revelation, *The Final Word*, Ray Stedman had this to say about one of our least revered political leaders:

Calvin Coolidge, our thirtieth president, was an extremely quiet and reserved man. When questioned, he rarely answered in more than two or three words—a tendency which earned him the nickname, "Silent Cal." The public saw him as a stiff and emotionless man ....

In 1933, the radio airwaves crackled with the news of Coolidge's death. Columnist Dorothy Parker was in her office at the *New Yorker* when a colleague flung open the door and blurted, "Dottie, did you hear? Coolidge is dead!"

Endowed with a quick but acid wit, she shot back, "How can you tell?"[9]

When looking for people who can disciple others, we shouldn't have to look too long for the needed evidence of spiritual life. A "discipler" should readily convey much evidence indicating truth has become a personal testimony and not just a compilation of learned abstractions.

Obvious though this principle should be, A. W. Tozer wrote, "After more than thirty years of observing the religious scene I have been forced to conclude that saintliness and church leadership are not often synonymous."[10] Paraphrasing Wordsworth, Tozer exclaimed:

Purest saints
Are often these of whom the noisy church
Hears least

Imagine, though, what it would be like for someone to invest himself or herself in your life. Consider the mistakes that might be avoided, the dry spells that might be averted, the increased progress that might be achieved, and the greater vision that might be transmitted. The encouragement that comes from a superior example would enable giant leaps in one's track record for obedience.

Perhaps the best structure for discipleship is small group fellowships that implement the "one another" principles of the Bible. Advancing this idea in his book, *Continuous Revival*, Norman Grubb writes:

> It is a simple fact that this openness before men does something in us. It sharpens us up concerning daily sin such as never before. It is part of the secret of daily revival. It is amazing how, when walking in the light with our brother as well as with God, we begin to come alive to attitudes, or actions, of sin in our lives which we never noticed to be sins before, or perhaps we always took for granted would always be a part of our make-up.[11]

If small groups focus on processing truth in specific, concrete ways with group support, most of discipleship can be done in this setting. If, however, the small group spends time teaching and then discussing God's Word, biblical fellowship will be sabotaged and effective discipleship will be undermined. This format, all too common in the church, will have made it so. The teaching and meditating of God's Word must *precede* the gathering for small group fellowship; it should not consume time once the group assembles.[12]

Being Blessed By Biblical Biographies

Another valuable resource we can draw on when looking for mentors and guides is Scripture itself. Hebrews, chapter 12, verse 1, speaks of being surrounded with a great cloud of witnesses. This doesn't mean that the saints who died generations ago are looking at us through a peephole in heaven, or that they're floating on a nearby cloud with an ability to see us even though we can't see them. No, this verse refers to the previous chapter that presented the lives of certain Old Testament greats, lives that can inspire us today, if we'll only take the time to be instructed from their stories. How often, and how much, we need to consider the testimonies from these witnesses!

For example, Hebrews, chapter 11, verse 5, talks about Enoch. Do you know about Enoch? Enoch lived a long time ago, during the very early days of the Old Testament, long before David and Moses and Noah. We are first introduced to this man while reading a genealogy in Genesis. And in reading this genealogy, where a long list of names are cited, the image comes to mind of a row of cradles over here and a row of coffins over there.

People with strange sounding names climbed out of their cradles and walked a few perfectly futile steps before finally toppling over into their respective coffins. This ever so brief summary—they were born, they lived this number of years, then they died—is somewhat disconcerting; for we would certainly hate for our lives to be so inconsequential this is all that could be said. In contrast to these apparently nondescript lives, we then come upon this man Enoch.

The Bible tells us that "Enoch walked with God three hundred years" (Genesis 5:22). Amazing! Most of us can't even make it through the week, but this man—without a Bible, without a church, without the indwelling Spirit—enjoyed a consistent fellowship with God for three centuries! And what makes this all the more impressive is he did this in a place, and at a time, that was so evil God was about to flood it out of existence.

The consistency of Enoch's walk inspired further commentary by Hannah More, the eighteenth-century writer from Bristol, England:

> The devout Christian endeavors to exemplify the emphatic description of the saint in the Old Testament: "he walks with God." He does not merely bow down at his footstool at stated intervals. He does not ceremoniously address him at great occasions only and then retreat and dwell at a distance. But he walks with him. His habitual intercourse, his natural motion, his daily converse, his intimate conversation is with his Redeemer.[13]

Commenting on the consistency of Enoch's walk with the Lord in contradistinction with our intermittent walk with him, F. B. Meyer wrote, "Better to walk with God every day in calm, unbroken fellowship, than to have occasional rapturous experiences, succeeded by long relapses and backslidings."[14]

In contrast to Enoch's experience of constant communication, people today think that God is like Carlyle's Philosopher who sits in his attic at midnight above the roar of the crowded streets, watching the teeming thousands below: men being born, dying, laughing, cursing, hoping, fearing, men herded and crammed together with nothing but a little masonry and carpentry between them. "But I," says the Philosopher, "I sit above it all. I am alone with the stars."[15]

Is that your picture of God—God above it all, distant and indifferent, inaccessible and aloof? Do you regard friendship with God as being (to use James Stewart's words) the cliché of a religion whose emotionalism is stronger than its logic? And, in your view, is such a friendship only possible to men whose fever has transported them into delirium? To such a perspective as this, Enoch would stand and say he was in no way guilty of unbridled rhetoric, or incredulity of thought, or distortion of fact, when he insisted that a deep and satisfying friendship walk with God *is* possible today.

Now to walk with God, in Enoch's day (and in ours), at least three things have to be true. First, there must be a *resolve*. Amos 3:3 asks, "Can two walk together unless be agreed?" Although identical thinking on every subject isn't required—even though this is more attainable than we might suppose (I Corinthians 1:10)—there must, at the very least, be this commitment to a shared fellowship.

James S. Stewart showed how the words of the prophet can search our souls to see if this kind of resolve really exists:

> ... we turn again, and think of our divided loyalties, our blurred and blundering compromises with temptation, our oscillating between the high things of our holy religion and the miserable earthbound tyrannies of self, our weak subservient acceptance of the monotony of defeat. And in our heart of hearts, in our dead honest moods, we know the remedy—if we would but take it: a stronger grasp of Christ's all-

conquering hand, a deeper reconciliation to the will divine, a truer, daily walk with God.[16]

How different our spiritual progress would be if resolve found its rightful place early on. Andrew Bonar, the nineteenth-century Scottish minister, once said, "We are decided men." Instead of equivocating with truth or negotiating with God, this man discovered how biblical resolve can eliminate that.

History and biography agree that Jonathan Edwards lived a splendid life, one that can never be explained apart from his resolve. Edwards even penned these words to convey this disposition of heart: "Resolved, that I will live so, as I shall wish I had done when I come to die."[17] One of the benefits of resolve is that it puts one on a trajectory the spirit of compromise cannot go.

In the beginning, Adam, the first man, enjoyed long fellowship walks with God. Then one day the Lord showed up for one of these walks, and Adam was nowhere to be found. Having just made the decision to discontinue these walks, Adam was hiding. Have you ever done that? Have you chosen to harbor a certain sin in your life, even though you knew it would break your fellowship with God?

A. B. Simpson wrote: "The faintest reservation is really the spirit of disobedience. And the failure to hearken to the full meaning of God indicates a spirit of unwilling obedience."[18]

To those who would vacillate and equivocate, Elijah asked, "How long halt you between two opinions?" Has this halting become a long season in your life? If so, we should remember: Resolve is required of the godly, especially those who live on the other side of the cross.

Speaking with directness to this issue, Simpson said:

God help you if you have been halting between two opinions, to yield the last reserve and give every power of your being and every moment of your life to him. Remember that on the cross Jesus gave you both hands, both feet and every drop of his precious blood.[19]

238

A second factor necessary to a fellowship walk with God is *reliance*. Galatians 5:25 says we are to "walk in the Spirit." This means we're to depend on the Lord to draw us to himself and to energize our worship, our fellowship, our ministry, and our obedience. True, the Holy Spirit never inhabited Enoch, but the Holy Spirit certainly was at work in his day (Genesis 6:5). For no man, not even Enoch, could get this close to God unless the Spirit of God first drew him and then enabled him to respond to the Lord's love.

Because the Bible says our old nature lacks the desire to fellowship with God (Romans 3:11), God has to make the first move, if a relationship with him is to begin. Once the Lord does open our minds, does touch our hearts, this resulting relationship can only be sustained if we'll lay hold, through faith, the needed grace for this relationship to grow (Colossians 2:6; Ephesians 2:8).

The alternative approach is trusting our brainpower, our willpower, and the fickle fluctuations of feelings. This Enoch didn't do, but have you? Has your relationship with God bogged down because you trusted resident capacities of the soul (mind, will and feelings) to sustain it? If so, I wonder if God would say to you what he said to those at Galatia: "Are you so foolish? Having begun in the Spirit, are you now being made perfect in the flesh?"

The strivings of well-intentioned flesh can never achieve what one's trusting in God's Spirit can do. We believers are Pneumatics, after all, people of the spirit! The Lord wants what he gave; and what he gave is his life in our born-again spirit. This is why all directives for improved behavior are preceded by a command to put on the new man. There must be a reliance on that, a victory already won, rather than a reliance on faculties of the soul, wherein we try to achieve victories of our own through earnest, honest, consecration and dedication.

The third factor essential to a worthy walk with the Lord is *restraint*. In II Corinthians, chapter 6, verses 14 through 16, the Spirit of God fires out five questions:

For what fellowship has righteousness with unrighteousness? And what communion has light

239

with darkness? And what accord has Christ with
Belial? Or what part has a believer with an
unbeliever? And what agreement has the temple
of God with idols?

Notice that in all these words—fellowship, communion,
accord, part, and agreement—the issue is one of nature. The
principle being: We are not to enmesh with those who don't
have the Lord's nature! Hence, verses 16 and 17 quote the
Lord God, "I will dwell in them and walk among them ...."
Therefore, "Come out from them and be separate," says the
Lord.

Do you see how walking with the Lord requires a
restraint from those attachments, those alliances, that leave
the Lord out? Enoch avoided all of this when it would have
been so easy for him not to. And if he did, with far less
resources, couldn't you and I do as much?

The Book of Hebrews pronounces this wonderful
benediction on Enoch's life when it declares that Enoch "had
this testimony, that he pleased God" (Hebrews 11:5).
Wouldn't you want to come to the end of your days and have
that said about you? Instead of having your name listed with
no commentary, wouldn't you want God to say something
approving about the way you lived your life?

In his commentary on the Apostle' Creed, Helmut
Thielicke took note of the differences between biblical
biographies from the biographies offered by the world. The
biographies the world offers display sensationalism, a fair
measure of psychological probing, a penchant to dig up
oddities, a footnoting of minutiae, a fixation on headlines,
and an assemblage of peer opinions. By contrast, biblical
biographies are remarkably concise. Typically, the core of
one's character is simply and summarily identified. We won't
have to dig to discover salient facts.

According to Thielicke:

A reader of the Old Testament will come across
long stretches where individual kings are noted
with the brevity of a telephone directory: "He was
born, did what pleased or displeased God and

died." Period! ... Do the biblical writers suffer from a lack of imagination or literary anemia?[20]

No, the cause of this brevity isn't that. Much more the reason is God's interest in what made a difference for eternity and not what produces tabloid fascination.

In the last book of the Old Testament, Malachi (1:8) asks one of the most important questions ever asked, "Will he (meaning God) be pleased with you?" This is a question of enormous importance, a question that each of us should answer in perfect candor. Who do we really want to please when we wake in the morning? Are we a part of the multitudinous many who are men-pleasers (Ephesians 6:6)? Or are we, like Jesus himself, not out to please ourselves (John 8:29) but to please God?

If Enoch were on the scene today, and if you and I had the privilege of being discipled by him, this straight up, bottom-line question would probably be the first question he'd ask us. Who are you most concerned about—*numero uno*? Others, and what they might do for you? Or God?

If your answer is God, then a review of a scriptural checklist might help authenticate your response. For example, Romans 8:8 says "... they that are in the flesh cannot please God." So if you can't say, "I'm a crucified man," or "I'm a crucified woman," you are not pleasing the Lord. No matter how principled and seemingly dedicated the flesh is, the Bible says those operating in this realm cannot please God. Only those who stay on the cross can please him.

Furthermore, Hebrews 11:6 says that without faith it is impossible to please God. So this thought prompts two questions for our personal inventory: 1) Are we trusting God in our daily transactions? Or, 2) is our reliance more on hard work and the resources we can obtain by networking with others?

If the unholy trinity of worry, fear, and depression are chronically operative in our life, then that means faith is being set aside. Moreover, if there is a lowering of goals, a reducing of vision, and a settling for a "settled for" life, that also indicates the setting aside of faith. For those who have their faith bridge in collapse can never please God, even though all their sincerity and industry may fool God's people. The deception may not be deliberate, but that is what it is.

II Timothy 2:4 also informs us that we can't please God if we're going to get entangled with the affairs of this life. Have you done that? Are you so involved with your school, your job, or your family, that you don't have enough time for God? Is this world, as the poet put it, too much with you, so that preoccupation with today blocks your view of eternity? Well, that will never please God!

Now as we gather all these points and questions up, we can more easily imagine a conversation between ourselves and Enoch. So, admiring what God admired, let's let the example of Enoch speak with conviction into our lives.

The concern about our resolve for fellowship—what we're relying on to produce it, what we must say no to in order to protect it—must be engaged with honest reflection and, if warranted, with proper redirection. The same holds true with the problem of our flesh, and the need for faith, and the importance of being less entangled with the affairs of daily life. All must be examined in the light of God, and then adjusted according to the will of God.

Additionally, to inspire us further, Enoch might very well offer this challenge: "Without interruption or interference, fellowship with God every day for a month and see if you're not going to have a powerful testimony of your own. I did it for 300 years, but you start for a month. And after a month, tell me if you want to continue this fellowship, just like I did."

Because Scripture tells us these examples were recorded for our benefit (I Corinthians 10:11), we must draw from them just as we would draw from a "discipler" in our church. And how do we do that? Well, after reading the story of one of these splendid characters, we must imagine what these biblical characters would say to us, given what the Bible says about them. Then we must take inventory so we can rightly answer the questions directed our way.

Some of what comes our way may be more direct and confrontational than we're used to, but that's to be expected! Remember, even a "discipler" within the church will sometimes get to the point with clarity and brevity, especially if there's enough strength of relationship to allow for this. The important point is: We should deal with the life-lessons these men and women of God have learned until what profited them profits us.

At times, it is true, the examples set forth in Scripture seem to describe attainments that are too high, aspirations that are too noble, achievements that are too grand. The spiritual heights these people ascended are so high, it seems, we can only get a brief glimpse of them before they disappear into the clouds of glory.

How fascinating and, at the same time, incriminating this view! But sometimes, in looking and longing, we feel so small, so far away, so incapable. It was in this regard that A. B. Simpson counseled wisely when he said: "Example alone cannot elevate human character and life beyond a fixed limitation. It can exalt our ideal, it can inspire our ambition, but it cannot energize our moral and spiritual weaknesses."[21]

For that outcome to occur, a different example is needed—the example of Jesus, who experienced every test, every temptation, with the same resources available to believers today, and yet lived in a way that surpassed the life of every person who walked this earth.

We are so blessed, because instead of standing on a summit of unequaled achievement and bidding us to follow, Jesus comes to where we are, in the valley far below, and takes us by the hand as he then imparts into our lives his faith, his wisdom, his strength. He does this because example alone—as worthy as it is—is never enough.

What we most need is a Shepherd who knows every particle of the treacherous terrain—the slopes and cliffs that suddenly appear, the forests that hide their predators, the waterholes that hide their poison. And what we also need is a Shepherd who knows the better way, a Shepherd who will guide and guard us until that distant land is finally reached.

Reflecting on the sure guidance God will give his own, F. B. Meyer wrote:

He who has opened eyes may read the Father's handwriting, and take the direction of his path, as though angels had flashed before his eyes to direct him. And the prepared path always leads to the vacant seat and the waiting portion. The road may be long, and the tax on patience and strength considerable; but the Father never leads his trustful child into a quagmire, or leads him out on the moorland to perish of exposure to the cold. There is always a destination to which the road leads, and it only awaits the quick eye, the ready ear, and the obedient heart, to detect the things that God hath prepared for them that love him.[22]

The very fact the Lord prepared them has to mean he wants us to *successfully* pursue them. And to that end, the Lord will aid in this pursuit.

When the Bible says Jesus is the Pioneer and Perfecter of our faith, it declares he is not only our example, having first done everything required of us while he dwelt among us, but that also Jesus will come to our side—and indeed into our hearts—infusing us with capacities no other shepherd could ever give his sheep.

And thus the journey, so difficult at first glance, can be made with tranquil assurance, due to the unique and wonderful blessings that come from the best example of our faith, the Lord Jesus Christ.

Reflection Questions

1. Have you ever had someone disciple you? If so, share your experience.

2. Of the three factors prerequisite for a successful walk with God, which one challenges you the most? Please explain.

3. After examining those Scriptures addressing the prerequisites for pleasing God, which one do you do the best? Please explain.

4. Are you willing to accept Enoch's challenge to fellowship every day with God for a month?

Chapter 16

Obedience's Opportunity–Part I

The fact our world is much more fascinated with evil than righteousness should come as no great surprise. Like Israel of old, the world has "cast off the thing that is good" (Hosea 8:3) and loved abomination instead (Hosea 9:10). In the same way pigs don't value pearls, the world doesn't value righteousness.

The sophisticates of our world—with trained brains and immoral minds—are much intrigued by that one who walks among the respectable during the day but then steals away at night to experience the darker side of life. While secularists of all types—ranging from intellectual elites to tabloid enthusiasts—revere that one who has a chink in the armor, they consider passé anyone who follows God with an unswerving loyalty. With a twinkle in their eye and a warm embrace, secularists will greet the complicated person. But with dismissing gestures and a turned back, they will ignore the simple person.

But why is "complicated" more esteemed than simple? What we call complicated, after all, is nothing more than a bundle of contradictions, the entanglements of sin and sin's consequences that weaken a man and render him common. Far more interesting is that one who refuses the compromises others couldn't resist and pursues purposes others couldn't find. Sin will always shrivel a man and make him ordinary; whereas obedience will distinguish a man and produce within a vast interior with awesome depths. Without Scripture, however, we won't learn how true that is.

We see such depths in the Lord Jesus as he committed himself to a task more important than any other. On the night of the great confrontation, when that battle of all battles would be fought, we see the disciples' support for him beginning to wane. One disciple had left to betray him; the other disciples were involved in a contentious rivalry of egos. But instead of bemoaning their insensitivity toward him, Jesus did precisely the opposite: He ministered to these men as he took on the role of a lowly servant.

With towel and washbasin in hand, Jesus moved on bended knee before each speechless disciple to wash their feet. Displaying the humility his kingdom required, Jesus stooped to lowliness in the Upper Room, which would become even lowlier in the garden that night, and lowlier still on the cross the next day.

Once the foot-washing was completed in the Upper Room, Jesus began to identify all the reasons and resources for obedience we've been examining in these chapters, at the conclusion of which Jesus stood to his feet and said, "Arise, let us go from here" (John 14:31b).

Knowing what you know now, wouldn't you have wanted to be there when Jesus left the Upper Room that night? Imagine the spine-tingling drama of the moment! As that slender figure came out into the night, you would have said, "There he is! Oh, my goodness, he's going to do it! He's on his way to battle the world's most dangerous enemy!"

Nothing in all of human history was as important as what was about to happen! Even so, there were no crowds to cheer when he left the Upper Room, and no throngs to welcome him when he arrived at the garden. There was darkness. There was silence. And only that, as Jesus moved against an empire of evil he was about to overcome.

Redeeming the Time

"Arise," Jesus said to his disciples, who, by now, had heard all they needed to know; for the time was at hand to convert principles into practice! There is always value in talking about truth—the need for obedience, the methods for obedience, the motivations for obedience. But at some point we must act! For unless we see and seize the opportunities to extend the Lord's kingdom, the teachings we received will have meant nothing.

What the Lord works into our lives must be implemented with a diligence motivated by the psalmist's words, "how short my time is." It seems the psalmist readily realized what most of us frequently forget—our time on this earth is remarkably short!

Many years ago a traveler to the state of Kentucky saw a statue of the famous racehorse, Man of War. At the base of that statue was the inscription, "This is the fastest horse the world has ever known." Underneath that inscription some wag wrote, "This is the fastest world the horse has ever known."

Illustrating the fast pace of modern life, Dr. Russell Bennett spoke of an incident that occurred at the Atlanta airport several years ago. An elderly gentleman approached a ticket agent to ask when the next flight departed for Montgomery, Alabama. The agent replied, "At 3:10 PM." Then the gentleman asked when this plane would arrive in Montgomery, Alabama. The agent answered, "At 3:12 PM."

The inquirer's eyes widened (for he had forgotten that Montgomery is in a different time zone than Atlanta). Breaking this silence, the agent finally asked, "Do you want to buy a ticket?" "No, Ma'am," the gentleman answered, "but I would sure like to see that thing take off!"

All this is old hat to the younger folks, though. One college student called to see how long it took to fly from Atlanta to New York, and when the agent said, "Just a minute," he thanked her and hung up!

Well, this *is* the fastest world the horse as ever known! As Alvin Toffler documented in his book, *Future Shock*, the metabolism of history has sped up to an incredible pace. The urgency to redeem the time, therefore, is especially needful in our generation.

Back in Sir Walter Scott's day, it was customary for people to have a sundial on their lawn, at the base of which would be inscribed some pithy saying. The saying Sir Walter selected originated not from a poet or philosopher but from

Scripture. So every time Sir Walter looked at his sundial he saw the words of our Savior, "Work for the night cometh." Because, yes, soon and very soon, our time will be over and the opportunity to labor for the Lord will be gone.

We all agree that an unfinished symphony is sad, and an unfinished manuscript is sad, but nothing is as sad as an unfinished life. Yet millions of people will get into their fourth decade of life without figuring out what God wants them to do. What a contrast this is with the Apostle Paul who declared, "I have finished the race" (II Timothy 4:7).

Instead of meandering through life, Paul did everything God wanted him to do. Glory! One can only imagine Paul's satisfaction—to have fought the good fight, and to have come to the end of his days with an awareness he achieved everything God purposed for him.

Many wonder and wander, without direction, and without any sense of urgency. C. E. Montague tells how he first realized the urgency of time. He heard a sermon in which the minister said, "I find it set down in the tables that the average duration of life after age 21 is 36 years. We may hope for a little more, we may fear a little less, but speaking generally 36 years or 13,000 days is the term in which our task must be accomplished."

For Montague, it was the reduction of this matter to days that brought the point home. Likewise, Thomas Chalmers experienced a dramatic turning to the Lord in his own life which he explained by saying, "Mathematician, though I was, I had forgotten two magnitudes—the shortness of time and the vastness of eternity."

Due to the marvels of modern medicine, the life expectancy we have today is significantly longer; but even so, from incubator to old age, our life expectancy is only about 28,000 days. That's it! So what are we going to do with the time we have? Are we going to fritter it away by overextending ourselves at work or by watching too much TV at home? Are we going to give big chunks of our time to entertainment as we neglect the assignment God intended us to fulfil? Leonard Ravenhill, the British evangelist, recalled an incident from European history that may well illustrate the predicament of many.

Napoleon Bonaparte made a lonely surprise visit one night to the outposts sentries on one of the vital positions of his battlefield. Stealthily he moved along in the gray light of the morning. One sentry after another immediately challenged him. Finally, the crafty warrior stole upon a strategic spot. There was no sentry to challenge him. The wily Napoleon moved closer and saw a pair of boots protruding from under a shock of corn and a rifle propped beside them. He made no comment—just picked up the rifle and himself stood guard, waiting for the awakening of the snoozing soldier. Finally the corn stirred, and up jumped the guilty defender and grabbed for the gun that was gone. Can you imagine his confusion and chagrin? What a bitter and shattering experience—caught napping by *Napoleon*![1]

Leonard Ravenhill then asked, "When the Lord of glory returns, will he find us Christians sleeping at our post of duty?"

Desiring a more faithful response from his people, Dr. Clarence McCartney, the well-known Presbyterian minister, often preached a sermon titled, "Come Before Winter." Once a year for forty years he preached this sermon, the title of which came from words Paul wrote to Timothy.

It was while Paul was jailed in Rome that he penned a request for his protégé Timothy to visit him. Accompanying this request was Paul's desire for a coat he had left to be brought, along with some old books. Then, adding urgency to his words, Paul concluded his letter with the petition to "come before winter." These latter words triggered by the fact the Mediterranean became impossible to navigate at that time of the year. Therefore, if Timothy were going to come, he needed to do it before winter.

Upon hearing Dr. McCartney preach this sermon, an alcoholic returned to his hotel room with those words "come before winter" ringing in his ears. When he later opened the refrigerator that day to get a can of beer, the Lord seemed to say him, "This is your hour! If you'll put that away, you'll gain a victory. But if you take a drink, the longed-for-victory will forever elude you. Come before winter!"

Rising to the challenge, the alcoholic began a journey that led to lifelong sobriety.

On another occasion, a young medical student heard this sermon and immediately felt impressed to write that long-overdue letter to his mother. Although he needed to study for an exam that day, those words, "come before winter," just wouldn't leave his mind. So he wrote the letter he knew he needed to write, telling his mother how much he loved her and how grateful he was for all she had done for him.

Within a week word came that his mother was taken to the hospital and that her situation was serious; so he needed to return home at once. Unfortunately, by the time he arrived, his mother had already died. But under her pillow was that letter he had written, a letter that had meant so much to her!

The words, "come before winter," declare God's message not to trivialize time, but to use it wisely and use it well.

Deciding to Serve

Yes, there is a time for *meditating*—the disciples surely benefited from that in the Upper Room. But there is also a time for *activating*—and it is this the Lord encouraged when he told his disciples to arise.

There was, it should be noted, considerable danger ahead—enough to make these disciples wonder where their leader was leading them! The decision to follow Jesus that night had certain similarities with the decision the Hebrews made when they followed Moses out of Egypt.

Put yourself in the ancient story. Here you are, one of the Hebrews recently set free from four centuries of Egyptian bondage. Feeling a mixture of elation and intimidation, you are following your leader, when suddenly you hear the sound of horse hooves thundering your way. The Egyptians!

So what are you feeling at this point? Your leader is marching you straight toward the river! Soon you will be trapped! So would thoughts of the coming massacre cause you to panic? Well, the disciples may have feared a similar entrapment, a fear that certainly increased when all those soldiers showed up! Hundreds of them, armed and dangerous!

The point here is that the decision to follow Jesus is a decision to join a fiercely-contested conflict. So fierce, in fact, that even Jesus asked these men to pray for him as they had never prayed before! But instead of watching and praying, these men ended up snoozing and snoring.

In his book, *Practical Christianity*, A. W. Pink spoke sternly about this scene: "Slumbering saints! What an incongruity! Taking their ease while threatened by danger ... Trifling away opportunities to glorify their Savior, instead of redeeming the time: rusting, instead of wearing out in his service."[2]

So what would *we* have said to these disciples had we come upon this slumber scene? Maybe we would have awakened them, saying, "Disciples, have you forgotten what happened to Samson when he slept, how the trap was set, how the plot was executed, how Samson went down to a terrible defeat? Have you also forgotten Sisera's fate when he slept? Have you forgotten that it was while this Canaanite captain slept that the Hebrew snuck in and hammered a tent peg through his brain? Disciples! How could you possibly go to sleep on *this* night, the night the Master needed you the most, the night the enemy would do his worst?"

Yes, Jesus had to arouse the very ones he earlier told to arise—and what a prophetic picture this is of today's church! Bud Wilkinson, the former coach of the Oklahoma Sooners and later the Saint Louis Cardinals, once described a football game as 50,000 people desperately needing exercise watching 22 players desperately needing rest. This scene bears remarkable resemblance to the church. Statistics show only fifteen percent of the congregation has an ongoing ministry, while the vast majority have joined the disciples in an undeserved rest.

This must not be! For the Lord has equipped us to do better! A. B. Simpson declared, "We must see in the Lord Jesus our infinite divine resources in the gifts and graces of the Holy Spirit, and all the equipment we need in every kind of ministry."[3] That part of the vineyard where the Lord calls us to labor may be nowhere near public view and in no way spectacular in the task assigned. Yet, there is truth in the observation that "the highest life consists not in doing magnificent things, but rather in doing common things in a magnificent way."

We all have assignments useful to the kingdom. And to the extent one task is great and the other is little is simply unknowable on this side of eternity. What may appear little may have an indispensable linkage with something great. Alexander Maclaren declared, "God has many tools in his tool chest, and he needs them all before the work is done. Joshua could no more have wielded Moses' rod than Moses could have wielded Joshua's sword."[4]

But why would the church shirk the work the Lord has given her to do? Doesn't she realize the Lord's labor assignments will greatly contribute to her satisfaction? We must remember that work not only preceded the curse but work will also be a part of heaven's joy.

In his own inimitable way, the well-known poet, Rudyard Kipling, envisioned a heaven that included in its glory an eternal satisfaction from a continuation of work.

When earth's last picture is painted,
and the tubes are twisted and dried;
The brightest colors have faded
and the youngest critic has died;
We shall rest and they that need it
shall lie down for an eon or two;
And the Master of all good workmen
shall put us to work anew.

There is certainly significance in the fact that we are laborers together with God. And given the knowledge that Revelation 1:6 says we are all priests, this has to mean that every Christian—not the seminary-trained professional only—is to have a sustained, sacrificial ministry that builds up the body of Christ. This is why we mustn't "hobby" ourselves with frivolous activities that preoccupy our souls with mind-numbing pursuits. And it is also why our life script should gain preapproval from God. We can't be making this up as we go along.

The exact ministry we are to undertake is so important God foreordained it before the foundations of the world! Can you fathom this? You are not an afterthought in the mind of God, some inconsequential planet-dweller who consumes and consumes until time finally runs out. No, God has a distinct and important assignment for you to undertake, one uniquely tailored to fit you. It is, indeed, an assignment so important for the enhancement of his kingdom he planned it all before you were even born.

At times, the way the Lord has orchestrated your preparation for this work may seem baffling to you, but F. B. Meyer counseled wisely when he wrote:

> Believe only that your circumstances are those most suited to develop your character. They have been selected out of all possible combinations of conditions and events in order to effect in you the highest finish of fruitfulness and beauty. They would have been the ones selected by you if all the wide range of omniscient knowledge had been within your reach.[5]

Once it dawns on our astonished souls the sacred significance God designed for us to experience, alertness and appreciation will keep us faithful to the task. As God unfolds his plan by increment for us to implement, each faithful response on our part we'll lead to further disclosures on God's part.

What we must guard against is the unsanctioned slumber the disciples took for themselves. Yet, too often, after beginning in earnest and setting our course with announced purpose, our eagerness wanes. James S. Stewart, Scotland's great preacher from the twentieth-century, described what may have happened.

> Somehow the high mood passed. The vision faded. The flame died upon the altar. Back crept the beloved temptation. Home came the

dethroned idol. Gradually, imperceptibly, Christ's standards were toned down. Steadily, the world's pressure worked its will.[6]

And before long, the test is over and our failure known. But why did this happen? Loss of vision! Without a vision the people, what—? Perish! And they may even perish without ever knowing what happened to them.

The lights go out! The conscience becomes dull! The immediate claims attention! The eternal is forgotten! Ignorance rules!

Edward Hastings, the twentieth-century Bible commentator, profiled such a person.

> The man who spends his life on earth in shallow enjoyments and selfish ease, careless of the world's sorrow and indifferent to its sins, blind to its fines beauties and most thrilling tragedies, moved by no great love, actuated by no great hope, stirred by no holy enthusiasm, is ignorant of all true life.[7]

One becomes a fool, if blinded by the god of this world and life is frittered away. But the words of Jesus that night, "Arise, let us go ..." summons something better. There is a high purpose for our life! Something great is in store! In commenting on this prospect Edward Hastings said: "It is one hallmark of greatness to be dominated by a single ruling passion. We recognize that hallmark on the lives on the lives of outstanding men of genius—the poets and prophets and captains of mankind."[8] Yet, one needn't be a genius to be under a ruling passion, and by that governing grip do mighty exploits for the Lord.

Just know that you don't have to make your opportunities; the Lord will do that. But when he says it's time to move, then move! Arise! Shine! For the glory of the Lord has come! That for which you were uniquely created awaits your response!

So *will* you redeem the time? And *will* you serve him well?

Reflection Questions

1. Is the gap between creed and deed, between what you know and what you grow, increasing or decreasing in your life?

2. Are you impressed with the urgency of time to get done what the Lord has called you to do?

3. What is the next needed step you should follow as you journey with the Lord? Has he previously told you to do something, but you haven't done it yet?

4. What is the strongest passion in your life?

Chapter 17

Obedience's Opportunity—Part II

Not every pledge of obedience is honored, not every vow is paid, not every commitment is completed. Often, there's a gap between well-intended words and poorly performed deeds. What we say and what we do may not always agree.

The disciples left the Upper Room that night sincere, but afraid; willing, but weak; well-taught, but deficient in their understanding. History is replete with evidence that other Christians have followed in their steps. Perhaps even your history includes such a chapter.

To counteract this outcome, any worthy strategy for obedience must include an assessment of failure, or, likely, that strategy will miss key points that need to be discussed.

In contrast to the perfect obedience of Jesus—so admirable because he did it as a man—we see these faltering disciples, of whom we may ask: Did they love the Lord? And the answer is, yes! Did they mean to fail? No! Yet they did fail, and in doing so opened a line of inquiry for us to pursue.

As we examine their failure (along with other failures followers of God have made), we see, prospectively, risk factors for failure and, retrospectively, conditions conducive to failure. One such condition relates to the difficulty of the assignment.

Just know that there is a God-ordained race set for each of us to run (Hebrews 12:2f.); and although your race will be different from my race, the one thing common about each race is the difficulty of its challenge. If you haven't discovered the flat-out impossibility of your race, it can be fairly deduced you're not on the right course. For the course God ordains always requires God himself to complete it!

Obviously, no one wants to undertake a commitment unprepared. The predisposition in most of us is to learn all we can so we won't be caught by surprise. If there are signs to watch for, problems to think through in advance, we want this information.

What we do not want is the pain that comes from avoidable failure. However, to see the pain of *others*, and what brought it on, is really good news and not bad news. Because getting advanced information helps us succeed when we might have otherwise failed.

In that frame of mind, we will next examine causes for compromise—that is, possible factors connected to failure and likely reasons for dereliction of duty.

Reasons for Dereliction of Duty

The dereliction of duty seen in the garden that night is in evidence still. A. W. Tozer asked, "What is the present condition of the evangelical church?" Then, answering his own question he wrote: "The bulk of Christians are asleep." In his book, *Rut, Rot, or Revival*, Tozer said of this lamentable lethargy, "It is possible to be spiritually asleep yet mentally, intellectually, physically and theologically alert."[1]

These apostles had been with Jesus for more than three years. They had even heard him explain what was going to happen to him, and to them, as the end drew near. But did they think they were going to fail him? No, trusting the emotion of their hearts and that willpower freshly flexed in the Upper Room, they went into the garden—too afraid to sleep? No, too confident not to sleep!

Their story is also our own! That fresh flush of emotion and new ripple of resolve have deceived us as well. We, too, have thought we will surely stand, at least for this hour. But, no, our flesh was weaker than we thought. Sooner than we thought, therefore, we failed, discovering too late that we had overestimated ourselves.

257

Dr. Arthur Gossip, the Scottish theologian, said that Jesus' words, "Apart from me you can do nothing," are the most hopeful words in Scripture. "For it is on the basis of that frank recognition of our utter fecklessness apart from him that Christ enters into his covenant with us and gives us his tremendous promises ...."[2]

Samuel Rutherford, another Scottish writer, said, "Unbelief may perhaps tear the copies of the covenant which Christ hath given you; but he still keeps the original in heaven with himself."[3]

For sure, God knows our weaknesses—their causes, their conduct, their consequences. But if we think our situation is not as bad as Jesus said it is, we will go forward like the disciples did that night, only to find ourselves succumbing to needless failure.

Another reason for dereliction of duty is simply a lack of faith. James said that faith without works is, what? Dead! Verbalized faith in the sanctuary means nothing, if home, work, and play don't see our words become observable deeds.

While it is true that good works do not save us, the Reformer Philip Melancthon had it right when he observed: Although we are saved by grace alone, if we are truly saved, grace won't be alone; there will be many good works!

We must remember that all God gives us—revelation, power, spiritual giftedness, and the support of fellow believers—were intended to translate faith into works. Leave works out of the equation and our faith is graveyard dead.

Still another reason for dereliction of duty is a lack of love. John Calvin said that "no man shall steadily persevere in the discharge of his ministry unless the love of Christ shall reign in his heart." Do you remember how Jesus put it to Peter? "If you love me"—what? "Feed my sheep."

To accept the ministry God gives us is an expression of love. And since one of the Greek words for serve, *laturo* (Romans 1:9), means worship, ministry is really an expression of the worshipping heart. It is axiomatic, then: The desire to serve the Lord flows from a heart that worships him. But should worship lose its frequency and fervor, failure to obey will be on display.

Guilt is another reason for dereliction of duty. This is what caused Peter to quit. Remember? Because Peter had so seriously failed the Lord, he felt he could never be used again. And many people today feel the same way. Despite what they've heard about grace, and despite what they've heard about forgiveness, their failure is ever before them!

Oh, they still come to church, but they keep a low profile there, having concluded that their opportunity to serve the Lord has been forfeited forever.

F. B. Meyer offered extensive counsel to people like this, and maybe you are one among them.

> Are you conscious of having marred God's early plan for yourself? His ideal of a life of earnest devotion to his cause has been so miserably lost sight of! Your career, as parent or child, as friend or Christian worker, has been such a failure! ... There seems to be no alternative but to go off into the rear and let others carry away the prizes that come so easily to them. While into the soul the conviction is burned: "I had my chance and missed it; it will never come to me again. The survival of the fittest leaves no place for the unfit. They must be flung amid the waste that is ever accumulating around the furnaces of human life." It is here that the gospel comes in with its gentle words for the outcast and lost. The bruised reed is made again into a pillar for the temple of God. The feebly smoking flax is kindled to a flame.[4]

The fallen Peter could see no hope for himself when he announced to his brethren that day, "I go a fishing." And when he said that he meant a lot more than "let's go down to the lake and catch a few." Peter's announcement meant a return to the old life, to the way it used to be before his monumental failure.

So out there in the wind and the waves and the salty night air, Peter drifted in more ways than one.

To freeze the scene at this point is to see guilt minimizing what Jesus had accomplished. Peter thought his sin was too great for redemption, and too terrible for restoration. However, no sin—Peter's or anyone else's—requires a higher cost than what Jesus paid on the cross. Jesus paid it all! Peter should have reckoned on that! Because to let failure have the final word is to deprive Jesus from seeing his victory applied.

In the book, *That Incredible Christian*, A. W. Tozer offered invaluable advice on this matter:

> There is an art in forgetting, and every Christian should become skilled in it. Forgetting the things which are behind is a positive necessity if we are to become more than mere babes in Christ. If we cannot trust God to have dealt effectually with our past, we may as well throw in the sponge now and have it over with. Fifty years of grieving over our sins cannot block out their guilt. But if God has indeed pardoned and cleansed us, then we should count it done and waste no more time in sterile lamentations.[5]

Yet another reason for dereliction of duty is cowardice. Like the man who kept his one talent and made no attempt to invest it for fear he would only lose it, many Christians today bury their talents, too. They do so, reasoning to themselves that they aren't as blessed as others in God's service—so why try? It was to Christians such as these, Andrew Murray spoke passionately:

> Oh, I come to you with this message: God does not ask you to make a full surrender in your strength or by the power of your will; God is willing to work it in you. Do you not read, "It is God that worketh in us, both to will and to do his good pleasure"? And that is our great need—to go on our faces before God until our hearts learn to believe that the everlasting God himself will come into our lives to change what is wrong, to conquer what is evil, and to work what is well pleasing in his blessed sight. God himself will work it in you.[6]

Remember, it is in weakness God makes us strong. The base, the vile, the foolish—these are the ones God chooses to use to confound the wise (I Corinthians 1:27, 28). True, there were others in the temple that day who gave more to the treasury, but which one did Jesus take special note of? The widow who gave her mite! The smallest of all coins earned the greatest of all appreciation because it was given and not withheld.

As we continue to inventory those reasons contributing to a dereliction of duty, we must take note of discouragement. This is what devastated Jeremiah. It seems, James Hastings said, as though Jeremiah's heart was at war with his duty. It was his assignment to declare God's message of impending doom. Monarchy, nation, temple—all were going to be cast in whirlwind of ruin! Disheartened by his task, Jeremiah sighed, "Oh, that I had in the wilderness a lodging place for wayfaring men that I might leave my people and go from them" (Jeremiah 9:2).

The feeling of wanting to get away, to lay the burden down, to vacation from the straight and narrow, is a very human feeling, from which not even the great men of God are immune. Jeremiah wanted to retire to the sidelines, to reside in one of these lodges where trader and traveler could be accommodated for the night. "There," thought Jeremiah, "I could be at home. I could keep in touch with the currents of the day without having to challenge its drift."

James Hastings is right: How the Jeremiah we find on Old Testament pages reminds us of ourselves: by nature timid, easily wearied, often impatient, distrustful of his own abilities, wanting to give up, to sit down, and to take his ease. But we mustn't do it! For God could never pronounce a benediction on a retirement like that. It was under his inspiration, after all, that an entirely different perspective was authored, "... be steadfast, unmovable, always abounding in your work for the Lord, knowing that your labor is not in vain in the Lord" (I Corinthians 15:58).

Sometimes we misread a situation. We think God has either forgotten us, or has no intention of using us. How easily this could have been done by Joseph, as he languished all those years in prison; and by Moses, while years passed in

261

obscurity there on the backside of the desert; and by David, while hunted down like a dog during those rag-tag years of cave-dwelling.

There are times when we can draw wrong conclusions from what seems indisputable evidence. But Jessie Penn-Lewis reminded us, "God's victories often look like defeats ... If we look for a life of continual outward success and desire to look prosperous and pleasing to the world, we have a wrong conception of God's way of working."[7] G. D. Watson wrote, "In order to have the abiding secret of power, we must consent to seeming failure for Jesus."[8]

We all know the story of Esther. Esther was told by Mordecai to do a daring deed that could cost her life. In accepting this assignment, Esther spoke these now-famous words, "If I perish, I perish." G. D. Watson observed, "That heart agreement to perish, to die and be buried in disgrace, was the key that unlocked a prison door, that let a whole nation out into liberty."[9]

There will be times when it appears we are a failure, and that God has forgotten us. But during these years when God hides us away and achieves much in our soul, a victory is being fashioned that one day will bring great glory to God. If we only know this, we can remain steadfast.

Years ago, when Averell Harriman, the former governor of New York, was about to leave for France where he was to serve as the United States Ambassador, someone asked him, "How's your French?" The governor answered, "My French is excellent, except for the verbs." And perhaps that is true for many Christians as well. We have wonderful nouns in our faith—encouragement, comfort, love, joy; and splendid adjectives in our faith—honorable, sacred, divine, inspiring. But as for the verbs—go, witness, give, and serve— we aren't as proficient.

At times, the slumbering disciples in the garden picture us all too well! We neglect the task the Lord gives us, only to disappoint him because we did.

Willing to Sacrifice

Years ago, E. Stanley Jones spent a night in what is believed to be the Garden of Gethsemane. In an attempt to identify with what Jesus encountered, this well-known missionary to India prayerfully entered not only the garden but soon after the very presence of God.

"About midnight," he wrote, "I read the gospel record of Gethsemane. Suddenly, I leaped up as the impact of that story hit me. For the end was not the blood drops of sweat and sorrow that weighed him to the ground, but the words, 'Arise. Let us be going.'" This, Stanley discovered, was a declaration to face suffering and death head-on! The surge of courage supplied by heaven had assured Jesus of the victory to come.

We all know what Jesus faced in the garden extended far beyond what any of us will experience. For example, when Scripture talks about Jesus "despising the shame," it wasn't talking about the ridicule, the nails, and the fact the cross that awaited him was for criminals. For *this* shame referred to the weight of all sin upon Jesus, and that contempt he bore when Father and Spirit turned away.

In this way the Lord's cross is not like our own. However, it is when we consent to die that the Lord does draw closer to us, purposing to give us himself through this experience.

Turning to the Lord by degree and installment is not the call Christ conveys. Hence, C. S. Lewis wrote:

> Christ says, "Give me *all*. I don't want so much of your money and so much of your work—I want *you*. I have come not to torment your natural self, but to kill it. No half measures are any good. I don't want to cut off a branch here and a branch there. I want to have the whole tree down. I don't want to drill the tooth or crown or stop it, but to have it out. Hand over the whole natural self, all the desires which you think innocent, as well as the ones you think wicked—the whole outfit. I will give you a new self instead. In fact, I will give you myself, my own will shall become yours."[10]

The clarion call to arise and go from here is a call to submit to the death of our self-life so we can then do what our self-life could never do, to suffer for Christ's sake.

Due to the necessity of such suffering, G. D. Watson offered extensive commentary on it in his book, *Pure Gold*:

> The Scriptures in multiplied forms of teaching set forth the truth that after believers are fully sanctified, they are led through processes of severe trials, hot furnace-testings which put to thorough proof every virtue and every grace of their hearts."[11]

Upon experiencing the thrill of being filled with the Spirit and the flow of these virtues suddenly manifesting, we may have assumed that the victory is now won and that the rest of life will be lived in the gush of glory. What we didn't realize, though, is that what God produces, he then tests, before he eventually honors. In his book, *God's First Words*, Watson declared, "Faith is always tested and then honored."[12]

G. D. Watson, the Virginian born in 1845 and sometimes called the apostle to the sanctified, added understanding where it had been missing from those testimonies that put the filling of the Spirit at the end of the story. This is not the end of the story! One will encounter needless bewilderment if this conclusion isn't corrected.

As Watson pointed out in his book, *White Robes*, some of the pain the saint will encounter will come directly from the hand of God. "The history of piety will show that thousands who seemed to suffer directly from the hand of God have been the very ones who loved God with a surpassing flame of devotion."[13] This is by design, Watson observed, for "every disappointment will cause us to lean harder on the unwavering arm; every shock will cause us to sink deeper into the unshakeable Rock ...."[14] And thus our love will grow!

In his book, *Bridehood Saints*, Watson declared, "Most Christians are for a long time seeking for various blessings, but when they enter the true death to self they become taken up with divine union, and find that God is their joy and their life."[15] And isn't this outcome far better than the blessings we've been seeking?

God knows how to use suffering as an advantage to his child. Hence, in his book, *Tribulation Worketh*, G. D. Watson wrote, "No nurse on earth can wean the soul from its old loves, its ambitions, its own good works, its manifold entanglements, like dear, old dusky sorrow."[16] Watson added, "Human biography is filled with instances which show that the men and women of great world-wide hearts have been those who were the children of deep sorrow."[17]

Those sorrows, designed for a destiny, will always yield a gain far greater than the pain. But at the time the stab of sorrow inflicts its wound, this may not seem possible.

Sometimes sorrow is inflicted to deal with a problem of the heart. In his book, *Soul Food*, G. D. Watson gave this illustration:

> If a cold, condemnatory saint is put through an unexplainable conflict of soul that makes him roll on the floor in agony for hours at a time, while his body is wet with perspiration, when he comes out of that sulphur bath, if he comes out on the Christ-side, there will be a tenderness in his judgments and a broadness in his compassion which no camp-meeting hallelujahs could ever impart.[18]

On some occasions, it must be pointed out, the sorrow inflicted may find its source in evil. II Timothy 3:12 declared that "all who desire to live godly in Christ Jesus will suffer persecution." And please notice the verb used here—not "might," "could" or "perhaps," but *will*!

We may not be sawed in half like Isaiah was, or be crucified upside down as Peter was, or boiled in oil as some said John was, but be assured: The enemy *will* attack! In mean and vindictive ways, he'll come against the godly person with both fists flying.

Yet for those Christians living compromised lives, no such evil is likely to befall them. And this makes sense, really, because why persecute a person who is attempting to blend with the world? Satan isn't upset with these people! To the contrary, may *their* number increase in God's church!

Ruing the fact that this has indeed happened, A. W. Pink wrote,

> Jesus Christ came into this world to glorify God and to glorify himself by redeeming a people unto himself. But what glory can we conceive that God has, and what glory would accrue to Christ, if there be not a vital and fundamental difference between his people and the world?[19]

Charles Spurgeon asked a similar question, "If God has given to you and to me an entirely new life in Christ, how can that new life spend itself after the fashion of the old life?"

Certainly, a major reason for this trend is Satan, whose influence extends widely—even in the church! Thus, provoking Alexander Maclaren to lament:

> ... there are many of us who feel that life is sufficiently comfortable and moderately happy, or at least quite tolerable, without any kind of reference to God at all ... more men are finding ... they can... have a fair share of gladness and satisfaction, without any need for a redeeming gospel and a forgiving Christ.[20]

If, however, a person will say what Jesus would have him say, and do what Jesus would have him do, then it doesn't matter how wise and sweet-spirited this person is, this person has just become a target the underworld wants destroyed!

It was for this reason that Peter said that we should not be surprised when attacks like these occur, "as though some strange thing happened to you" (I Peter 4:12). There's nothing strange about this! Since Satan hates God, he's going to try to hurt God by hurting you.

"Arise," said Jesus, "for *this* is the direction I want you to walk—straight into persecution." But, in walking this way, please know that blood and tears aren't going to be your final destination. Because remember: Jesus endured the cross "for the joy that was set before him" (I Peter 2:21; Hebrews 12:2,

3). So suffering wasn't his last port of call—joy was! And since he is our example, joy will be our destiny, too!

This truth is no doubt the premise for Alexander Maclaren's observation that "radiant optimism is the only fitting attitude for Christian people in looking into the future."[21]

It may have looked like Jesus had lost all when he went to the cross. But then what happened? After becoming obedient even unto death, Philippians 2:8 said, the next verse, Philippians 2:9, declares God highly exalted him and gave him a name which is above every name. This means God isn't calling us only to suffering, he is also calling us to glory (I Peter 5:10).

The Bible declares, and even decrees, that we will be "heirs with God and joint heirs with Christ, if indeed we suffer with him ...." (Romans 8:17). Oswald Chambers wrote, "There will come one day a personal and direct touch from God when every tear and perplexity, every oppression and distress, every suffering and pain will have a complete and ample and overwhelming explanation."[22]

This is a promise so marvelous it isn't comprehensible. The very idea we will have all Jesus possesses extends grace to limits unknown! The Apostle Paul exclaimed, "For I consider the suffering of this present time are not worthy to be compared with the glory which shall be revealed in us" (Romans 8:18). What an extraordinary declaration! Imagine: However gross and gruesome the suffering, the resulting glory will far outweigh it! The principle being: With growing opposition comes glowing opportunities!

And so it was with anticipated triumph that Jesus declared, "Blessed are you when men hate you, and when they exclude you, and revile you, and cast out your name as evil, for the Son of Man's sake. Rejoice in that day and leap for joy! For indeed your reward is great in heaven" (Luke 6:22, 23).

True, in the day of suffering you may not feel so blessed. And when oppression bears down, you may not feel like leaping for joy. But you would—you would!—if the words of Jesus have become a revelation to you! To have only a brief and partial glimpse of what it is you'll receive for suffering for his sake (II Corinthians 1:7) is to cause you, too, to "be glad with exceeding joy" (I Peter 4:13).

Taking the whole scene in, A. B. Simpson said:

> Someday, even you, trembling, faltering one, shall stand upon those heights and look back on all you passed through, all you have narrowly escaped, all the perils through which he guided you, the stumblings through which he guarded you and the sins from which he saved you; and you shall shout, with a meaning you cannot understand now, "Salvation belongs to our God ...."[23]

Yet, the suffering we deliberately choose for ourselves because we love God more than life itself will result in further rejoicing and an even greater reward. In his book, *The Root of the Righteous*, A. W. Tozer described this suffering well:

> ... there is another kind of suffering, known only to the Christian: it is voluntary suffering deliberately and knowingly incurred for the sake of Christ. Such is a luxury, a treasure of fabulous value. And it is rare as well as precious, for there are few in this decadent age who will of their own go down into this dark mine looking for jewels. God will not force us into this kind of suffering; He will not lay this cross upon us nor embarrass us with riches we do not want. Such riches are reserved for those who apply to serve in the legions of the expendables, who love not their lives unto death, who volunteer to suffer for Christ's sake and who follow up their application with lives that challenge the devil and invite the fury of hell.[24]

Considering this coming reward, might not the Lord's word's, "Let us arise and go from here" motivate a determination to get God's best—the joy, the glory, the jewels, as Dr. Tozer so imaginatively speaks of it here?

Can you now see the opportunities that obedience affords? And on that basis, will you now "arise" and "go from here"—that is from the level of living where you have been living, to that higher and costlier level where these obedience opportunities do exist? To these questions, which couldn't be plainer, should come answers that couldn't be clearer.

You should know, and remind yourself often, there is a continuity between this world and the next. Our progress in obedience here will factor into the level of our living there. G. D. Watson said that "you and I may live on forever and forever in heaven, and God may use us in distant worlds and distant ages, but all through eternity we will but be carrying out the lessons of the obedience of the lives we are now living."[25]

Our starting place there, and the trajectory of triumphs that will be ours to enjoy, is based on the obedience lessons mastered in this life. Again, it is only those who arise to serve the Lord in obedience who will rise in the next life to levels of glory their humble hearts never could have imagined.

The opportunity to obey is precisely that, an opportunity. And once you see this opportunity for what it is, your heart will gladly respond to Finney's challenge: "You must fully set your heart to obey God in all things—at all times—under all circumstances ...."[26]

Fix that goal in your heart and not only will all the resources of God be yours for the victory, but one day the stupendous rewards of God will be lavished upon you.

Reflection Questions

1. After reviewing reasons cited in this chapter for the church's dereliction of duty, which reason resonated with you the most?

2. After contemplating the suffering obedience involves, what thoughts triggered first in your mind? And what were the settled conclusions you eventually embraced?

3. If there is continuity between your obedience in this life and the level of living you will enjoy in the next, what motivation does this thought provide you?

Endnotes

Chapter 1—There's No Other Way

1. *The Barna Report, The Journal for the Scientific Study of Religion, The Pew Forum U. S. Religious Landscape Survey* and other sources of investigative study provide extensive documentation to show that the differences in behavior between Christians and non-Christians are negligible.

2. This optimism applies to the micro-perspective, wherein for a given instance sin's solution seems apparent. However, it doesn't reflect the macro-perspective of most Christians, wherein it is assumed that over the longer haul sin is inevitable and many defeats are unavoidable.

3. Fullness of joy is promised by Jesus in John 16:24 as the byproduct of a successful prayer life. However, a successful prayer life requires obedience (Isaiah 59:2; Psalm 66:18), without which prayer will fail and joy will elude.

4. Andrew Murray, *The Believer's Secret of Holiness*, (Minneapolis, Bethany Publishing House, 1984), p.142.

5. It is true that joy and feelings are not equitable. Nevertheless, the impact joy has on feelings—what the Bible calls "gladness of heart"—is indispensable to those feelings.

6. Steven Barabas, *So Great Salvation*, (Eugene, OR., Wipf & Stock, 2005), p.178.

7. James Stewart, *The Gates of New Life*, (Edinburgh, T. & T. Clark, 1956), p.165.

8. Hannah Whitall Smith, *The Christian's Secret of a Happy Life*, (Old Tappan, NJ., Fleming H. Revell Company, 1974), p.17.

9. A. W. Tozer, *The Root of the Righteous*, (Harrisburg, Christian Publications, 1955), p.52.

10. E. M. Bounds, *Winning the Invisible War*, (Springdale, Whitaker House, 1984), p.129.

11. J. C. Ryle, *Practical Religion*, (Kindle Edition, 2010; Kindle location, p.107).

12. G. D. Watson, *Love and Duty*, (Salem, Ohio, Schmul Publishing Company, Inc. 1984), p.84.

13. A. W. Tozer, *Gems From Tozer*, (Harrisburg, Christian Publications, 1969), p.51.

14. Andrew Murray, *The Spirit of Christ*, (Springdale, Whitaker House, no date cited), p.14.

15. A. W. Tozer, *That Incredible Christian*, (Harrisburg, PA., Christian Publications, Inc., 1964), p.134.

16. Andrew Murray, *The Believer's Secret of Holiness*, p.52.

17. Oswald Chambers, *Our Brilliant Heritage*, (Grand Rapids, MI., Discovery House Publishers, 1998), p.186.

Endnotes

18. G. D. Watson, *Bridehood Saints*, (Hampton, TN., Harvey and Tait Publishers, 1988), p.142.

19. Thomas Watson, *The Great Gain of Godliness*, (Carlisle, PA., The Banner of Truth Trust, 2008), p.43.

20. Thomas Goodwin, *The Works of Thomas Goodwin, Volume 1*, Lafayette, IN., Sovereign Grace Publishers, Inc., 2000), p.362.

21. Charles Finney, *How to Experience the Higher Life*, Kindle Edition, 2010, Kindle location: 1337.

22. A. B. Simpson, *Wholly Sanctified*, (Camp Hill, PA., Christian Publications, 1991), p.83.

23. F. B. Meyer, *Christ in Isaiah*, (Fort Washington, PA., CLC Publications, 2001), pp. 10, 11.

24. Samuel Chadwick, *Humanity and God*, (Salem, Ohio, Schmul Publishing Company, 1982), pp.178-179.

25. Jessie Penn-Lewis, *The Story of Job*, (Ft. Washington, PA., CLC Publications, 1996), p.232.

Chapter 2—The Spirit's Strength

1. David C. K. Watson, *My God is Real*, (New York, The Seabury Press, 1970). p.78.

2. Ibid., p.74.

3. Charles Finney, *How to Experience the Higher Life*, (Kindle Edition: 2010; Kindle location: 419).

4. F. B. Meyer, "The Anointing with the Holy Spirit," located under Sermon Texts on the website sermonindex.net

5. There is reason to believe that the language of Romans 7 is fictive and dialogical, employed for the purposes of personalizing and dramatizing truth and not for disclosing biographical information. Extending Paul's language, instead of explaining it, I will focus on core thoughts in Romans 7, to the extent they have some relevancy for the believer.

6. Andrew Murray, *The Collected Works and Sermons of Andrew Murray*, Christian Miracle Foundation Press, (Kindle Edition, 2011; Kindle location:1782-1783).

7. I am indebted to Bill Gillham, author of the book, *Lifetime Guarantee*, (Brentwood, Wolgemuth and Hyatt Publishers, 1987) for this term.

8. Jack R. Taylor, *The Key to Triumphant Living*, (Nashville, Broadman, 1971), p.78.

9. Miles J. Stanford, *The Complete Green Letters*, (Grand Rapids, Zondervan, 1983), p. 217.

10. Jerry Bridges, *The Pursuit of Holiness*, (Colorado Springs, Navpress, 1978), p 87.

Endnotes

11. Ibid., p. 87.
12. Stephen Charnock, *The Works of Stephen Charnock*, (Kindle Edition, 2011; Kindle locations: 3631-3632.
13. Andrew Murray, *The Believer's Secret of the Master's Indwelling*, (Minneapolis, Minnesota, Bethany House Publishers, 1977), p 35.
14. Ruth Paxson, *Life on the Highest Plane*, (Grand Rapids, Baker Book House, 1928), p.220.
15. Hannah Whitall Smith, *The Christian's Secret of a Happy Life*, pp.133, 134.
16. John E. Hunter, *Let Us Go Onto Maturity*, (Grand Rapids, MI., Zondervan, 1974), p.83.
17. Charles Finney, *How to Experience the Higher Life*, Kindle Edition: 2110; Kindle locations: 2806-2807.
18. A. B. Simpson, *The Christ in the Bible Commentary*, Volume Two (Camp Hill, PA., WingSpread Publishers, 2009), p.270.

Chapter 3—Heaven's Hope—Part I

1. A. W. Tozer, *The Radical Cross*, (Camp Hill, PA., WingSpread Publishers, 2005), p.133.
2. Dave Hunt, *Whatever Happened to Heaven?*, (Eugene, OR., Harvest House Publishers, 1988). p. 11.
3. G. D. Watson, *Holiness Manual*, (Salem, Ohio, Schmul Publishing Company, 2007), p.81.
4. *The Speaker's Bible, The Gospel of Matthew*, Volume 29, Edward Hastings, ed., (Aberdeen Scotland, Morrison and Gibb Ltd., 1938), p.82.
5. Herbert Lockyer, *All God's Comfort*, (Peabody, Massachusetts, Hendrickson Publishers, 2004), p.124.
6. C. S. Lewis, *Mere Christianity*, (New York, MacMillan Publishing Company, 1977), p.119.
7. A. W. Tozer, *I Call it Heresy*, (Harrisburg, PA., Christian Publications, 1974), p. 80.
8. Ibid., p.80.
9. Blaise Pascal, *Pensees*, (New York, NY., Washington Square Press, 1963), p.61.
10. Ibid., p.62.
11. James Stewart, *The Gates of New Life*, p.29.
12. Dave Hunt, *Whatever Happened to Heaven?* pp.40, 41.
13. E. J. Carnell, *The Case for Biblical Christianity*, (Grand Rapids, William B. Eerdmans Publishing Company, 1969), p.180.
14. W. A. Criswell and Paige Patterson, *Heaven*, (Wheaton, IL., Tyndale House, 1991), pp.6, 7.

Endnotes

15. In setting forth these two pictures, I have used some concepts and wording offered in E. M. Bounds' wonderful little book, *Heaven*, (Grand Rapids, Baker Book House, 1975).

16. W. T. H. Richards, *God's Great Promises*, (Abingdon Press, Nashville and New York, 1973), pp.107, 108.

17. John MacArthur, *The Glory of Heaven*, (Wheaton, Il., Crossway Books, 1996), p.106.

18. Charles Finney, *How to Experience the Higher Life*, Kindle Edition, 2010; Kindle Locations: 1275-1276.

19. Serious Christian thinkers like C. S. Lewis have concluded that there will be animals in heaven. This somewhat philosophical/biblical topic is called vivisection. On page 192 of his book, *God's Eagles* (Salem, Ohio, Schmul Publishing Company, 1989), G. D. Watson offered a sprightly reflection on this topic. "Many of the ablest Bible expositors and the most godly saints in past generations have believed that God will raise from the dead those horses that have been very useful to men in this life, and glorify those horses and continue to use them in the coming ages for the saints to ride upon. That may be true, or may not, but one thing is certain: everything belongs to God, and he has the absolute right and law and power to raise any dead creature he pleases, and use it in any way he may choose for his glory, and he will not stop to consult the higher critics or an infidel church or an ungodly world as to what he may do in the glorious age that is to come." In some ways, this perspective seems to fit the nineteenth-century man, and does not include the woman who wants her cat or bird in heaven and the little boy who holds in reserve the most intense desire to get his dog back.

20. On page 246 of his book, *God's Eagles*, (Salem, Ohio, Schmul Publishing Company), 1989) G. D Watson observed: "The Tree of life will yield twelve manner of fruits, and yield its fruit every month, and the leaves of the tree are for healing the nations. This word 'healing' more literally should be translated 'health preserving'; it does not imply that the nations will get sick ... the leaves of the tree will be used to preserve the perfect health of the nations throughout the ages that are to come."

Chapter 4—Heaven's Hope—Part II

1. Thomas Watson, *The Lord's Prayer*, Kindle Edition, 2010; Kindle locations: 1657-1658.

2. G. D. Watson, *Heavenly Life*, (Salem, Ohio, Schmul

Endnotes

Publishing Company, 1994), p.98.

3. Ibid., p.99.
4. Ibid., p.99.
5. J. C. Ryle, "Heaven," found under Sermon Texts on the website sermonindex.net
6. Thomas Watson, *The Lord's Prayer*, Kindle locations: 1688-1689.
7. G. D. Watson, *Heavenly Life*, p.103.
8. G. D. Watson, *God's Eagles*, p.31.
9. Thomas Watson, *The Lord's Prayer*, Kindle locations: 1705-1706.
10. On page 105 of *The Tozer Pulpit*, Volume 6 (Harrisburg, PA., Christian Publications, 1975) Tozer pointed out, "When the followers of Jesus Christ lose their interest in heaven ...they cannot be a powerful force in a sad and sinful world."
11. Author's inclusion within quote indicated by brackets throughout this book.
12. E. M. Bounds, *Winning the Invisible War*, p.148.
13. David Brainerd, *The Life of David Brainerd*, (Grand Rapids, Baker Book House, 1978), p 51.
14. E. M. Bounds, *Heaven*, p.35.
15. J. C. Philpot, "More Pearls From Philpot,": found under Sermon Texts on the website sermonindex.net
16. F. J. Huegel, *The Cross of Christ, The Throne of God*, (Dixon, MO., Rare Books, n.d.), p.99.
17. F. B. Meyer, *Christ in Isaiah*, (Fort Washington, PA., CLC Publications, 2002), p.26.
18. G. D. Watson, *Spiritual Feasts*, (Salem, Ohio, Schmul Publishing Company, 1991), p.38.
19. A. W. Tozer, *Who Put Jesus on the Cross?* (Harrisburg, PA., Christian Publications, 1975), p.105.
20. S. D. Gordon, *Quiet Talks on Power*, (New York, Grosset & Dunlap, 1903), p. 178.
21. Amy Carmichael, *Whispers of His Power*, (Ft. Washington, PA., CLC Publications, 2001), p.64.
22. Thomas Goodwin, *The Works of Thomas Goodwin, Volume 1*, p.324.
23. G. D. Watson, *Love and Duty*, p.86.
24. A. W. Tozer, *Jesus, Author of Our Faith*, (Camp Hill, PA., WingSpread Publishers, 1998), p.94.
25. C. S. Lewis, *The Problem of Pain*, (New York, The Macmillan Company, 1962), p.61.
26. E. M. Bounds, *Heaven*, p.87.
27. Charles Spurgeon, *Faith's Checkbook*, (South Plainfield, New

Endnotes

Jersey, Bridge Publishing, 1987), p.352.

28. G. D. Watson, *The Seven Overcomeths*, (Salem, Ohio, Schmul Publishing Company, 2007), p.109.
29. James S. Stewart, *Walking with God*, (Vancouver, British Columbia, Regent College Publishing, 1996), p.21.
30. A. W. Tozer, *The Tozer Pulpit*, Volume 6, p.171.

Chapter 5—Identity's Influence

1. A. W. Tozer, *Whatever Happened to Worship?*, (Camp Hill, PA., Christian Publications, 1985), p. 107.
2. Andrew Murray, *The Ministry of Intercessory Prayer*, (New Kensington, PA, Whitaker House, 1984), p. 117.
3. F. J. Huegel, *Forever Triumphant*, (Minneapolis, Minnesota, Bethany Fellowship, 1955), p.66.
4. John E. Hunter, *Limiting God*, (Grand Rapids, MI., Zondervan, 1966), p.19.
5. Charles Hodge, *The Way of Life*, (Grand Rapids, Baker Book House, 1977), p.330.
6. Ibid., p.324.
7. A. B. Simpson, *Standing on Faith*, Kindle Edition, 2010; Kindle locations: 203-204.
8. F. J. Huegel, *Forever Triumphant*, p. 66.
9. Ruth Paxon, *Rivers of Living Waters*, (Chicago, Moody, 1984), p. 24.
10. A. B. Simpson, *The Christ in the Bible Commentary*, Volume Six (Camp Hill, PA., WingSpread Publishers, 2009), p.102.
11. Andrew Murray, *The Believer's Secret of the Master's Indwelling*, p. 86.
12. G. D. Watson, *Soul Food*, (Hampton, TN., Harvey Christian Publishers, 2000), p.47.
13. Jessie Penn-Lewis, *Life in the Spirit*, (Forth Washington, PA., 1991), p.53.
14. Ibid., p.9.
15. G. D. Watson, *Tribulation Worketh*, (Hampton, TN., Harvey Christian Publishers, 2000), p.33.
16. Philip Yancey, *What's So Amazing About Grace?*, (Grand Rapids, Michigan, Zondervan, 1998), p.69.
17. D. Martyn Lloyd-Jones, *Romans, The New Man*, (Edinburgh, UK., The Banner of Truth Trust, 2008), p.203.

Chapter 6—The Father's Fellowship—Part I

1. E. M. Bounds, *Winning the Invisible War*, p.79.
2. A. B. Simpson, *The Christ in the Bible Commentary*, Volume

Endnotes

Five, (Camp Hill, PA., WingSpread Publisher, 2009), p.316.

3. Robert Raines, *Soundings*, (New York, Evanston, and London, Harper and Row, 1970), pp. 94, 95.
4. A. W. Pink, *Gleanings from Paul*, Public Domain, (Monergism Books, Kindle locations: 135-136).
5. John Owen, *John Owen on the Holy Spirit*, (Kindle Edition, 2010; Kindle location: 18127).
6. Horatius Bonar, *Rent the Veil*, Public Domain, published 1874, Edinburgh, (Pensacola, FL., Mt. Zion Publications), p.8.
7. Alexander Maclaren, *Expositions of Holy Scripture, Isaiah and Jeremiah*, Public Domain Books, Kindle location: 638.
8. Samuel Chadwick, *Humanity and God*, p.16.
9. Hannah Whitall Smith, *God of All Comfort*, (Gainesville, FL., Bridge-Logos, 2006), p.57.
10. Frederick W. Faber, *All for Jesus*, (London, Richardson and Son, 1854), p.284.
11. G. D. Watson, *Our Own God*, (Hampton, IN., Harvey Christian Publishers, 2008), p.17.
12. Miriam Huffman Rockness, *A Passion for the Impossible*, (Grand Rapids, MI., Discovery House Publishers, 2003), p.150.
13. G. D. Watson, *Our Own God*, p.153.
14. A. W. Tozer, *And He Dwelt Among Us*, (Ventura, CA., Regal, 2009), p.50.
15. John Henry Jowett, *Friend on the Road and Other Studies in the Gospels*, Kindle Edition, 2010; Kindle locations: 861-862.
16. J. H. Jowett, *Brooks by the Traveler's Way*, (New York A. C. Armstrong and Son; London, H. R. Allerson,1902), p.51.
17. A. B. Simpson, *The Christ in the Bible Commentary*, Volume Five, pp.549, 550.
18. J. H. Jowett, *Brooks by the Traveler's Way*, p.22.

Chapter 7—The Father's Fellowship—Part II

1. Clyde E. Fant, Jr. and William M. Pinson, Jr., *20 Centuries of Great Preaching, Volume 8,* (Waco, Word Books, 1971), p. 236.
2. James S. Stewart, *A Man in Christ*, (Vancouver, Regent College Publishing, 2002), p.238.
3. Samuel Chadwick, *Humanity and God*, p.22.
4. Alexander Maclaren, *Expositions of Holy Scripture, Psalms*, Public Domain Books, Kindle locations: 2571-2572.

Endnotes

5. Helmut Thielicke, *The Waiting Father*, (New York, Evanston, San Francisco, London, Harper and Row, 1975), p.80.
6. Henry Scougal, *The Life of God in the Soul of Man*, (Harrisonburg, VA: Sprinkle Publications, 1986), p.121.
7. Thomas Watson, *The Godly Man's Picture*, (Carlisle, PA., The Banner of Truth Trust, 2009), p.28.
8. Alexander Maclaren, *Expositions of Holy Scripture, Isaiah and Jeremiah*, Kindle locations: 44-45.
9. A. B. Simpson, *The Christ in the Bible Commentary*, Volume Four, (Camp Hill, PA., WingSpread Publishers, 2009), p.26.
10. A. B. Simpson, *The Christ in the Bible Commentary*, Volume Five, p.50.
11. A. B. Simpson, *The Christ in the Bible Commentary*, Volume Six, (Camp Hill, PA., WingSpread Publishers, 2009), p.26.
12. A. B. Simpson, *The Christ in the Bible Commentary*, Volume Two, p.135.
13. A. B. Simpson, *The Christ in the Bible Commentary*, Volume Four, p.72.
14. A. W. Tozer, *Jesus, Our Man in Glory*, (Camp Hill, PA., WingSpread Publishers, 2009), p.29.
15. Thomas Goodwin, *The Works of Thomas Goodwin, Volume 1*, p.328.
16. A. B. Simpson, *Standing on Faith*, Kindle location: 1276.
17. Thomas Watson, *The Lord's Prayer*, Kindle location: 528.
18. Thomas Manton, *A Treatise of Self-Denial*, Monergism epub, p.14.
19. Ibid., p.15.

Chapter 8—Divinity's Direction—Part I

1. G. D. Watson, *Soul Food*, p.60.
2. Miles. J. Stanford, *The Complete Green Letters*, p.197.
3. A. W. Tozer, *Gems From Tozer*, (Harrisburg, Christian Publications, 1969), p.75.
4. James S. Stewart, *A Man in Christ*, p.39.
5. A. B. Simpson, *Present Truths or the Supernatural*, Worthy Christian Library (online), chapter 2, paragraph 2.
6. Erich Sauer, *The King of the Earth*, (Grand Rapids, Wm. B. Eerdmans Publishing Co., 1967), p.210.
7. A. W. Tozer, *That Incredible Christian*, p.81.
8. A. W. Tozer, *Man, The Dwelling Place of God*, (Camp Hill, PA., WingSpread Publishers, 1997), p.120.
9. A. B. Simpson, *The Christ in the Bible Commentary*, Volume Five, p.401.

Endnotes

10. A. B. Simpson, *When God Steps In*, (Camp Hill, PA., Christian Publications, 1997), pp.70, 71.
11. G. D. Watson, *Spiritual Feasts*, p.82.
12. A. B. Simpson, *The Christ in the Bible Commentary*, Volume Three, (Camp Hill, PA., WingSpread Publishers, 2009), p.289.
13. Ibid., p.291.
14. F. F. Bosworth, *Christ the Healer*, (Old Tappan, N. J., Fleming H. Revell Company, 1973), p.40.
15. A. W. Tozer, *Gems From Tozer*, p.57.
16. Thomas Watson, *A Body of Divinity: Contained in Sermons upon the Westminster Assembly's Catechism*, (Kindle Edition, 2010), p.30.
17. G. D. Watson, *Coals of Fire*, (Salem, Ohio, Schmul Publishers, n. d.), p.78.
18. Ibid., p.78.
19. Ibid., p.78.

Chapter 9— Divinity's Direction—Part II

1. A. B. Simpson, *Behind the Veil*, chapter 5, paragraph 7.
2. Jessie Penn-Lewis, *Life out of Death*, (Fort Washington, PA., CLC Publications, 1991), p.73.
3. A. B. Simpson, *The Christ in the Bible Commentary*, Volume 6, (Camp Hill, PA., WingSpread Publishers, 2009), p.99.
4. Alexander MacLaren, *Expositions of Holy Scripture Isaiah and Jeremiah*, Public Domain Books, Kindle Edition, 2005; (Kindle Locations: 3449-3450).
5. G. D. Watson, *Spiritual Feasts*, p.26.
6. G. D. Watson, *Holiness Manual*, p.72.
7. A. B. Simpson, *Present Truths or the Supernatural*, Introduction, paragraph 8.
8. Alexander Maclaren, *Expositions of Holy Scripture Deuteronomy, Joshua, Judges, Ruth, and First Book of Samuel, Second Samuel, First Kings, and Second Kings chapters I to VII*, Public Domain Books. Kindle Edition, 2005; Kindle location, p.128.
9. Vance Havner, *Reflections on the Gospels*, (Ft. Washington, PA., CLC Publications, 2004), p.103.
10. *Spurgeon's Expository Encyclopedia*, Volume 15, (GrandRapids, Michigan, Baker Book House, 1978), p.208.
11. Samuel Brengle, *Helps to Holiness*, (Shoals, IN., Old Pathe Tract Society, n. d.), p.74.
12. Miriam Huffman Rockness, *A Passion for the Impossible*, p.332.

Endnotes

13. Thomas Watson, *A Body of Divinity: Contained in Sermons upon the Westminster Assembly's Catechism*, p.31.

Chapter 10—Peace's Protection–Part I

1. Ian Barclay, *Living and Enjoying the Fruit of the Holy Spirit*, (Chicago, Moody Press, 1975), p.50.
2. G. D. Watson, *Tribulation Worketh*, p.27.
3. Ibid., pp.27, 28.
4. Ibid., p.28.
5. G. D. Watson, *Heavenly Life*, p.61.
6. John Henry Jowett, *Friend on the Road and Other Studies in the Gospels*, Kindle Edition, 2010; Kindle locations: 795-798.
7. Ibid., Kindle locations: 1007-1009.
8. F. B. Meyer, *Our Daily Homily*, Volume 1 (Redding, CA., Pleasant Places Press, 2009), p.44.
9. Ibid., p.44.
10. A. W. Tozer, *The Warfare of the Spirit*, (Camp Hill, PA., Christian Publications, 1993), p.56.
11. John Henry Jowett, *Friend on the Road and Other Studies in the Gospels*, Kindle locations: 1096-1097.
12. Alexander Maclaren, *Expositions of Holy Scripture Isaiah and Jeremiah*, Public Domain Books, Kindle Edition, Kindle locations: 4311-4313.
13. John Edmund Haggai, *How to Win over Worry*, (New York, Pirimand, 1969), p.16.
14. Watchman Nee, *The Spiritual Man*, (New York, Christian Fellowship, 1968), p. 157.
15. A. B. Simpson, *The Christ in the Bible Commentary*, Volume Five, p.405.
16. A. B. Simpson, *Apostolic Testimony*, Telfair, PA., Worthy Christian Library (online), chapter 8, paragraph 9.

Chapter 11—Peace's Protection–Part II

1. John Owen, *Communion with God*, ed. R. K. Law (Edinburgh, Scotland, The Banner of Truth Trust, 1991), p.13.
2. C. S. Lewis, *The World's Last Night*, (New York: Harcourt, Brace and Janovich, 1960), p. 109.
3. Hannah Whitall Smith, *God of All Comfort*, p.155.
4. Ibid., p.103.
5. F. B. Meyer, *Elijah and the Secret of His Power*, (Chicago, Moody, 1976), p.110.
6. Bruce Wideman, *Flee, Follow, Fight*, (Jackson, MISS.,

Endnotes

Hederman Brothers, 1984). p.57.

7. Ray C. Stedman, *The Ruler Who Serves*, (Word Books, Waco, Texas, 1976), p.2.

Chapter 12—Gratitude's Goal

1. George MacDonald, *The Best of George MacDonald*, (Colorado Springs, CO., Cook Communications Ministries, 2006), p.113.
2. Frederick W. Faber, *All for Jesus*, p.216.
3. A. B. Simpson, *The Christ in the Bible Commentary*, Volume Three, (Camp Hill, PA., WingSpread Publishers, 2009), p.365.
4. James S. Stewart, *Walking with God*, p.62.
5. Thomas Watson, *The Godly Man's Picture*, p.131.
6. James S. Stewart, *A Faith to Proclaim*, (Grand Rapids, MI., Baker Book House, 1972), p.54.
7. James S. Stewart, *Walking with God*, p.57.
8. A. W. Tozer, *Gems From Tozer*, p. 35.
9. Paul E. Billheimer, *Destined for the Throne*, (Minneapolis, Bethany House Publishers, 1975), p.120.
10. Ibid. p.120.
11. Watchman Nee, God's *Plan and the Overcomers*, (New York, Christian Fellowship, 1977), p. 71.
12. F. J. Huegel, *Forever Triumphant*, pp.91, 92.

Chapter 13—The Problem's Proportions—Part I

1. The Speaker's Bible, *The Second Epistle to the Corinthians*, Edward Hastings, ed., (Edinburgh, Turnbull & Spears), 1933, p.198.
2. John Henry Jowett, *Friend on the Road and Other Studies in the Gospels*, Kindle locations: 696-699.
3. C. S. Lewis, *The World's Last Night*, (New York, Hartcourt, Brace and Javanovich, 1960), p.11.
4. C. S. Lewis, *The Problem of Pain*, (New York, New York, The Macmillan Company, 1972), p.124.
5. A. B. Simpson, *The Christ in the Bible Commentary*, Volume Five, p.300.
6. G. D. Watson, *Love Abounding*, (Cincinnati, Ohio, God's Revivalist Press, n. d.), p.213.
7. G. D. Watson, *Pure Gold*, (Hampton, TN., Harvey Christian Publishers, 1996), p.9.
8. G. D. Watson, *Soul Food*, p.48.
9. G. D. Watson, *Tribulation Worketh*, p.14.

Endnotes

10. G. D. Watson, *The Secret of Spiritual Power*, (Nicholasville, Kentucky, Schmul Publishing Company, 2009), p.37.
11. Amy Carmichael, *Learning of God*, compiled by Stuart and Brenda Blanch, (Ft. Washington, PA., CLC Publications, 2000), p.120.
12. Jessie Penn-Lewis, *The Story of Job*, p.49.
13. Ibid., p.94.
14. F. B. Meyers, *Jeremiah*, (Fort Washington, PA. CLC Publications, 2002), p.68.
15. G. D. Watson, *White Robes*, (Hampton, TN., Harvey Christian Publishers, 2000), p.42.
16. G. D. Watson, *Our Own God*, (Hampton, TN., Harvey Christian Publishers, 2008), pp.17, 18.
17. James. S. Stewart, *The Strong Name*, p.185.
18. A. B. Simpson, *Behind the Veil*, Soul Food, chapter 11, paragraph 13.
19. F. B. Meyer, *Christ in Isaiah*, (Fort Washington, PA., CLC Publications, 2001), p.39.
20. J. H. Jowett, *The Preacher—His Life and Work*, Kindle Edition, 2011; Kindle locations: 356-357.
21. Hannah Whitall Smith, *The Christian's Secret of a Happy Life*, p.89.
22. Thomas Manton, *A Treatise of Self-Denial*, p.20.
23. James S. Stewart, *The Wind of the Spirit*, (Grand Rapids, MI., Baker Books, 1984), p.70.
24. G. D. Watson, *Coals of Fire*, (Salem, Ohio, Schmul Publishers, n. d.), p.150.
25. Thomas Goodwin, *Patience and Its Perfect Work*, (Kindle Edition: 2010; Kindle location: 808).
26. J. H. Jowett, *Brooks by the Traveler's Way*, p.72.
27. G. D. Watson, *The Secret of Spiritual Power*, p.39.
28. Ibid., p.39.
29. A. B. Simpson, *The Christ of the Bible Commentary*, Volume Two, p.125.
30. Ibid., p.229.
31. Richard Sibbes, *The Bruised Reed*, (Carlisle, PA., The Banner of Truth Trust, 1998), p.58.
32. G. D. Watson, *The Secret of Spiritual Power*, p.46.
33. J. H. Jowett, *Brooks by the Traveler's Way*, p.114.
34. G. D. Watson, *The Secret of Spiritual Power*, p.165.
35. F. B. Meyer, *Tried by Fire*, (Fort Washington, PA., CLC Publications, 2001), p.33.
36. G. D. Watson, *Soul Food*, p.47.

Endnotes

Chapter 14—The Problem's Proportions—Part II

1. Thomas Goodwin, *The Works of Thomas Goodwin*, Volume I, (Lafayette, IN, Sovereign Grace Publishers, 2000), p.367.
2. Arthur W. Pink, *Practical Christianity*, (Grand Rapids, MI., reprinted by Baker Book House, 1975), p.159.
3. C. S. Lewis, *God in the Dock*, William B. Eerdmans Publishing Company, (Grand Rapids, Michigan, 1970), p.73.
4. Erich Sauer, *The King of the Earth*, p.63.
5. E. M. Bounds, *Winning the Invisible War*, p. 27.
6. Jack Taylor, *Victory Over the Devil*, (Nashville, Broadman, 1973), p.19.
7. E. M. Bounds, *Winning the Invisible War*, p.78.
8. Bill Gillham, *What God Wishes Christians Knew about Christianity*, (Eugene, OR., Harvest House Publishers, 1998), p.111.
9. J. N. D. Anderson, *Christianity: The Witness of History*, (Wheaton, Intervarsity, 1970), p.46.
10. Robert A. Pyne, *Humanity and Sin*, p. 150.
11. A. W. Tozer, *The Tozer Pulpit Volume 8*, (Harrisburg, PA., Christian Publications, 1981), p.47.
12. A. W. Tozer, *The Root of the Righteous*, pp.90, 91.
13. A. W. Tozer, *Leaning into the Wind*, (Lake Mary, Florida, Creation House, 1984), p.69.
14. Stephen Charnock, *The Works of Stephen Charnock*, Kindle location: 3493.
15. Paul Billheimer, *Destined For the Cross*, (Illinois, Tyndale, 1982), p. 13.
16. Abraham Kuyper, T*he Practice of Godliness*, (Grand Rapids, Baker, 1977), p.70.
17. F. J. Huegel, *The Mystery of Iniquity*, (Dixon, MO., Rare Books, n. d.), p.14.
18. *The Speaker's Bible, The Gospel of Matthew*, Volume 29, Edward Hastings, ed., p.166.
19. Andrew Murray, *In Search of Spiritual Excellence*, (Springdale, Whitaker House, 1984), p. 35.
20. Thomas Watson, *The Godly Man's Picture*, p.31.
21. Ruth Paxson, *Life on the Highest Plain*, (Grand Rapids, Baker Book House, 1928), p.242.
22. Miles J. Stanford, *The Complete Green Letters*, p.38.
23. Ray C. Stedman, *Body Life*, (Texas, Word, 197), p.117.
24. Roy Hession, *When I Saw Him*, (Fort Washington, PA., CLC Publications, 1975), p.22.

Endnotes

Chapter 15—Example's Encouragement

1. Samuel Chadwick, *Humanity and God*, p.170.
2. Andrew Murray, *The School of Obedience*, (Chicago, Moody Press, 1990), p.41.
3. G. D. Watson, *Our Own God*, p.34.
4. A. Boyd Leuter, Jr., "A Theological Evaluation of 'Christ Model' Disciple-Making", *The Journal of Pastoral Practice*, Vol. 5, No. 4, (Phillipsburg, Presbyterian and Reformed Publishing, 1982), p.11.
5. Ibid., p.15.
6. A. W. Tozer, *Christ the Eternal Son*, (Harrisburg, PA., Christian Publications, 1982), p.110.
7. James S. Stewart, *Walking with God*, p.156.
8. Samuel Chadwick, *Humanity and God*, p.189.
9. Ray C. Stedman, *God's Final Word*, (Grand Rapids, Discovery House Publishers, 1991), p. 69.
10. A. W. Tozer, *Man, the Dwelling Place of God*, p.106.
11. Norman Grubb, *Continuous Revival*, (Fort Washington, Christian Literature Crusade, 1971), p.30.
12. See chapter two of the author's book, *Pursuing Fellowship*, Volume One, for an explanation of why such a small group format is necessary.
13. Hannah More, *The Spirit of Prayer*, (Grand Rapids, Zondervan, 1986), p.112.
14. F. B. Meyer, *Our Daily Homily*, p.5.
15. James S. Stewart, *The Strong Name*, (New York, Charles Scribner's Sons, 1941), p.125.
16. James S. Stewart, *Walking with God*, p.17.
17. Jonathan Edwards, *The Works of Jonathan Edwards*, ed, Edward Hickman, (Edinburgh, Scotland, The Banner of Truth Trust, 1974), Volume one, p. xxi.
18. A. B. Simpson, *The Christ in the Bible Commentary*, Volume Two, p.248.
19. A. B. Simpson, *The Christ in the Bible Commentary*, Volume Three, p.57.
20. Helmut Thielicke, *I Believe*, (Philadelphia, Fortress Press, 1968), p.95.
21. A. B. Simpson, *Seeing the Invisible*, (Camp Hill, Christian Publications, 1994), p. 235.
22. F. B. Meyer, *Samuel the Prophet*, (Fort Washington, PA., Christian Literature Crusade, 1978), pp.105-106.

Endnotes

Chapter 16—Obedience's Opportunity–Part I

1. Leonard Ravenhill, *Revival Praying*, (Minneapolis, Minnesota, Bethany House Publishers, 1984), p.151.
2. A. W. Pink, *Practical Christianity*, p.115.
3. A. B. Simpson, *The Christ in the Bible Commentary*, Volume Five, p.291.
4. Maclaren, Alexander, *Expositions of Holy Scripture Deuteronomy, Joshua, Judges, Ruth, and First Book of Samuel,Second Samuel, First Kings, and Second Kings chapters I to VII*, Maclaren, Alexander (2005-05-01). Expositions of Holy Scripture Deuteronomy, Joshua, Judges, Ruth, and First Book of Samuel, Second Samuel, First Kings, and Second Kings chapters I to VII, Public Domain Books. Kindle Edition, 2005; Kindle location, p.92.
5. F. B. Meyer, *Elijah and the Secret of His Power*, p.25.
6. James S. Stewart, *The Gates of New Life*, (Edinburgh, T & T Clark, 1937), p.118.
7. The Speaker's Bible, *The Second Epistle to the Corinthians*, ed., Edward Hastings, p.128.
8. Ibid., p.96.

Chapter 17—Obedience's Opportunity–Part II

1. A. W. Tozer, *Rut, Rot, or Revival*, (Camp Hill, PA., 1992), pp.29, 30.
2. *The Interpreter's Bible*, Volume 8, (Nashville, Abingdon-Cokesbury, 1952), p.715.
3. A. J. Gordon, *In Christ*, (Grand Rapids, MI., Baker books, 1964), p.122.
4. F. B. Meyer, *Jeremiah*, pp.85, 86.
5. A. W. Tozer, *That Incredible Christian*, pp.45, 46.
6. Andrew Murray, *The Believer's Absolute Surrender*, (Minneapolis, Minnesota, Bethany House, 1985), p.77.
7. Jessie Penn-Lewis, *Prayer and Evangelism*, (Fort Washington, PA., CLC Publications, 1995), p.15.
8. G. D. Watson, *The Secret of Spiritual Power*, p.21.
9. Ibid., p.23.
10. C. S. Lewis, *Mere Christianity*, p.167.
11. G. D. Watson, *Pure Gold*, p.9.
12. G. D. Watson, *God's First Words*, (Hampton, TN., Harvey Christian Publishers, 1992), p.92.
13. G. D. Watson, *White Robes*, (Hampton, TN., Harvey Christian Publishers, 2000), p.42.
14. Ibid., p.43.

Endnotes

15. G. D. Watson, *Bridehood Saints*, (Hampton, TN., Harvey Christian Publishers, 1988), p.143.
16. G. D. Watson, *Tribulation Worketh*, p.17.
17. Ibid., p.17.
18. G. D. Watson, *Soul Food*, (Hampton, TN., Harvey Christian Publishers, 2000), pp.48, 49.
19. A. W. Pink *Regeneration Or the New Birth*, Monergism Books, Kindle locations: 123-125.
20. Alexander Maclaren, *Expositions of Holy Scripture, Isaiah and Jeremiah*, Public Domain Books. Kindle Edition, 2005; Kindle locations:6137.
21. Ibid., Kindle locations: 4064-4065.
22. Oswald Chambers, *Shade of His Hand*, (Grand Rapids, MI., Discovery House, 1991), pp.57, 58.
23. A. B. Simpson, *The Christ in the Bible Commentary*, Volume Two, p.137.
24. A. W. Tozer, *The Root of the Righteous*, p.133.
25. G. D. Watson, *Tribulation Worketh*, p.34.
26. Charles Finney, *How to Experience the Higher Life*, Kindle Edition, 2010; Kindle locations: 1319-1320.

www.ingramcontent.com/pod-product-compliance
Lightning Source LLC
LaVergne TN
LVHW051623080426
835511LV00016B/2132